D R Y D E N
AND THE TRADITION OF
PANEGYRIC

DRYDEN

and the Tradition of Panegyric

JAMES D. GARRISON

University of California Press
Berkeley   Los Angeles   London

University of California Press
Berkeley and Los Angeles, California
University of California Press, Ltd.
London, England
Copyright © 1975, by
The Regents of the University of California
ISBN 0–520–02682–9
Library of Congress Catalog Card Number: 73–91676
Printed in the United States of America

For Brendan O Hehir

Contents

Preface

THIS STUDY originated in curiosity about a passing remark made by Dryden in his "Account" of *Annus Mirabilis*. There he observes that "the same images serve equally for the epic poesy, and for the historic and panegyric, which are branches of it . . ." Wondering what connection Dryden saw between a major genre like epic and a minor one like panegyric, I began to investigate the status of panegyric in the seventeenth century and to examine works claiming to belong to this genre. I gradually discerned the outlines of a literary tradition that deserves to be taken seriously, especially by readers of Dryden. The purpose of this book is, then, to recover the tradition of panegyric (chapters 2 and 3) and to consider its impact on the poetry of Dryden (chapters 4 and 5).

Because many of the works under consideration here are not well known, I have liberally excerpted passages for discussion. All quotations from Dryden's poetry are from *The Poems of John Dryden*, edited by James Kinsley, Oxford, 1958, cited in the notes as *Poems*. For classical authors I have used the texts and translations of The

Loeb Classical Library, with the permission of the Harvard University Press and William Heinemann, Ltd. For neo-Latin authors I have used the following editions: *The Poems of Desiderius Erasmus*, edited by C. Reedijk, Leiden, 1956, with the permission of the E. J. Brill company; *The Latin Epigrams of Thomas More*, edited and translated by Leicester Bradner and C. Arthur Lynch, Chicago, 1953, with the permission of the University of Chicago Press; *The Poetry of Walter Haddon*, edited by Charles J. Lees, The Hague and Paris, 1967, with the permission of Mouton and Company, Publishers. I also wish to thank the editors at Holt, Rinehart and Winston for permission to quote from Robert Frost's poem "For John F. Kennedy His Inauguration."

One further note on quotation from Latin writers. Except in the introductory chapter, where all quotations are given in English, I have adopted a simple rule of thumb regarding translations. Excerpts from Latin panegyrics are cited in the original, followed by prose translations. Excerpts from Latin criticism or commentary on panegyric, however, are given only in translation. The responsibility for all unidentified translations is mine, but much of the credit belongs to Salle Ann Schlueter, who helped me prepare the English versions of quotations from the neo-Latin poets.

It is a pleasure to thank those who have given me guidance, criticism, and encouragement. I am especially grateful to Hugh M. Richmond and Thomas G. Barnes, who read the dissertation from which this book evolved, and to Leo Hughes, who read the manuscript in its final form. I am also obliged to friends and colleagues who gave me valuable suggestions on individual chapters—Larry

Carver, Anne Englander, Joseph Englander, Blair Labatt, and Steven N. Zwicker. Most of all, I wish to thank Brendan O Hehir for the encouragement and direction he has so generously given to my work.

J. D. G.
Austin, Texas
September 1974

Short Titles

Claudian, *III Cons.*	*Panegyricus De Tertio Consulatu Honorii Augusti*
Claudian, *IV Cons.*	*Panegyricus De Quarto Consulatu Honorii Augusti*
Claudian, *VI Cons.*	*Panegyricus De Sexto Consulatu Honorii Augusti*
Claudian, *Manlio Theodoro*	*Panegyricus Dictus Manlio Theodoro Consuli*
Daniel, *A Panegyrike Congratulatorie*	*A Panegyrike Congratulatorie Delivered to the Kings most excellent majesty, at Burleigh-Harrington in Rutlandshire*
Drummond, *Forth Feasting*	*Forth Feasting. A Panegyricke To the Kings most excellent Majesty*

Erasmus, *Gratulatorium Carmen*	*Illustrissimo principi Philippo feliciter in patriam redeunti gratulatorium carmen Erasmi sub persona patriae*
Haddon, *In auspicatissimum*	*In auspicatissimum serenissimae Reginae Elisabethae regimen*
Jonson, *A Panegyre*	*A Panegyre, on The Happie Entrance of James Our Soveraigne, To His first high Session of Parliament in this his Kingdome, the 19. of March, 1603*
More, *Carmen Gratulatorium*	*In Suscepti Diadematis Diem Henrici Octavi, Illustrissimi Ac Faustissimi Britanniarum Regis Ac Catherinae Reginae Eius Felicissimae Thomae Mori Londoniensis Carmen Gratulatorium*
Waller, *A Panegyric To My Lord Protector*	*A Panegyric To My Lord Protector, Of The Present Greatness, And Joint Interest Of His Highness, And This Nation*

1: Panegyric

WHEN ASKED by President-elect Kennedy to participate in the inaugural ceremonies of January 1961, Robert Frost responded with a poem which begins:

> *Summoning artists to participate*
> *In the august occasions of the state*
> *Seems something artists ought to celebrate.*
> *Today is for my cause a day of days.*
> *And his be poetry's old-fashioned praise . . .*[1]

Interpreting the significance of this "day of days" for the president and the public, Frost concludes with a prophecy of a new golden age.

> *It makes the prophet in us all presage*
> *The glory of a next Augustan age*
> *Of a power leading from its strength and pride,*
> *Of young ambition eager to be tried,*
> *Firm in our free beliefs without dismay,*

1. Robert Frost, *For John F. Kennedy His Inauguration*, lines 1–5, *The Poetry of Robert Frost*, ed. Edward Connery Lathem (New York, 1969), p. 422. Copyright © 1961, 1962 by Robert Frost. Copyright © 1969 by Holt, Rinehart and Winston, Inc. Reprinted by permission of Holt, Rinehart and Winston, Inc.

> *In any game the nations want to play.*
> *A golden age of poetry and power*
> *Of which this noonday's the beginning hour.*[2]

Shortly before his assassination Kennedy revealed his understanding of these lines in his address at the dedication of the Frost library. "[It is] hardly an accident that Robert Frost coupled poetry and power. For he saw poetry as the means of saving power from itself. When power leads man toward arrogance, poetry reminds him of his limitations. When power narrows the areas of man's concern, poetry reminds him of the richness and diversity of his existence. When power corrupts, poetry cleanses."[3] Frost's poem names the general subject of this book, "poetry and power," while Kennedy's interpretation suggests the emphasis, poetry as a check on power.

Frost's inaugural poem recalls the poetry of John Dryden. The public theme, expressed in couplets mingled with an occasional triplet, is reminiscent of Dryden's addresses to the later Stuart kings. The closing prophecy echoes in particular *Astraea Redux*, the poem Dryden wrote to celebrate the Restoration of Charles II in 1660.

> *Oh Happy Age! Oh times like those alone*
> *By Fate reserv'd for Great* Augustus *Throne!*
> *When the joint growth of Armes and Arts foreshew*
> *The World a Monarch, and that Monarch* You.[4]

2. Frost, *For John F. Kennedy His Inauguration*, lines 70–77.

3. "From the Address of President John F. Kennedy at the Dedication of the Robert Frost Library, Amherst College, October 26, 1963," *Of Poetry and Power: Poems Occasioned by the Presidency and by the Death of John F. Kennedy*, ed. Erwin A. Glikes and Paul Schwaber (New York, 1964), app., pp. 135–136.

4. John Dryden, *Astraea Redux. A Poem On the Happy Restora-*

Both Frost and Dryden revive the famous prophecy in book 6 of Vergil's *Aeneid* to proclaim an Augustan ideal of civilization, the union of "poetry and power," of "Armes ánd Arts." The resemblance perhaps explains why Frost refers to his poem as "old-fashioned praise." Writing three centuries after Dryden, Frost evokes an old tradition of public poetry which Dryden would have called "panegyric."

At the height of its popularity and importance in the Stuart period, panegyric is a literary genre that has since fallen not only out of fashion, but virtually out of existence. Moreover, the word "panegyric" itself has changed in meaning and in connotation since the seventeenth century. We must begin, therefore, by tracing the historical evolution of the term and establishing its critical meaning for Dryden and his contemporaries.

HISTORICAL DEFINITION

To appreciate the special significance of the term "panegyric" in Dryden's day, it is helpful to distinguish this term from its common twentieth-century synonym, "encomium." In a modern English dictionary, Webster's Third International, for example, the words "panegyric" and "encomium" are given as synonyms for each other and both are defined by a mutual synonym, "eulogy." In

---

tion and Return Of His Sacred Majesty Charles the Second, lines 320–323, *The Poems of John Dryden*, ed. James Kinsley, 4 vols. (Oxford, 1958), I, 24. Unless otherwise specified, all citations from Dryden's poetry are repeated from this edition and noted as *Poems*.

seventeenth-century English dictionaries, on the other hand, the two terms are not given as synonyms. The distinction between them, preserved throughout the Stuart period, is expressed shortly after Dryden's death in John Kersey's *Dictionarium Anglo-Britannicum*. Kersey defines "encomium" as "a Speech, or Song, in Commendation of a Person; Praise." His definition of "panegyrick" is more detailed: "a Speech deliver'd before a solemn and general Assembly of People, especially in Praise of a great Prince."[5] "Encomium" is thus a general term synonymous with "praise," whereas "panegyrick" denotes a specific kind of public occasion (a "general Assembly of People"), a specific mode ("a Speech"), and a specific subject of praise ("a great Prince"). Kersey's distinction between these two terms, lost in modern English, accurately summarizes the definitions given by the lexicographers of the preceding century.

But there is more to this distinction than the difference between a general and a specific term. In the seventeenth-century dictionaries of John Bullokar, Henry Cockeram, Thomas Blount, Edward Phillips, and Elisha Coles, the definitions of "encomium" are consistent in denotation and neutral in connotation, whereas the definitions of "panegyric" are inconsistent and sometimes charged with emotion.[6] A comparative table reveals this difference.

---

5. John Kersey, *Dictionarium Anglo-Britannicum* (London, 1708).

6. John Bullokar, *An English Expositor* (London, 1616); Henry Cockeram, *The English Dictionarie* (London, 1623); Thomas Blount, *Glossographia* (London, 1656); Edward Phillips, *The New World of English Words* (London, 1658); Elisha Coles, *An English Dictionary* (London, 1676).

Bullokar (1616)	*Panegyricall.* That which is spoken flatteringly in praise of some great person: Also it signifieth, stately, honorable, magnificent, or a speech made of many great matters together.	*Encomium.* A praise
Cockeram (1623)	*Panegyricall.* That which is flatteringly spoken, in the praise of some great person.	*Encomion.* Praise.
Blount (1656)	*Panegyrick.* A licentious kind of speaking or oration, in the praise and commendation of Kings, or other great persons, wherein some falsities are joyned with many flatteries.	*Encomium.* A praise or song in commendation of any person.
Phillips (1658)	*Panegyrick.* A solemn convention of people, at some publick solemnity; also an Oration in the praise of some great person.	*Encomium.* speech made in praise of another.
Coles (1676)	*Panegyrick.* a general assembly or Solemnity, also an Oration in praise of Great Personages.	*Encomium.* a speech in the Praise or Commendation of any.

"Encomium," praise of "any person," does not arouse the same emotions as "panegyric," praise of "great persons." Panegyric, unlike encomium, touches a political nerve.

Political differences cannot, however, entirely account for the inconsistencies among these definitions of "panegyric." Although the political views of the author may influence the tone of his definition, the fundamental discrepancies on this list are inherited from earlier lexicographers, as a closer look at Thomas Blount's *Glossographia* reveals. The first edition of this dictionary, published during the interregnum, was followed by a second in 1661, the same year as Dryden's *To His Sacred Majesty, A Panegyrick on his Coronation*. Possibly reflecting the changing spirit of the times, Blount here reduces the antimonarchical emphasis in his definition of "panegyrick" by lopping off the phrase "wherein some falsities are joyned with many flatteries." In its place, however, Blount adds a second definition, which suggests that he was motivated to make the alteration more by the competition of his rival Edward Phillips than by political considerations. At least, Blount's second definition corresponds to the primary definition given by Phillips in 1658: "Also any Feast, Game or Solemnity exhibited, before the General Assembly of a whole Nation."[7]

Blount's two different explanations of 1661, which capture the basic discrepancy in seventeenth-century dictionary definitions of "panegyric," reflect two different sources of information. His secondary definition is condensed from the glossary to Philemon Holland's translation of Plutarch's *Morals* (1603). "*Panegyricke*. Feasts, games, faires, marts, pompes, showes, or any such solemnities, performed or exhibited before the general assembly of a whole nation; such as were the Olympick, Pythick, Isthmick, and Nemian games in Greece."[8] His primary definition, on the other hand, is appropriated from Thomas Thomas's *Dictionarium Linguae Latinae et Anglicanae* (1587). "Panegyricum. A licentious and lascivious kinde of speaking or oration in the praise and

7. Blount, *Glossographia;* 2d ed. (London, 1661).
8. Philemon Holland, trans. *The Philosophie, commonlie called, The Morals Written By the learned Philosopher Plutarch of Chaeronea* (London, 1603), app.

commendation of Kings, wherein men do ioyne many lyes with flatterie."[9] In short, one source is Greek (*panegyrikos*) and the other Latin (*panegyricus or panegyricum*).

As Philemon Holland's definition suggests, panegyric originates in the festivals of ancient Greece. Derived from the word *panegyris*, meaning "a general assembly," the panegyric was a speech delivered before a mass audience on a festival occasion. Gorgias, Hippias, and Lysias are all known to have delivered panegyrics, but the most famous and influential of these festival orations is the *Panegyrikos* of Isocrates.[10] Although never actually delivered as a speech, the oration was circulated among those who attended the Panathenaic festival in 380 B.C. The festival provided Isocrates not only with an occasion and an audience, but also with a serious subject: national reconciliation. The oration emphasizes the conciliatory purpose of the festival itself.

Now the founders of our great festivals are justly praised for handing down to us a custom by which, having proclaimed a truce and resolved our pending quarrels, we come together in one place, where, as we make our prayers and sacrifices in common, we are reminded of the kinship which exists among us and are made to feel more kindly towards each other for the future, reviving old friendships and establishing new ties.[11]

9. Thomas Thomas, *Dictionarium Linguae Latinae et Anglicanae* (London, 1587).

10. For a brief discussion of festival oratory and an extended consideration of Isocrates, see George Kennedy, *The Art of Persuasion in Greece* (Princeton, 1963), pp. 166–167, 174–206.

11. Isocrates, *Panegyricus*, sec. 43, *Isocrates*, trans. George Norlin, Loeb Classical Library, 3 vols. (London and New York, 1954), I, 145.

The impulse behind both the festival and the festival oration, or panegyric, is the desire to promote domestic peace and national unity. When English lexicographers define "panegyric" as a "general assembly or Solemnity," they are at least indirectly referring to the Greek custom thus described by Isocrates.

When, on the other hand, they define "panegyric" as an "oration, in the praise and commendation of Kings, or other great persons," they are referring to Roman custom and literature. A late addition to the Latin language, the word *panegyricus* occurs only rarely in the Republican period and still infrequently in the early years of the empire.[12] Cicero, for example, does not use the word except to refer specifically to Isocrates' oration, while Quintilian finds only three occasions to use it in the entire course of the *Institutio Oratoria*.[13] By the fourth century, however, the word is commonly used to designate an oration, either in prose or verse, addressed to a public figure, usually the emperor. The most important and enduring examples of late Roman panegyric are by the poet Claudian. Between 395 and 404, Claudian attached the *panegyricus* label to five poems, each of which celebrates the beginning of a new year and the installation of a new consul. Three of these poems are addressed to the emperor Honorius, including the *Panegyricus De Quarto Consulatu Honorii Augusti*, which begins: "Once more the year opens under royal auspices and enjoys in fuller

12. Edouard Galletier, ed. and trans., *Panégyriques latins*, 3 vols. (Paris, 1949), Introduction, I, vii.

13. Galletier, I, vii, and Edward Bonnell, *Lexicon Quintilianeum* (Hildesheim, 1962).

pride its famous prince . . ."[14] The public occasion, here an inaugural ceremony, now calls for eulogy of the emperor.

Combining the Greek example of Isocrates with the Roman example of Claudian produces a composite definition of "panegyric" like Kersey's: "a Speech deliver'd before a solemn and general Assembly of People, especially in Praise of a great Prince." If Kersey had a specific author in mind, however, it was probably neither Isocrates nor Claudian, but rather Pliny the Younger. Elected consul for the year 100, Pliny acknowledged the honor in a speech delivered before the senate. Titled an *actio gratiarum*, this speech includes expressions of gratitude and promises of faithful service to the senators. But these remarks are only tiny appendages to the body of the speech, an elaborate idealization of Trajan, who was present to hear himself praised as the *optimus princeps*. Although Pliny did not call the speech a *panegyricus*, later orators viewed it as a model of the genre. In fact, when Pliny's oration was rediscovered for the Renaissance in the fifteenth century, it was not alone but rather at the head of a collection of panegyrics that came to be known as the *panegyrici latini* or *panegyrici veteres*. Modeled directly on Pliny's *actio gratiarum*, these other orations (eleven in number) publicly celebrate the Roman emperors from Diocletian to Theodosius. All of the

14. Claudius Claudianus, *Panegyricus De Quarto Consulatu Honorii Augusti*, lines 1–2, *Claudian*, trans. Maurice Platnauer, Loeb Classical Library, 2 vols. (London and New York, 1963), I, 287. Unless otherwise specified, all citations of Claudian's poems are repeated from this edition; all English translations of the poems are by Maurice Platnauer.

orations in this collection fit Kersey's definition of "panegyric." They all praise a "great Prince" before a "general
Assembly of People."

The general assembly that gathered to hear the eulogies of the later Roman emperors was not, however,
necessarily restricted to the senate. On the contrary, the
surviving panegyrics indicate that one of the most common occasions for this kind of oratory was an imperial
visit to a provincial town. When the emperor decided to
visit Autun or Trèves, for example, the town showed its
appreciation by having its most distinguished orator
(usually a professor at the local school) deliver an address. The speech was an essential part of the ceremony,
like the decorations, the festive games, and the military
salute.[15]

The attendant atmosphere, perhaps not altogether different from the atmosphere in Athens during the Panathenaic festival, more obviously suggests the progresses of the Tudor and Stuart monarchs, especially those
of Elizabeth and James I. The fourth-century orators
might have felt almost at home in Cambridge on August
9, 1564, for example, when Elizabeth paid a visit to the
university. "This daie, about IX^{ne} of the clock, before
dinner, her Highness, with her train, rode from Colledge to Colledge; and at every House where her Grace
staid was receaved with a short Oracion, two in Greeke,
the residue in Latin . . ."[16] Even when such orations were

15. For a discussion of the historical context of these orations,
see René Pichon, *Les Derniers Ecrivains profanes* (Paris, 1906),
especially chap. 1.
16. *The Progresses and Public Processions of Queen Elizabeth*,
ed. John Nichols, 3 vols. (London, 1823), I, 186.

delivered in English, the speaker often paused to establish a classical precedent. In 1572 the recorder of Warwick carefully opened his speech to Elizabeth by defining the term *panegyricae* (shorthand for *orationes panegyricae*).

The manner and custome to salute Princes with publik Oracions hath bene of long tyme usid, most excellent and gracious Sovereigne Ladie, begonne by the Greeks, confirmed by the Romaynes, and by discourse of tyme contynued even to thies our daies: and because the same were made in publike places and open assemblies of senators and counsaillors, they were callid both in Greek and Latyn *panegyricae*.[17]

By incorporating the Latin word into his English speech, the recorder expresses a sense of continuity with the classical past and identifies himself with the orators of the Roman empire, in particular with the "noble senator, Caius Plinius."[18]

There was, however, another good reason for borrowing the Latin word on this occasion. It was not until the 1590's that the English vocabulary contained an equivalent of either *panegyricus* or *oratio panegyrica*. The first appearance of any form of the word in English is a translation of the latter expression: "Panegyricall Oration." The innovator was Gabriel Harvey and his innovation was met with predictable abuse from Thomas Nashe. In

17. *The Progresses . . . of Queen Elizabeth*, I, 311. This passage is cited by Ernest W. Talbert, "The Interpretation of Jonson's Courtly Spectacle," *PMLA*, LXI (1946), 457, and by Warren L. Chernaik, *The Poetry of Limitation: A Study of Edmund Waller* (New Haven and London, 1968), p. 134. I am particularly indebted to Professor Chernaik, whose book offers valuable perspectives on the tradition of panegyric. See especially pp. 115–123.
18. *The Progresses . . . of Queen Elizabeth*, I, 312.

one of his attacks on Nashe, Harvey had referred to "a plausible discourse" or "a Panegyricall Oration."[19] In his answer Nashe condenses this to "plausible Panegyricall Orations" and then comments sarcastically: "Soft, ere I goe anie further, I care not if I draw out my purse, and change some odde peeces of olde Englishe for new coyne; but it is no matter, upon the Retourne from *Guiana,* the valuation of them may alter, and that which is currant now be then copper."[20] This, as it turns out, is a remarkably prescient statement. A turn-of-the-century neologism, "panegyric" continues to be used infrequently and carefully well into the seventeenth century.[21] When it eventually gains currency as an English word, its "valuation" does indeed begin to change from gold coin to copper.

By tracing this changing "valuation" of "panegyric" through the titles of seventeenth- and eighteenth-century poems, we can begin to establish the literary context of Dryden's addresses to the later Stuart kings. The first recorded use of the noun "panegyric" in the English language occurs in the title of Samuel Daniel's poem on the Stuart succession: *A Panegyrike Congratulatorie Delivered to the Kings most excellent majesty, at Burleigh-*

19. Gabriel Harvey, *Pierce's supererogation,* in *The Works of Gabriel Harvey, D.C.L.,* ed. Alexander B. Grosart, 3 vols. (London, 1884), II, 326.

20. Thomas Nashe, *Have with you to Saffron-Walden,* in *The Works of Thomas Nashe,* ed. Ronald B. McKerrow, 5 vols. (Oxford, 1958), III, 52.

21. My authority for the first recorded uses of the term is the *Oxford English Dictionary.* Looking up the full contexts of the seventeenth-century entries under "panegyric" reveals that writers often italicized the word and sometimes even defined it for their readers.

Harrington in Rutlandshire (1603). The title indicates
that Daniel not only conceived of his poem as a verse
oration, but also that he actually read the poem directly
to the king.[22] Ben Jonson's title of one year later also recalls the Roman background by stressing the public, occasional nature of the genre: *A Panegyre, on the Happie
Entrance of James Our Soveraigne, To His first high Session of Parliament in this his Kingdome, the 19. of March,
1603* [1604]. The ancient significance of the term is also
expressed in the title of a poem written by William
Drummond of Hawthornden to welcome James I to Scotland in 1617: *Forth Feasting. A Panegyricke to the Kings
most excellent Majesty*. The word "feasting" suggests in
particular the kind of ceremonial occasion, or festival, described by Isocrates. "Panegyric" for these early Stuart
poets means: an address to a monarch on some public,
ceremonial occasion.

This definition survives even the experience of the interregnum. Although royal, ceremonial occasions ceased
to exist during the struggles of the mid-century, panegyrics continued to be written. The best example from the
1650's is Edmund Waller's poem to Cromwell: *A Panegyric To My Lord Protector, Of The Present Greatness,
And Joint Interest, Of His Highness, And This Nation*.
Like his predecessors, Waller conceives of the genre as
an address, if not to a king, then at least to a "great person." Moreover, although his poem responds to no public
ceremony, his title emphasizes the traditional purpose
of such ceremony, national reconciliation, or as he ex-

22. It is not known for certain, however, that Daniel read the
poem to James. See Cecil Seronsy, *Samuel Daniel* (New York,
1967), p. 111.

presses it, the "Joint Interest, Of His Highness And This Nation." Imported from Greece through Rome, panegyric in England clings to its classical heritage even when historical circumstances would seem to be most inimical to this particular kind of oratory.

When circumstances changed in 1660, the simultaneous impulse to express the idea of reconciliation and to recapture the forms, ceremonies, and rituals of the past produced a large number of panegyrics. The titles of these poems, although usually not as expansive and revealing as those written earlier in the century, nevertheless reassert the classical significance of the term. Thomas Fuller's *A Panegyric to His Majesty, on His Happy Return* (1660), Dryden's *To His Sacred Majesty, A Panegyrick on his Coronation* (1661), Sir Francis Fane's *A Panegyrick to the King's most excellent Majesty, upon his happy accession to the crown, and his more fortunate marriage* (1662), all preserve the occasional, oratorical, and courtly characteristics associated with the Latin term *panegyricus*. Robert Wild's panegyric of a decade later is also consistent with the classical derivation of the term: *A Panegyrick to the King's Majesty . . . on his auspicious meeting of his two Houses of Parliament, February 4ᵗʰ– 5ᵗʰ, 1672*. Right to the end of the seventeenth century, in fact, we find poem titles that closely resemble the titles of Daniel and Jonson written a hundred years earlier. In 1697, for example, an anonymous writer celebrated William III in *A Panegyrick on His most excellent Majesty King William III. Occasioned by the happy conclusion of the general peace, September the 20ᵗʰ, 1697*.

During the later Stuart period, however, we find more and more titles that lack one or another of the identifying characteristics of classical panegyric. Although Charles Cotton's *A Panegyric to the King's most excellent Majesty* (1660) celebrates the Restoration, the ceremonial occasion is omitted from the title. Other titles (including the anonymous panegyric "on" William III mentioned above) give no indication of the oratorical origins of the genre, as increasingly we find panegyrics "on . . ." rather than panegyrics "to . . .," like Elkanah Settle's *A Panegyrick on the loyal and Honourable Sir George Jefferies* (1683). In still other titles, praise of the king is replaced by praise of those who only barely qualify as "great persons," as in *A Panegyric upon Nelly* (1681), formerly attributed to Rochester. Perhaps the prize title of the period, however, belongs to one Samuel Austin, who reveals a unique combination of knowledge and ignorance of the classical tradition: *A panegyrick on His Sacred Majesties royal person, Charles IId, by the grace of God, king of England, Scotland, France, and Ireland, defender of the faith, etc., and coronation* (1661). This clumsy attempt to combine the occasional and courtly dimensions of panegyric, while entirely ignoring its oratorical mode, indicates a waning awareness of the precise classical significance of the term. In short, a gap appears during the later Stuart period between *panegyricus* and "panegyric."

Gradually losing its original significance, "panegyric" acquires a general meaning and a pejorative connotation that eventually make it an unsuitable designation for a serious poem. Indeed, in the early eighteenth century the term virtually disappears as a generic title for an important or serious poem. Certainly no poet of stature equal to Jonson or Dryden, or even Waller for that matter, now cared to label a serious poem as a "panegyric." Even the

laureate poets neglect or disdain the term. William White-
head, the most prolific of the eighteenth-century laure-
ates, wrote some fifty poems on state occasions, none of
them titled "panegyric." Thomas Warton, perhaps the
most talented of these poets, wrote only one "panegyric,"
A Panegyric on Oxford Ale (1750). As this title suggests,
"panegyric" is appropriated in the eighteenth century for
a variety of new and usually comic, ironic, or satiric purposes. Warton's poem could be placed in a list including
such poems as *A Panegyric upon that familiar animal by
the vulgar called a louse* (1707), *A Panegyric upon Silence*
(1709), *A Panegyric on Cuckoldum* (1732), *A panegyric
upon riddles* (1742), and *A Panegyric on Cork Rumps*
(1777).[23] By the end of the Stuart period, the term "panegyric" has been domesticated as an English word with its
own cluster of overtones, with its own characteristic uses.

Once the "valuation" of "panegyric" has thus changed
from gold to copper, as Nashe had accidentally predicted,
the term means: exaggerated praise of almost anyone or
anything. Moreover, it is used consistently as a term of
ridicule or opprobrium. This is strikingly evident in the
prose of the eighteenth century. For example, in 1711
Steele light-heartedly uses the term to ridicule book
dedications.

In these Cases, the Praise on the one Hand and the Patronage
on the other, are equally the Objects of Ridicule. . . . Panegy-

23. These titles all appear on the list of paradoxical encomia
provided by Henry Knight Miller, "The Paradoxical Encomium
with Special Reference to Its Vogue in England, 1600–1800," *MP*,
LIII (1956), 145–178. For further discussion, see below under
"Critical Definition," and for consideration of this problem in a
different context, see Alexander H. Sackton, "The Paradoxical Encomium in Elizabethan Drama," *TSE*, xxviii (1949), 83–104.

rick generally implies no more than if the Author should say to the Patron, My very good Lord, You and I can never understand one another, therefore I humbly desire we may be intimate Friends for the future.[24]

Although Steele generalizes the term, equating "Panegyrick" with "Praise," he at least preserves the original idea of direct address to some "great person," in this case a prospective patron. Later in the century this vestige of the classical tradition is lost, and the term comes to include even self-praise. Thus, in 1748 Lord Chesterfield cautions his son:

If you are intent upon your own subject, neither envy, indignation, nor ridicule will obstruct or allay the applause which you may really deserve; but if you publish your own panegyric, upon any occasion, or in any shape whatsoever, and however artfully dressed or disguised, they will all conspire against you, and you will be disappointed of the very end you aim at.[25]

Less seriously, Goldsmith in 1762 complains to the readers of *The Citizen of the World* about "this season of panegyric, when scarce an author passes unpraised either by his friends or himself."[26] Three years later Johnson uses the term with equal generality and even greater disdain in his cutting reference to Theobald's victories over

24. Richard Steele, "Spectator 188," *The Spectator*, ed. Donald F. Bond, 5 vols. (Oxford, 1965), II, 240.

25. Philip Dormer Stanhope, Fourth Earl of Chesterfield, "Letter 1598 To His Son (Stanhope CLXVI)," *The Letters of Philip Dormer Stanhope, Fourth Earl of Chesterfield*, ed. Bonamy Dobrée, 6 vols. (London, 1932), IV, 1248.

26. Oliver Goldsmith, "The Editor's Preface to *Letters From a Citizen of the World To His Friend in the East*," in *Collected Works of Oliver Goldsmith*, ed. Arthur Friedman, 5 vols. (Oxford, 1966), II, 14.

previous editors of Shakespeare: "I have sometimes
adopted his restoration of a comma, without inserting
the panegyrick in which he celebrated himself for his
atchievement."[27] This general trend is summed up by
Puff in Sheridan's play *The Critic* (1779). In his first appearance on stage, Puff announces his profession: "I
make no secret of the trade I follow—among friends and
brother authors . . . I am, Sir, a Practitioner in Panegyric,
or to speak more plainly—a Professor of the Art of
Puffing . . ."[28]

Given this contemporary pattern of usage, it is no
wonder that Reynolds declined to give a "panegyric" on
Gainsborough in 1788, commenting: "It is not our busi-
ness here, to make panegyricks on the living, or even on
the dead who were of our body. The praise of the former
might bear the appearance of adulation; and the latter,
of untimely justice . . ."[29] Boswell, in his introductory
remarks to the *Life of Johnson*, makes a similar declaration: "And he will be seen as he really was; for I profess
to write, not his panegyrick, which must be all praise,
but his Life; which, great and good as he was, must not
be supposed to be entirely perfect."[30] Both Reynolds
and Boswell, typically, use "panegyric" as a pejorative
and elaborate synonym for "praise." It is essentially this

27. Samuel Johnson, "Preface to Shakespeare," *Johnson on
Shakespeare*, ed. Arthur Sherbo, the *Yale Edition of the Works of
Samuel Johnson*, 9 vols. to date (New Haven, 1958–), VII, 96.

28. Richard Sheridan, *The Critic, or A Tragedy Rehearsed*, act
1, scene 2, *The Dramatic Works of Richard Brinsley Sheridan*, ed.
Cecil Price, 2 vols. (Oxford, 1973), II, 511.

29. Joshua Reynolds, "Discourse XIV," *Discourses on Art*, ed.
Robert R. Wark (San Marino, Cal., 1959), pp. 247–248.

30. James Boswell, *The Life of Samuel Johnson*, ed. G. B. Hill,
rev. L. F. Powell, 6 vols. (Oxford, 1934), I, 30.

general and negative conception of the term that has survived into the twentieth century.

To summarize, the seventeenth-century distinction between "panegyric" and "encomium" disappears in the eighteenth century. Johnson authoritatively confirms contemporary usage when, in 1755, he defines "panegyric" as "An eulogy, an encomiastick piece." The interchangeability of the two terms is even more obvious in his definition of "encomium" as "Panegyrick, praise; elogy."[31] Johnson's definition of "panegyric," which is much closer to Webster's than to Blount's or Kersey's, reflects the general meaning of the word current in the eighteenth century. In fact, Johnson almost seems to echo Fielding's association of "panegyric" and "encomium" in an early passage of *Tom Jones*. When Dr. Blifil is attempting to deceive Squire Allworthy, Fielding tells us: "He then launched forth into a panegyric on Allworthy's goodness; into the highest encomiums on his friendship . . ."[32] This equation between "panegyric" and "encomium," implicit in the best prose of the eighteenth century, explicit in Fielding, and sanctioned by the authority of Johnson, extends to our own day.

Before attempting to place Dryden against the historical background of panegyric, we first need to supplement the evolving dictionary definition of "panegyric" as a word with the evolving critical definition of panegyric as a literary genre.

31. Samuel Johnson, *A Dictionary of the English Language*, 2 vols. (London, 1755).

32. Henry Fielding, *The History of Tom Jones, A Foundling*, book 1, chap. 12, *The Works of Henry Fielding*, ed. William Ernest Henley, 12 vols. (New York, 1903), III, 58.

CRITICAL DEFINITION

During the Renaissance the classical tradition of panegyric attracted a body of critical commentary, not large
but nevertheless influential. The general direction of this
criticism is indicated by the Warwick recorder, who completes his definition of *panegyricae* by outlining the purpose of this kind of oratory.

. . . and because the [orations] were made in publike places
and open assemblies of senators and counsaillors, they were
callid both in Greek and Latyn *panegyricae*. In thies were sett
fourth the commendacions of Kings and Emperors, with the
sweet sound whereof, as the ears of evil Prynces were de-
lightid by hearing there undeservid praises, so were good
Princes by the plesaunt remembrance of their knowen and true
vertues made better, being put in mynde of their office and
government.[33]

Elizabeth responded to these words when she answered
her subject: "It was told me that youe would be fraid to
look upon me, or to speak boldly; but you were not so
afraid of me as I was of youe; and I now thank you for
putting me in mynd of my duety, and that should be in
me."[34] The recorder's speech and the queen's response
suggest that the Renaissance found a serious purpose behind panegyric: instruction of the monarch.

Perhaps the most cogent of didactic appreciations of
panegyric was written early in the sixteenth century by
Erasmus. Engaged to compose a panegyric to Philip of
Burgundy, Erasmus fortified himself in his labor by re-

33. *The Progresses . . . of Queen Elizabeth*, I, 311.
34. *The Progresses . . . of Queen Elizabeth*, I, 315–316. Elizabeth's response is cited and emphasized by both Talbert, p. 457,
and Chernaik, p. 134.

calling ancient examples. In a letter to the official orator of the University of Louvain, Erasmus writes:

Those persons who think Panegyrics are nothing but flattery, appear not to know with what design this kind of writing was invented by men of great sagacity, whose object it was, that by having the image of virtue put before them, bad princes might be made better, the good encouraged, the ignorant instructed, the mistaken set right, the wavering quickened, and even the abandoned brought to some sense of shame. Is it to be supposed that such a philosopher as Callisthenes, when he spoke in praise of Alexander, or that Lysias and Isocrates, or Pliny and innumerable others, when they were engaged in this kind of composition, had any other aim but that of exhorting to virtue under pretext of praise?[35]

Erasmus, somewhat uncomfortable in the role of panegyrist, sets up two lines of defense against the charge of flattery: (1) panegyric presents an "image of virtue," not simply praise, and (2) panegyric has been written by respectable men and therefore must itself be respectable. Among these "men of great sagacity," Pliny stands out, for later in the same letter Erasmus mentions the panegyric to Trajan explicitly. And yet the name of Isocrates is the most revealing addition to this list. As Isocrates' *Panegyrikos* does not include celebration of a prince, Erasmus must also have another oration in mind. Possibly he is alluding to the *Philip,* where Isocrates transposes material from the *Panegyrikos,* thus shifting responsibility for national reconciliation to the shoulders of the prince he is praising, Philip of Macedon. More likely, however, Erasmus has in mind *To Nicocles.* At least external evidence points toward this particular model.

35. Erasmus, "Epistle 177," *The Epistles of Erasmus,* trans. Francis Morgan Nichols, 3 vols. (London, 1901), I, 366.

Erasmus's *Panegyricus,* presented to Archduke Philip of Burgundy on the sixth of January 1504, and published shortly thereafter, was not immediately forgotten, at least not by its author. References to the work occur periodically in subsequent correspondence, and in 1516 he appended the *Panegyricus* to the first edition of the *Institutio Principis Christiani.* The preface to this volume, moreover, is his own Latin translation of an extract from Isocrates' *To Nicocles.* This oration, a compendium of advice concerning a ruler's obligations to his subjects, is a perfect companion (as well as model) for Erasmus's own tract on the education of the prince. The inclusion of the *Panegyricus* in the same volume implies that Erasmus considered it also to have educational value. The republication of the panegyric a dozen years after the occasion for which it was written, in a volume that includes two tracts on royal education, is strong circumstantial evidence that Erasmus meant what he said when he defined the function of panegyric as "exhorting to virtue under pretext of praise."

The close connection between panegyric and the Renaissance tract on royal education can also be demonstrated by reference to interpretations of Claudian. In the first chapter of the second book of Sir Thomas Elyot's *The Book named The Governour* (1531), where the author discusses the works necessary for a prince to read and "premeditate," we find a translation from "the verses of Claudian, the noble poet, which he wrote to Theodosius and Honorius, emperors of Rome."[36] Elyot proposes that

36. Thomas Elyot, *The Book named The Governour,* book 2, chap. 1, ed. S. E. Lehmberg, Everyman's Library Edition (New York and London, 1962), p. 98. This passage is cited and briefly dis-

the prince read selections from Claudian's panegyrics every day.

These verses of Claudian, full of excellent wisdom, as I have said, would be in a table, in such a place as a governor once in a day may behold them, specially as they be expressed in Latin by the said poet, unto whose eloquence no translation in English may be equivalent. But yet were it better to con them by heart . . . [37]

Elyot's advice is later affirmed by none other than James VI (and I), who also quotes from Claudian in *Basilikon Doron* (1599), urging his son Prince Henry to follow the precepts of the *Panegyricus De Quarto Consulatu Honorii Augusti*. When James himself came to the English throne four years later, he rode to his coronation through an arch inscribed with a citation from this very poem, meaning (according to Ben Jonson) that "no watch or guard could be so safe to the estate, or person of a Prince, as the love and natural affection of his subjects . . ."[38] Underlying this citation (one of several extracts from Claudian appropriated for this occasion) is the traditional ideal of national reconciliation, here defined as harmony between the prince and the people.

As the above *sententia* from Claudian implies, pane-

---

cussed by Alan Cameron, *Claudian: Poetry and Propaganda at the Court of Honorius* (Oxford, 1970), p. 433.

37. Elyot, book 2, chap. 1.

38. Ben Jonson, *Part of the Kings entertainment in passing to his coronation*, in *Ben Jonson*, ed. C. H. Herford and Percy and Evelyn Simpson, 11 vols. (Oxford, 1941), VII, 89. For a contemporary account of the event, see Stephen Harrison, *The Archs of Triumph* (London, 1604). For a brief note on the particular citations from Claudian, see Cameron, p. 434.

gyric is addressed not only to the monarch, but also to his subjects. Renaissance commentators saw in classical panegyric admonitions to the people as well as instructions to the prince. This second, but obviously complementary, purpose of the genre emerges most clearly from interpretations of Pliny. The panegyric to Trajan, which went through numerous Latin editions during the Renaissance, was twice translated into English during the seventeenth century, first by Robert Stapylton in 1644 and then by White Kennet in 1686. Kennet introduced his version with a lengthy critical preface which demonstrates the durability of didactic interpretation, while emphasizing the function of panegyric as an address to the people.

As the date of his translation suggests, Kennet undertook the project with the accession of James II in mind. He devotes a significant part of the preface to declaring, first, a historical parallel between James and Trajan, and second, his dismay and surprise that his contemporaries have not come forward with Plinyesque celebrations of their new prince. He attributes this failure to the fear of being accused of "flattery." "Silence on this subject, where there may be so many temptations to be eloquent, can upon that caution onely be accounted for. However, what we dare not imitate, we may at least rehearse: And may apply a translation where we must not venture at a like Original."[39] As Kennet proceeds to explain the significance of panegyric, we begin to see more clearly why he troubled to translate Pliny's speech at this particular time.

39. White Kennet, trans., *An Address of Thanks To a Good Prince Presented in the Panegyrick of Pliny upon Trajan, The Best of the Roman Emperors* (London, 1686), p. vi.

Since it is an impulse of Nature to celebrate that goodness by which we are influenced, and an universal instinct disposes to extoll our Benefactours; since too the infinite obligations of providence have now made subjection our happiness, as much as Religion has always assign'd our duty, and we have a Monarch so indulging, that our onely yoke is a pressure of inability to raise him a deserved commendation: It is obvious to reflect on this gratulatory Speech of *Pliny,* and to conclude that nothing pen'd at so wide a distance comes so nearly up for an application to our times.[40]

Here the emphasis is not on the obligations of the prince, but on the duties of the subject. Kennet's translation of Pliny is his panegyric to James II, and its primary purpose is to solicit the allegiance of the people to this new Trajan. In his conclusion, Kennet expresses this purpose unequivocally.

And now I ask the Reader no other mercy, but that when he has run through this Character of a *Roman Emperour,* he would bless the Divine Providence for living under the protection of a more *Gratious Monarch,* who wants nothing but the united Allegiance of his Subjects to make him happier than Augustus, since Heaven's and his own goodness have already made him even Better than Trajan.[41]

Whether James will actually be "Happier than Augustus" thus depends on the public audience of the panegyric.

Whether James will actually prove to be another Trajan, however, depends only on the king himself. Although Kennet directs his interpretive preface primarily to the people, he does not neglect the traditional advice to the

40. Kennet, p. v. It is incidentally amusing and slightly ironic to notice Kennet refer to James as a "Monarch so indulging," in light of the famous Declaration of Indulgence issued in 1687.

41. Kennet, p. xx.

prince. He describes the didactic "intent" of Pliny's panegyric in such a way that James could hardly miss the point.

The intent of [the panegyric] . . . was first a deserv'd commendation of the good Trajan, and then the offer of a kind of winning Lecture to future Princes, (not by way of assertory instructions, which he was sensible would have look'd saucy and pedantick) by recommending the best of Precedents to insinuate upon their imitation, which had a more taking resemblance of modesty, and promis'd a stronger influence.[42]

Whatever Pliny's intention in the original address to Trajan, Kennet's intention is quite evidently to use the translation as a means of instructing James. The phrase, "winning Lecture to future Princes," explains to the king how he should interpret Pliny's idealization of Trajan. Thus, by directing the responses of both the prince and the people, Kennet attempts to achieve domestic peace and national unity. In effect, he attempts to accomplish the traditional purpose of the Greek *panegyrikos* by translating a Roman *panegyricus*.

From the early sixteenth century to the end of the seventeenth, general discussion of panegyric as a literary genre is derived from commentary on particular classical authors, above all Isocrates, Pliny, and Claudian. The influence of these three ancient writers extends to Dryden and is reflected in his criticism. Toward the conclusion of his well-known discussion of Vergil and Ovid in the preface to the *Sylvae*, Dryden compares the latter poet with Claudian.

42. Kennet, p. vii.

Ovid and Claudian, though they write in styles differing from each other, yet have each of them but one sort of music in their verses. All the versification and little variety of Claudian is included within the compass of four or five lines, and then he begins again the same tenor; perpetually closing his sense at the end of a verse . . .[43]

The reference to Claudian is slighting, to be sure, but the remarkable fact is that Dryden mentions him at all, as his criticism of Latin literature is concentrated on the golden and silver ages. Justifying his own poetry by comparison with the great Augustan poets, Vergil above all, Dryden had little need to invoke the relatively obscure name of Claudian. As this reference indicates, however, it is entirely probable, if not certain, that Dryden had read Claudian's panegyrics. It has been fifty years since Mark Van Doren first suggested similarities between Claudian and Dryden, and yet, to my knowledge, no one has ever pursued the idea. Van Doren wrote: "The last great Roman poet, Claudian, was a professional panegyrist; his verses in praise of Honorius and Stilicho . . . look forward to the poetry of Dryden in respect to their fertility, ingenuity, and general temper."[44] Whether or not Claudian directly influenced Dryden, the two poets are at least indirectly linked (as Van Doren implies) by the tradition of panegyric.

43. John Dryden, "Preface to *Sylvae: or, the Second Part of Poetical Miscellanies*," in *John Dryden: Of Dramatic Poesy and Other Critical Essays*, ed. George Watson, 2 vols. (New York, 1962), II, 21–22. Unless otherwise specified, all citations from Dryden's criticism are repeated from this edition and noted as *Essays*.

44. Mark Van Doren, *John Dryden: A Study of His Poetry* (Bloomington, Indiana, 1946), p. 109. Originally published as *The Poetry of John Dryden* (New York, 1920).

That Dryden was conscious of this tradition is quite emphatically demonstrated in the critical dedication to *Eleonora*, which he subtitled a "panegyrical poem."

And on all occasions of praise, if we take the Ancients for our patterns, we are bound by prescription to employ the magnificence of words, and the force of figures, to adorn the sublimity of thoughts. Isocrates amongst the Grecian orators, and Cicero, and the younger Pliny, amongst the Romans, have left us their precedents for our security . . . [45]

Although Dryden emphasizes style rather than purpose, his list recalls the very similar one penned by Erasmus almost two centuries earlier. The addition of Cicero's name (probably a reference to an oration like the *Pro Marcello*) only confirms Dryden's recognition of the oratorical origins of the genre. But Dryden extends his list of "patterns" by alluding to a fellow poet, not Claudian in this instance, but Pindar. "I think I need not mention the inimitable Pindar who stretches on these pinions out of sight, and is carried upward, as it were, into another world."[46] Although Dryden's allusion almost certainly owes something to the seventeenth-century revival of the "Pindaric" ode, his identification of Pindar with the tradition of panegyric is, for its time, still unusual. Before Dryden, criticism of panegyric emphasizes its oratorical mode, illustrated most often by the Roman example of Pliny. Dryden, by coupling Pliny and Pindar in his list of models for panegyric, suggests a broader notion of the genre, one that unites the Greek ode with Roman oratory.

Because Pindar's odes celebrate men as heroes rather

45. "Dedicatory letter prefixed to *Eleonora*," *Essays*, II, 61.
46. "Dedicatory letter prefixed to *Eleonora*," *Essays*, II, 61.

than as rulers, Dryden's allusion also contains the implication that panegyric too is a heroic genre. In fact, years earlier Dryden had explicitly acknowledged his heroic conception of the genre by linking panegyric and epic. Attempting to find a generic niche for *Annus Mirabilis*, Dryden observes that the "same images serve equally for the epic poesy, and for the historic and panegyric, which are branches of it . . ."[47] The inclusion of panegyric in this comparison is an important, if cryptic, piece of criticism. It is important because it places a traditionally oratorical genre within the highest genre of poetry, cryptic because Dryden offers no explanation that would justify such a lofty comparison.[48] The context does indicate, however, that the main point of comparison is in the "images." By this Dryden seems to mean the portrayal (or image) of the hero, for he goes on to speak of two types of heroic image: (1) "heroes drawn in their triumphal chariots, and in their full proportion," and (2) "others [in which] . . . there is somewhat more of softness and tenderness to be shown . . ."[49] In either case, Dryden concludes that the purpose of heroic "images" is to "beget admiration," in contrast to the images of the burlesque mode, which "beget laughter." Panegyric, then, like epic, will inspire the reader's admiration.

47. "An account of the ensuing Poem, in a Letter to the Honorable, Sir Robert Howard," *Essays*, I, 101.

48. Earl Miner has recognized the importance of this critical comment, although he does not explore its theoretical basis. Earl Miner, *Dryden's Poetry* (Bloomington, Indiana and London, 1967), p. 8. See also Professor Miner's introduction to *Selected Poetry and Prose of John Dryden*, Modern Library College Edition (New York, 1969), p. xxvi.

49. "An account of the ensuing Poem," *Essays*, I, 101.

But admiration, as seventeenth- (and eighteenth-) century writers were quick to point out, may be tinged with envy. Sir William Davenant, for example, saw this as a particular problem in shaping his idea of *Gondibert*.

I was likewise more willing to derive my Theme from elder times, as thinking it no little mark of skilfulness to comply with the common Infirmity; for men, even of the best education, discover their eyes to be weak when they look upon the glory of Vertue, which is great actions, and rather endure it at distance then neer, being more apt to beleeve and love the renown of Predecessors then of Contemporaries, whose deeds, excelling theirs in their own sight, seem to upbraid them, and are not reverenc'd as examples of Vertue, but envy'd as the favours of Fortune.[50]

Although Davenant finds this distinction between past and present a necessary one, if the reader's admiration is not to degenerate into envy, he goes on to point out an important connection between past heroes and contemporary princes. "Princes and Nobles, being reform'd and made Angelicall by the Heroick, will be predominant lights, which the people cannot chuse but use for direction, as Gloworms take in and keep the Suns beams till they shine and make day to themselves."[51] Here, then, is a dual theory of admiration: princes admire and emulate the epic hero and thus become worthy of such admiration themselves. In this account of epic theory Davenant approaches Erasmus's defense of panegyric,

50. William Davenant, "Preface to *Gondibert, An Heroick Poem*," *Critical Essays of the Seventeenth Century*, ed. J. E. Spingarn, 3 vols. (Oxford, 1908), II, 11.

51. Davenant, "Preface to *Gondibert*," Spingarn, II, 45. This passage is cited by Ruth Nevo, *The Dial of Virtue: A Study of Poems on Affairs of State in the Seventeenth Century* (Princeton, 1963), pp. 28–29.

the main difference being that the "Theme" of epic comes from "elder times," whereas panegyric is concerned directly with the present.

Thomas Hobbes takes for granted this connection between ancient heroes and contemporary royalty in his answer to Davenant's preface. "For there is in Princes and men of conspicuous power, anciently called *Heroes*, a lustre and influence upon the rest of men resembling that of the Heavens . . ."[52] Whereas Davenant sees in the epic hero a model for the modern prince, Hobbes looks at the modern prince and sees an ancient hero. Hobbes derives his view from his familiar geographical scheme of poetic genres. Court, city, and country all have their appropriate "kinds" of poetry: heroic, satiric, and pastoral, respectively. Heroic poetry, the poetry associated with the court, would naturally include panegyric as one of its "branches." When Dryden calls panegyric a "branch" of epic, he perceives and acknowledges the fundamental similarity between contemporary criticism of epic and contemporary criticism of panegyric.

When Dryden speculated about his own proposed epic of Arthurian or Plantagenet Britain, he stated plainly that the leaders of his own day would be honored in the poem. Indeed, it was partly on this basis that he sought patronage for the project. Addressing the Earl of Mulgrave, he writes: "Your Lordship has been long acquainted with my design, the subject of which you know is great, the story English, and neither too far distant from the present age, nor too near approaching it. Such it is, in my opinion, that I could not have wished a nobler

52. Thomas Hobbes, "Answer to Davenant's Preface to *Gondibert*," Spingarn, II, 55.

occasion to do honor by it to my king, my country, and
my friends; most of our ancient nobility being concerned
in the action."[53] Dryden thus conceived of his epic in
Vergilian-Spenserian terms, as presenting an analogy between past and present. An epic about an ancient king
and nobility would also be an epic about a contemporary
king and nobility. As Dryden never wrote the epic, his
panegyrics to "men of conspicuous power" (to borrow
Hobbes's phrase) assume a special importance in his
career as a partial substitute for the great poem he long
aspired to write.

Although regrettably terse, Dryden's criticism of panegyric describes a more complex and more significant genre
than previous critics would have led us to expect. By
invoking Isocrates and Pliny, Dryden places his criticism
of panegyric in the Renaissance tradition initiated by
Erasmus. By placing panegyric in the same constellation
of genres as the Pindaric ode and the epic, he dignifies
the genre as a kind of heroic poetry. This implicit accommodation between classical oratory and classical
poetry is, however, shadowed by a recognition that it is
"difficult to write justly on any thing, but almost impossible in praise."[54] In the preface to *The Spanish Friar*
(1681), Dryden even remarks indignantly on "the stale,
exploded trick of fulsome panegyrics" which are not
"worthy of a noble mind."[55] Although it is possible to
dismiss this remark as a device Dryden uses to free him-

53. "To John, Earl of Mulgrave" [Dedicatory Epistle to *Aureng-
Zebe*], *Essays*, I, 191.

54. "To the Right Honourable John, Lord Haughton" [Dedi-
catory Epistle to *The Spanish Friar*], *Essays*, I, 279.

55. "To . . . Lord Haughton," *Essays*, I, 279.

self from the customary tributes required in dedications (thus allowing him to write a critical preface instead), it clearly forecasts eighteenth-century criticism of the genre. From the time of Erasmus to the time of Dryden, appeals to classical authority and precedent prevail over the persistent charge of flattery, but in the eighteenth century a rapid reversal takes place and criticism of the genre becomes universally an opportunity for ridicule.

From this chorus of voices speaking against panegyric we can distinguish those of Swift, in *A Tale of a Tub*, and Pope, in *The Dunciad Variorum*. Starting from the assumption that panegyric is mere flattery, "Bundles of Flattery," in fact, Swift makes two important observations: (1) that panegyric is difficult to write and dull to read, and (2) that it is never well received by the general public. The difficulty and dullness of the genre are due to the lack of variety found in the form.

For, the Materials of Panegyrick being very few in Number, have been long since exhausted: For, as Health is but one Thing, and has been always the same, whereas Diseases are by thousands, besides new and daily Additions; So, all the Virtues that have been ever in Mankind, are to be counted upon a few Fingers, but his Follies and Vices are innumerable, and Time adds hourly to the Heap. Now, the utmost a poor Poet can do, is to get by heart a List of the Cardinal Virtues, and deal them with his utmost Liberality to his Hero or his Patron.[56]

The cool public reception Swift, echoing Davenant, attributes to envy.

56. Jonathan Swift, *A Tale of a Tub To which is added The Battle of the Books and the Mechanical Operation of the Spirit*, ed. A. C. Guthkelch and D. Nichol Smith, 2d ed. (Oxford, 1958), pp. 49–50.

BUT, tho' the Matter for Panegyrick were as fruitful as the Topicks of Satyr, yet would it not be hard to find out a sufficient Reason, why the latter will be always better received than the first. For, this being bestowed only upon one or a few Persons at a time, is sure to raise Envy, and consequently ill words from the rest, who have no share in the Blessing.[57]

Extending Swift's conception of the genre as dull flattery, Pope makes Elkanah Settle the prince of dullness precisely because he wrote panegyrics.

Settle was alive at this time, and Poet to the City of *London*. His office was to compose yearly panegyricks upon the Lord Mayors, and Verses to be spoken in the Pageants: But that part of the shows being by the frugality of some Lord Mayors at length abolished, the employment of City Poet ceas'd; so that upon *Settle's* demise, there was no successor to that place. This important point of time our Poet has chosen, as the Crisis of the Kingdom of *Dulness* . . . [58]

In the eighteenth century to write panegyrics is, almost by definition, to be acclaimed a dull author.

The most significant criticism of panegyric in the eighteenth century, however, was written between the time of Swift's tale and Pope's epic. In the second edition of his *Characteristics* (1714), the third Earl of Shaftesbury discusses the problems of the genre in some detail.

Our ENCOMIUM or PANEGYRICK is as fulsome and displeasing; by its prostitute and abandon'd manner of Praise. The worthy Persons who are the Subjects of it, may well be esteem'd Sufferers by the Manner. And the Publick, whether it will or

57. Swift, *A Tale of a Tub*, Guthkelch and Smith, p. 50.
58. Alexander Pope, *The Dunciad Variorum*, note to book 1, line 88, *The Dunciad*, ed. James Sutherland, 3rd ed. rev. (New Haven and London, 1963), in the Twickenham Edition of Pope's *Poetical Works*, V, 69.

no, is forc'd to make untoward Reflections, when led to it by such *Satirizing Panegyrists*. For in reality the Nerve and Sinew of modern *Panegyrick* lies in a dull kind of Satire; which the Author, it's true, intends shou'd turn to the advantage of his Subject; but which, if I mistake not, will appear to have a very contrary Effect.[59]

By equating "encomium" and "panegyric," by implicitly distinguishing "modern *Panegyrick*" from ancient panegyric, Shaftesbury places his criticism in the immediate context of contemporary literature. Instead of conjuring up ancient examples to justify the practice of writers like Settle, Shaftesbury concentrates on the actual "Effect" of reading such modern verse, with the result that panegyric is perceived as a form of satire. When the author intends praise, "a dull kind of Satire" emerges. When, we might add, the author does not intend praise, the formulas of panegyric can provide a framework for a very sharp kind of satire.[60]

There is of course nothing new about ironic or paradoxical praise. As Henry K. Miller's study of the subject has shown, the tradition is an ancient one and even includes works by authors of serious panegyrics. But Isocrates did not call his ironic praise of Helen a "panegyric" and Erasmus, who celebrates Philip of Burgundy in a "panegyric," praises folly in an "encomium." Moreover, Miller's list of English paradoxical encomia from 1600 to

59. Anthony Ashley Cooper, Third Earl of Shaftesbury, *Characteristicks of Men, Manners, Opinions, Times*, 2d ed. (London, 1714), I, 226. This passage is cited and discussed by Aubrey Williams, *Pope's Dunciad: A Study of Its Meaning* (New York, 1968), p. 13. Originally published under the same title in 1955.

60. Williams makes this point very nicely with special reference to Pope; Williams, pp. 12–13.

1800 includes no work titled "panegyric" before 1660, only four from 1660 to 1700, and twelve from 1700 to 1800. Although this list is not exhaustive, it is indicative of the trend. The term "panegyric" is not only generalized in the eighteenth century to mean the equivalent of "encomium," it also comes generically to imply its opposite, satire. It is this paradoxical conception of the genre that motivates Swift to propose *A Panegyrical Essay upon the Number THREE* and *A Panegyrick upon the World*, Gay to write *A Panegyrical Epistle to Mr. Thomas Snow, Goldsmith, near Temple-Barr,* Henry Carey to ridicule Ambrose Philips in *Namby-Pamby; or a Panegyric on the new versification,* Pope to do the same for George II in the "Panegyric strains" of the epistle "To Augustus," and Fielding to compose "a Panegyric or rather Satire on the Passion of Love, in the sublime Style" in *Joseph Andrews.*[61] Just as Fielding's equation of "panegyric" and "encomium" in *Tom Jones* confirms the evolution of "panegyric" from a specific to a general term, so his equation of panegyric and satire in *Joseph Andrews* confirms the evolution of panegyric from a serious to a comic genre.

We can conclude this introductory chapter by tentatively placing Dryden against this evolutionary background. Dryden's career bridges the gap between the

61. See Swift, "Treatises wrote by the same Author . . . which will be speedily published," *A Tale of a Tub,* Guthkelch and Smith, p. 2; Pope, *The First Epistle of the Second Book of Horace Imitated,* line 405, *Imitations of Horace,* ed. John Butt (New Haven and London, 1939), in the Twickenham Edition of Pope's *Poetical Works,* IV, 231; Fielding, *Joseph Andrews,* book 1, chap. 7. ed. Martin C. Battestin (Middletown, Conn., 1967), in the *Wesleyan Edition of The Works of Henry Fielding,* p. 34.

serious Renaissance appreciation of panegyric and its comic inversion in the eighteenth century. Consideration of Dryden and the tradition of panegyric will put us in touch not only with the genre he most wanted to write, epic, but also with the genre he actually did write with most success, satire. To understand Dryden's own unique accommodation of panegyric, epic, and satire, however, we must first establish with greater care the classical heritage of panegyric, defined as: an oration addressed to a monarch, or other figure of "conspicuous power," on a public, ceremonial occasion.

2: Backgrounds

IN HIS panegyric on the coronation of Charles II, John Evelyn acknowledges an apparent debt to literary theory by referring to the "laws of *Panegyric*."

[We] have received a Prince, but such a Prince, whose state and fortune in all this blessed change, we so much admire not, as his mind; For that is truly felicity, not to possesse great things, but to be thought worthy of them: And indeed Great Sir, necessity constrains me, and the laws of *Panegyric*, to verifie it in your Praises, by running over at least those other Appellations, which both your vertue has given to your Majesty, and your Fortune acquir'd. For he is really no King who possesses not (like you) a Kingly mind be his other advantages what they may . . . [1]

Although Renaissance commentators from Erasmus to Dryden provide a convincing defense of panegyric, they do not prescribe any "laws" governing the genre. To outline the "laws of *Panegyric*" alluded to by Evelyn, we

1. John Evelyn, *A Panegyric to Charles the Second. Presented to His Majesty On the Day of His Inauguration* (London, 1661), pp. 8–9. I have used the facsimile reprint in the Augustan Reprint series, no. 28 (Los Angeles, 1951).

must turn first to the rhetoric books, then to the tradition of panegyrical oratory, and finally to the derivative tradition of panegyrical poetry.

RHETORIC

In the passage cited above, Evelyn elaborates a distinction between praise of virtue and praise of fortune. The source of this distinction is probably Aristotle. In the *Rhetoric*, Aristotle distinguishes between the honor derived from external circumstances and the happiness that comes from the habit of virtue.[2] Cicero expresses a similar idea in the *De Inventione*. "[It] is foolish to praise one's good fortune and arrogant to censure it, but praise of a man's mind is honourable and censure of it very effective." Years later, in the *De Oratore* Cicero lends a prescriptive emphasis to this idea when he observes that the orator engaged in praise may begin by mentioning the favors of fortune, but should conclude by commending the proper use of those favors.[3] These related statements, which lie very close to the surface of Evelyn's panegyric, belong to the theory of demonstrative oratory. Evelyn advertises his debt to this branch of rhetoric when he later pauses to recollect "all partitions of the Demonstrative."[4] Evelyn evidently saw a connection between the

2. Aristotle, *Rhetoric*, book 1, chap. 9, *Aristotle, The "Art" of Rhetoric*, trans. John Henry Freese, Loeb Classical Library (London and New York, 1926), p. 103.

3. Cicero, *De Inventione*, book 2, chap. 59, trans. H. M. Hubbell, Loeb Classical Library (Cambridge, Mass., 1960), p. 345; Cicero, *De Oratore*, book 2, chap. 85, trans. E. W. Sutton and H. Rackham, Loeb Classical Library (Cambridge, Mass., 1959), pp. 461–463.

4. Evelyn, p. 5.

"laws" of panegyric on the one hand, and the "partitions" of demonstrative oratory on the other. The first goal of this chapter is to determine as precisely as possible the nature of this connection.

According to Aristotle, who is usually cited as the authority for the division of oratory into three kinds, the demonstrative is concerned with praise and blame, its object being to assign honor or disgrace.[5] The crucial difference between demonstrative and both deliberative and judicial oratory is that in the latter kinds the audience must make a decision on the basis of what is said. The deliberative (or political) speech usually requires a decision as to the expedience of a certain policy, while the judicial (or forensic) speech demands a decision of guilty or not guilty. Because the demonstrative (or epideictic) oration makes no such demands on its audience, it is considered by Aristotle, and later by Cicero, as a display piece designed mainly to please or to entertain.

It is for this reason that Cicero disdains the third branch of oratory and refuses to discuss it with patience in any of his treatises on rhetoric. He quickly dismisses the demonstrative from his discussion in the *Orator*, for example, because these orations "were produced as showpieces . . . for the pleasure they will give, a class comprising eulogies, descriptions, histories, and exhortations like the *Panegyric* of Isocrates, and similar orations by many of the Sophists . . . and all other speeches unconnected with battles of public life."[6] For Cicero de-

5. Aristotle, *Rhetoric*, book 1, chap. 9.
6. Cicero, *Orator*, chap. II, sec. 37, trans. H. M. Hubbell, Loeb Classical Library (Cambridge, Mass., 1952), p. 333.

monstrative oratory is an alien type, suitable for the Greeks perhaps, but out of place in the Forum.

The demonstrative nevertheless occupies an important place in the later tradition of Ciceronian rhetoric. This is true partly because Cicero's name was often linked to the influential *Rhetorica ad Herennium*.[7] In this handbook the demonstrative does take a backseat to the other kinds of oratory, but it is not ignored or disdained. The author would divide this kind of speech into three parts, an *exordium, divisio,* and brief *peroratio*. He makes three "partitions" in the *divisio*: (1) external circumstances, (2) physical attributes, and (3) character. The first category includes such topics as ancestry, education, wealth, titles, and sources of power, while the second is concerned with the subject's agility, strength, beauty, and health. The third and most important part of the argument should focus on four cardinal virtues: wisdom (or prudence), fortitude, temperance, and justice. The topics thus defined in the *Rhetorica ad Herennium* are reiterated during the imperial period by Quintilian, who offers in addition two general (and more flexible) approaches to this kind of speech. One approach calls for the orator to proceed through a list of the subject's virtues, while the alternative is to allow these virtues to emerge from a chronological survey of the subject's life. To look ahead, in these two plans we have the outline for panegyric exposed by Swift and the theory of biography rejected by Boswell.[8]

7. In the Renaissance, the *Rhetorica ad Herennium* was commonly ascribed to Cicero. See Wilbur Howell, *Logic and Rhetoric in England, 1500–1700* (New York, 1961), pp. 66, 80, 108.

8. For a discussion of the shifting importance of the delibera-

If the demonstrative, at least in its positive form of praise, has fallen out of favor for serious writers by the eighteenth century, it is nevertheless very popular and important during the English Renaissance. The rhetoric books published in England between 1550 and 1650 usually devote substantially more attention to the demonstrative than they do to the deliberative.[9] This basic pattern is established by Thomas Wilson's English *Arte of Rhetorique,* published in 1553. Wilson, who does not share Cicero's contempt for the third branch, follows the *Rhetorica ad Herennium* quite closely in his discussion of the demonstrative, dividing the topics of praise into the traditional three categories, "fortune," "body," and "character."[10] Adopting Quintilian's suggestion, moreover, Wilson recommends a biographical plan of organization, which he illustrates with a speech in praise of a "noble personage."[11]

Although Wilson's focus on praise of a "noble personage" anticipates later dictionary definitions of "panegyric," Wilson does not use this term nor does he offer any details that would suggest interest in or knowledge of this particular type of speech. Later English rhetoricians, however, including Charles Butler, John Clarke, and John Newton, do list panegyric under the demonstrative heading. Although these writers apparently conceived

---

tive and demonstrative branches in the eighteenth century, see Wilbur Howell, *Eighteenth-Century British Logic and Rhetoric* (Princeton, 1971), pp. 444–445.

9. Howell, *Logic and Rhetoric in England, 1500–1700,* pp. 106–107.

10. Thomas Wilson, *The Arte of Rhetorique* (London, 1553), p. 6.

11. Wilson, pp. 14–17.

of panegyric as a subtype of demonstrative oratory, they do not bother to discuss the matter, probably because they could find no precedent for such discussion in either Cicero or Quintilian. If the "partitions" of demonstrative oratory can be adequately described from Roman sources, the "laws of *Panegyric*" must be sought elsewhere.

The theory of panegyric comes, in fact, from comparatively obscure Greek rhetorics of the second and third centuries A.D. Two such rhetorics stand out, one supposedly by Dionysius of Halicarnassus, the other by Menander of Laodicea (sometimes distinguished as Menander Rhetor). Although these two authorities often appear side by side in Renaissance discussions of panegyric, the Dionysius rhetoric was probably the more influential, at least in England.[12] This art of rhetoric, long attributed to Dionysius of Halicarnassus but now believed to have been written after his death, opens with a chapter devoted exclusively to panegyric.[13] According to this author, a panegyric is a speech designed for a festival occasion, and it has six parts: (1) an opening prayer to the god or gods most closely connected with the particular festival, (2) praise of the city where the celebration is being held, (3) further consideration of the place, its myths, its agriculture, its weather, etc., (4) discussion of the contests being held, (5) celebration and elaboration on the nature of the victor's crown by ref-

12. This inference is based primarily on the influence of the Dionysius rhetoric evident in Thomas Farnaby's *Index Rhetoricus et Oratorius*, and on the appearance of a Latin translation of the work just four years after Dryden's death. See below.

13. The text I have used is the London edition and Latin translation of 1704. *Dionysii Halicarnassensis Quae Exstant Rhetorica et Critica*, ed. and trans. John Hudson, 2 vols. (London, 1704), II.

erence to history and mythology, and (6) praise of the
king, who is the judge of the festival contests.[14] Although
essentially an outline for a Greek festival oration, this
prescription does include praise of the king.

Even so, however, Renaissance writers either discard
or radically change the Greek theory of panegyric in order
to bring it into more perfect agreement with Roman practice. Faced with the task of reconciling the theory of
festival oratory with the practice of political eulogy,
Renaissance rhetoricians nod respectfully in the direction
of Dionysius and Menander, and then establish a new
theoretical basis for panegyric by describing Pliny's address to Trajan.[15]

In England a typical example of this approach is found
in Thomas Farnaby's *Index Rhetoricus et Oratorius*
(1625.) One of the most durable and popular rhetorics
of the seventeenth century (it went through ten editions
between 1625 and 1700), the *Index Rhetoricus* includes a
useful and provocative discussion of panegyric. Farnaby
initially defers to Greek authority, incorporating the
above outline into his text and duly providing a shoulder
note which refers the reader to the Dionysius rhetoric.
Having done this much, Farnaby then abandons the outline in order to describe a different kind of panegyric,
which he distinguishes as the *panegyrica nova*.[16] The

14. For more details on this plan for a panegyric, see George
Kennedy, *The Art of Persuasion in Greece* (Princeton, 1963), p. 167;
Kennedy, *The Art of Rhetoric in the Roman World* (Princeton,
1972), pp. 634–636.

15. The best example of this approach is by Gerhard Vossius,
*Commentariorum rhetoricorum; sive, Oratoriarum institutionum.
Libri sex,* 3rd ed. (Lyon, 1630), pp. 44ff., 89–91, 409–410.

16. Thomas Farnaby, *Index Rhetoricus et Oratorius* (London,
1646), pp. 10–16. For a discussion of the importance and popularity

basic difference between these two kinds of panegyric is the relative space devoted to praise of the king. Whereas the *laus regis* is simply an appendage to the old panegyric outlined first, it is central to the new panegyric as discussed by Farnaby. Although he says nothing about praise as a form of royal education, Farnaby does insist that the *panegyrica nova* functions as an exhortation to the people, urging them to "joy, obedience, and concord."[17] In effect, Farnaby distinguishes Greek (old) and Roman (new) panegyric, and then assigns to the Roman form the Greek purpose. Like White Kennet sixty years later, Farnaby implies that the Roman form has, for all practical purposes, replaced the Greek, but one of those purposes remains national reconciliation. Something of Isocrates thus survives in the later tradition of panegyric dominated by Pliny.

By abstracting Farnaby's definition of the *panegyrica nova*, we can finally answer the question posed at the beginning of this chapter. According to the author of the *Index Rhetoricus*, the new panegyric begins with consideration of the public occasion at hand and then proceeds to praise the monarch "from the places of demonstrative [rhetoric]."[18] Here, then, is the connection, assumed by Evelyn, between the "laws" of panegyric and the "partitions" of demonstrative oratory. The demonstrative topics are used to elaborate the *laus regis*. This at least is the theory. In practice, as the tradition of panegyrical oratory reveals, the *laus regis* depends not

---

of this rhetoric, see Howell, *Logic and Rhetoric in England, 1500–1700*, pp. 280, 321–324, 335, 340.

17. Farnaby, p. 13.
18. Farnaby, p. 13.

only on the demonstrative but also on the deliberative
branch of classical rhetoric.

When Evelyn referred to the "laws" of panegyric, he
had in mind not only the "partitions" of a demonstrative
oration, but also the specific example of Pliny the Younger. "Thus what was once applyed to *Trajan,* becomes due
to your Majesty."[19] It is hardly surprising that Evelyn
should choose to model his address to Charles II on Pliny's
address to Trajan, for this speech was regarded throughout the Renaissance as the supreme model of panegyric.
From 1500 to 1700, when the topic is panegyric, Pliny's
oration is almost invariably offered as the classical para-
digm. For example, the famous Dutch scholar and rheto-
rician Gerhard Vossius, whose work was well known in
seventeenth-century England, considered Pliny's speech
"the most beautiful example" of panegyric; it behooves
us, he says, to study this panegyric carefully, for "no
other can teach us better."[20]

There were those in England who apparently agreed
with this assessment, as Pliny's oration was required
reading in some seventeenth-century English schools. We
know for certain that by mid-century the *Panegyricus*
(as it was always titled during this period) was required
of students at Rotherham school, at Merchant Taylors',
and probably at several others.[21] In 1659, therefore,

19. Evelyn, p. 7.

20. Vossius, pp. 409–410.

21. Martin L. Clarke, *Classical Education in Britain 1500–1900*
(Cambridge, 1959), pp. 38, 41.

Obadiah Walker could take familiarity with Pliny's panegyric for granted in *Some Instructions concerning the Art
of Oratory*. Discussing his choice of illustrations, he
writes: "Examples (which for the great part I have taken
out of Plinius Secundus his *Panegyrick* and *Epistles*
being an Author you are well acquainted with . . ."[22]
Those who were not acquainted with the speech were
urged to become so in Thomas Holyoke's *Large Dictionary in Three Parts* (1677). Defining the Latin word *panegyricum*, Holyoke adopts Thomas Thomas's definition
with a significant proviso.

Panegyricum. A lascivious kind of speaking, wherein men do
join in praising one, many lyes with flattery, but this was
the abuse of it, the word itself signifies no such infamous
kind of speaking. See Plinies Panegyrick to Trajan.[23]

We can follow Holyoke's advice and consider not only
Pliny's speech but also the tradition of oratory that is
founded on it.

Although Pliny develops his eulogy from the places
of demonstrative rhetoric, the speech is not organized
according to either of the patterns recommended by his
master Quintilian. Neither a biography nor a catalog of
virtues, Pliny's sometimes rambling speech is structured
by a contrast between past and present, between *prius*
. . . and *nunc* . . . . Pliny gives this temporal contrast
thematic significance by juxtaposing the irresponsibility,
effeminacy, triviality, weakness, and licentiousness of
previous emperors, and the piety, abstinence, and forti-

22. Obadiah Walker, *Some Instructions concerning the Art of
Oratory* (London, 1659), p. 19.
23. Thomas Holyoke, *Large Dictionary in Three Parts* (London,
1677).

tude of the current emperor. Translated into specific political contexts, these contrasting sets of qualities account for the administrative blunders of Domitian and Nero, on the one hand, and for Trajan's judicious administration of the army, the treasury, and the courts, on the other. In sum:

Omnia, patres conscripti, quae de aliis principibus a me aut dicuntur aut dicta sunt, eo pertinent ut ostendam, quam longa consuetudine corruptos depravatosque mores principatus parens noster reformet et corrigat. Alioqui nihil non parum grate sine comparatione laudatur. Praeterea hoc primum erga optimum imperatorem piorum civium officium est, insequi dissimiles; neque enim satis amarit bonos principes, qui malos satis non oderit.[24]

All that I say and have said, Conscript Fathers, about previous emperors is intended to show how our Father is amending and reforming the character of the principate which had become debased by a long period of corruption. Indeed, eulogy is best expressed through comparison, and, moreover, the first duty of grateful subjects towards a perfect emperor is to attack those who are least like him: for no one can properly appreciate a good prince who does not sufficiently hate a bad one.

Pliny's panegyric thus posits a bold and sweeping contrast between political good and evil, as the vicious past is superseded by the virtuous present.

The structural and thematic pattern of Pliny's panegyric is elaborated and particularized by his imitators. In the fourth century, for example, Latinus Drepanius Pacatus

24. Pliny the Younger, *Panegyricus*, sec. 53, *Pliny, Letters and Panegyricus*, trans. Betty Radice, Loeb Classical Library, 2 vols. (Cambridge, Mass., and London, 1969), II, 440–442. All translations from Pliny's panegyric are by Betty Radice.

shapes the contrast between past and present into a contrast between usurpation and restoration. In his panegyric to Theodosius, Pacatus identifies the evil past with Maximus, the usurping tyrant, and the joyous present with Theodosius, the perfect prince. The orator takes special delight in his narration of the rise and fall of the usurper. The effects of usurpation and tyranny are vividly portrayed in a passage where Maximus, dressed in the purple, is seen surveying the fruits of his (temporary) triumph:

Hic aurum matronarum manibus extractum, illic raptae pupillorum cervicibus bullae, istic dominorum cruore perfusum appendebatur argentum.[25]

Here one was weighing the gold torn from the hands of matrons, there the ornaments ripped from the necks of orphans, elsewhere the silver drenched with the blood of its owners.

No less vivid is the bloody description of the final defeat of Maximus's forces:

Datur debito rebelle agmen exitio, volvuntur impiae in sanguine suo turbae, tegit totos strages una campos continuisque funeribus cuncta late operiuntur.[26]

The army of rebellion is delivered to its due destruction, the impious battalions roll in their own blood, the whole plain disappears under a single heap of bodies and, without end, corpses cover the earth.

The contest between political good and evil is resolved, by war in this case, and political equilibrium is restored. By violating the ideals of peace, stability, and order, the

25. Latinus Drepanius Pacatus, *Panegyricus Latini Pacati Drepani Dictus Theodosio*, sec. 26, *XII Panegyrici Latini*, ed. R. A. B. Mynors (Oxford, 1964), pp. 102–103.

26. Pacatus, sec. 34.

"impious" Maximus becomes the characteristic villain of panegyrical oratory, a villain of far more dangerous proportions than either Nero or Domitian.

Renaissance imitators of Pliny preserve the basic historical pattern of the panegyric to Trajan, although they naturally vary the circumstantial details. Erasmus, who acknowledges Pliny as his master in this kind of oratory, organizes his panegyric around the absence and return of Archduke Philip, to whom the oration is addressed. As Erasmus shows in great detail, the return of the prince brings national rejuvenation: in art, in commerce, in public morality, in religion, in scholarship, even in nature. Indirectly, however, celebration of the monarch's return involves criticism of his absence; Erasmus implicitly associates Philip with the dislocated past as well as the glorious present. In one extended passage, for example, he offers a list of the prince's responsibilities, all of which Philip has shirked by voluntarily leaving the country.[27] Later in life, moreover, Erasmus used Philip's irresponsibility as a negative moral exemplum in the *Institutio Principis Christiani*.

[There] is nothing more harmful and disastrous to a country, nor more dangerous for a prince, than visits to far-away places, especially if these visits are prolonged; for it was this, according to the opinion of everyone, that took Philip from us and injured his kingdom. . . . The king bee is hedged about in the midst of the swarm and does not fly out and away. The heart is situated in the very middle of the body. Just so should a prince always be found among his own people.[28]

27. Erasmus, *Panegyricus*, in *Opera Omnia*, ed. J. LeClerc, 10 vols. (Hildesheim, 1962), IV, 548F.

28. Erasmus, *The Education of the Christian Prince*, trans. Lester K. Born (New York, 1936), p. 208. In his excellent introduction,

As the first edition of the *institutio* was followed in the same volume by the *panegyricus*, it is possible to regard this passage as a gloss on the earlier work. Instead of contrasting Philip with some Renaissance Domitian, Erasmus finds in Philip's absence a perfect foil for celebrating his return.

The flexibility of the *prius . . . nunc . . .* pattern is demonstrated in a panegyric addressed to James I in 1604, John Gordon's *England and Scotlands Happinesse . . . A Panegyrique of Congratulation for the concord of the realmes of great Brittaine, in unitie of religion under one King.* Gordon considers Elizabeth and James as ideal monarchs in contrast to the Pope, who is indicted for "usurping upon the Kings of the Western Empire."[29] James consolidates the achievement of Elizabeth, "restoring . . . the true Church" and crushing "heresie and Romish Idolatry."[30] The contrast between evil and good, past and present, is focused by Gordon's elaboration on the union of the two crowns.

The people (Sire) of the Ilands of great Brittaine, were not united in religion, in peace, in concorde, in like affections and will under one King, but they have beene long banded one agaynst an other, in a Sea of discordes, discentions, and cruell

---

Professor Born recognizes the importance of Latin panegyric in shaping Erasmus's conception of the ideal monarch. See also Lester K. Born, "The Perfect Prince According to the Latin Panegyrists," *American Journal of Philology*, IV (1934), 20–35.

29. John Gordon, *England and Scotlands Happinesse . . . A Panegyrique of Congratulation for the concord of the realmes of great Brittaine, in unitie of religion under one King* (London, 1604), p. 5. I have used the facsimile reprint in The English Experience series, no. 461 (Amsterdam, 1972).

30. Gordon, p. 47.

warres, against the decree and lawe of God. . . . But now that
the light of the Gospell, the true worshippe of one God hath
taken lively and sure roote in their hartes under the fortunate
raygne of the deceased Queene, and under your happy and
lawefull succession in these Realmes, they are become of one
heart, of one affection, and finally beeing made the true people
of God, they have obtained blessing, grace and mercie.[31]

As in Latin and neo-Latin panegyric, so now in English
panegyric, historical events are shaped into an ideal pattern of restored order, concord, and peace.

Although Evelyn claims to offer his panegyric to
Charles II "spontaneously, and by Instinct, without Arti-
fice,"[32] in actual fact he has conflated the traditional vari-
ations on the original pattern established by Pliny. Past
degeneration, usurpation, absence, and discord are suddenly and miraculously replaced in the present by regeneration, restoration, return, and concord.

Let us then call to mind (and yet for ever cursed be the
memory of it) those dismal clouds, which lately orespread us,
when we served the lusts of those immane Usurpers, greedy of
power, that themselves might be under none; Cruel, that they
might murther the Innocent without cause; Rich, with the
public poverty; strong, by putting the sword into the hands
of furies, and prosperous by unheard of perfidie. . . . But I
will not go too far in repeating the sorrowes which are van-
ish't, or uncover the buried memory of the evils past; least
whilst we strive to represent the vices of others, we seem to
contaminate your Sacred purple, or alloy our present rejoyc-
ing; since that only is sign of a perfect and consummate felicity, when even the very remembrance of evils past, is quite
forgotten.[33]

31. Gordon, pp. 3–4.   32. Evelyn, p. 3.
33. Evelyn, p. 4.

If there is anything besides circumstantial detail that distinguishes Evelyn's panegyric from those of his predecessors, it is his repeated allusion to "Providence" and divine "miracle." The contrast between prince and usurper, for example, here becomes a contrast between heavenly and earthly power. "But whilst Armies on earth fought for the Usurper, the Hosts of Heaven fought in their courses for your Majesty."[34] The return of the divinely sanctioned king is a "Miraculous Reverse" that initiates a whole new era of human history. "And let it be a new year, a new *Aera*, to all the future Generations, as it is the beginning of this, and of that immense, *Platonic* Revolution . . ."[35] In Evelyn's panegyric the traditional theme of restoration, inherited from Pliny and transmitted by panegyrists like Pacatus, Erasmus, and Gordon, assumes cosmic overtones.

If the monarch is sanctioned by divine authority, however, he is also subjected to human restraint. This aspect of traditional panegyric often called for special comment in Evelyn's day. In the preface to his translation of Pliny, for example, White Kennet struggled to reconcile his own idea of divine right with Pliny's emphatic restriction on the emperor's power. Early in the oration Pliny insists that Trajan owes his eminent position to the goodwill of the senate and the consent of the people:

audiebas senatus populique consensum: non unius Nervae iudicium illud, illa electio fuit.[36]

[You] were told that the Senate and people approved, and this choice and decision were not Nerva's alone, but the heart-felt prayer of the whole country.

34. Evelyn, p. 7.   35. Evelyn, pp. 4–5.
36. Pliny, sec. 10.

Responding to this passage, and particularly to the word *electio,* Kennet counters with criticism of Trajan.

After all, the most natural deduction, which I conceive this passage capable of, is this, that such flashes of good nature in a Prince may be of very hurtful consequence, they prostitute his honour, Alienate his Authority, and make all the rabble an execrable High Court of Justice. . . . Whereas 'tis at the best an unwary vapour, an undigested slant of popularity, to the quest whereof this Prince was too abundantly addicted . . . [37]

In the next English version of the speech, on the other hand, this passage is translated with the added emphasis of italics. "[You] had the Consent of the Senate and People: 'twas not the single Judgment of *Nerva,* but *their Election* . . ."[38] The translator, George Smith, pointedly dedicated this translation to the Electress Sophia of Hanover, then heir to the English throne occupied by Queen Anne. From their different political perspectives, both Kennet and Smith perceived the limiting force of Pliny's statement. From the time of Pliny to the time of Evelyn, the theme of restoration coexists in panegyric with the theme of limitation.

Pliny provides the basis for the development of this theme when he observes that the emperor is subject to the law:

Quod ego nunc primum audio, nunc primum disco; non est princeps super leges sed leges super principem . . . [39]

37. White Kennet, trans., *An Address of Thanks To A Good Prince Presented in the Panegyrick of Pliny upon Trajan, The Best of the Roman Emperours* (London, 1686), p. xvii.

38. George Smith, trans., *Pliny's Panegyrick Upon the Emperor Trajan,* 2d ed. (London, 1730), p. 42.

39. Pliny, sec. 65.

There is a new turn of phrase which I hear and understand for the first time—not "the prince is above the law" but "the law is above the prince."

This passage also upset Kennet, who comments that such a notion would destroy "the prime and fundamental prerogative of Princes, their being unaccountable to any but God."[40] Although earlier in his preface Kennet had derided the principle as "unheard of," he concludes by warning that it was "the very Principle our late Regicides proceeded on."[41] That Kennet could find in Pliny's panegyric anything so patently subversive as a theoretical prescription for regicide indicates a degree of complexity in this form that we might not at first have suspected. Indeed, Pliny himself raises at least the specter of regicide when he compares Trajan to Lucius Junius Brutus.[42] Following Pliny's example, Pacatus asserts that during the reign of Theodosius, even Brutus—in this case Marcus Junius Brutus—would be content with the institution of kingship.[43] Both allusions, whether to the fate of Tarquinius Superbus or to that of Julius Caesar, suggest the ultimate human restraint on kingship: assassination. Although the note of warning in these classical panegyrics is indirect and subdued, it is unmistakably present, as Kennet's reading of Pliny demonstrates.

Although Renaissance panegyrists do not ignore the exemplum of assassination, they normally are more practical, more forceful, and yet less extreme in defining the limits of monarchical power. Erasmus, for example, guides Philip of Burgundy toward patronage of the arts by restricting him to a peaceful foreign policy. Erasmus

40. Kennet, p. xviii.
41. Kennet, p. xviii.
42. Pliny, sec. 55.
43. Pacatus, sec. 20.

insists that a prince who fritters away his energies in foreign wars (or even in foreign journeys) denies himself the greatest tribute the world has to pay a prince: recognition as one who fosters the spirit of scholarship and literature. Erasmus rises eloquently to this theme in his peroration.

Litteraturae . . . quae quoniam jam olim in Graecia, jam pridem in Italia, nuper etiam in Gallia . . . incommode coeperunt haberi, nimirum propter tumultum bellorum, et clangorem tubarum, a quibus vehementer abhorrent, quippe pacis filiae, tranquillitatis alumnae, fortassis in hanc tuam ditionem non invite demigrabunt.[44]

Because long before now in Greece, a long time ago in Italy, and even recently in France, the literary arts began to be held in less than proper esteem, undoubtedly on account of the tumult of warfare and the blare of war-trumpets from which they shrink back in horror—these literary arts which are in truth the daughters of peace and the children of tranquility perhaps will change their abode not unwillingly to the land of your sway.

By thus championing the twin causes of peace and literature, Erasmus attempts to channel monarchical power in fruitful rather than wasteful directions.

Just as Erasmus presses his own interests on Archduke Philip, so John Gordon presses his on James I. But Gordon is more devious in developing the theme of limitation. To persuade James that the "restoring and reformation of the auncient Church," begun by Elizabeth, "must be finished by you," Gordon makes the king's power contingent on the completion of this task.[45] If, instead, James

44. Erasmus, *Panegyricus*, LeClerc, IV, 549C.
45. Gordon, pp. 42–43.

should "cleave unto . . . that great whore of *Babilon*" (the Catholic church), he will become a slave.[46]

> Most humbly beseeching your Majesty to remember that the Popes pretend to be the true kings of *England* and *Ireland* houlding the Kinges of the said kingdoms for their vassals and tributaries; who now under colour to free you from their said pretensions, would draw you unto them, and impose upon you a most heavy and servile yoake.[47]

In effect, Gordon prescribes a modest limitation on the king's power by carefully envisioning the alternative, severe limitation, even slavery. In their different ways, then, Renaissance panegyrists like Erasmus and Gordon follow their ancient predecessors and attempt to restrict, or at least channel, the exercise of monarchical power.

It is in light of this persistent theme that we can appreciate a crucial *sententia* of Evelyn's panegyric: "If the Republick belong then to *Caesar*, *Caesar* belongs much more to the Republick . . ."[48] It is worth noting that just one decade earlier essentially the same "sentence" had been used to justify revolution against the Stuart monarchy. In his first defense of the English people, Milton writes that "a king exists for the people, not the people for the king."[49] It is even possible that Milton would have agreed with Evelyn's explanation of the idea, an explanation which aptly summarizes the significance

46. Gordon, p. 45.
47. Gordon, p. 45.
48. Evelyn, p. 9.
49. John Milton, *A Defence of the People of England*, trans. Donald Mackenzie, *Complete Prose Works of John Milton*, ed. Don M. Wolfe, 4 vols. to date (New Haven and London, 1953–), IV, i, 470. Milton also cites the panegyrics of both Claudian and Pliny in defense of the English people, pp. 389, 445–446, 466.

of the limitation theme by returning us to Pliny's *leges super principem.*

Nor indeed do you desire any thing should be permitted your Majesty, but what is indulg'd your Vassals, subjecting even your self to those Lawes by which you oblige your Subjects; For as it is a great felicity to be able to do what one will, so is it much more glorious, to will only what is just and honourable.[50]

The same king whom Evelyn celebrates as the divine "restorer" of his country is limited by human laws and by human concepts of what is "just and honourable." Central to the tradition of panegyric is the attempt to reconcile in one oration the themes of restoration and limitation.

The significance of this thematic reconciliation cannot be explained away or dismissed as "mere flattery." Although the panegyrist is patently vulnerable to the charge of ignoble purpose, the orators who follow Pliny persistently attempt to refute this charge. Pliny, to begin with, makes the candor of his speech a tribute to the freedom allowed under the new administration, rejecting the servile blandishments that were previously the custom.[51] Erasmus goes further, citing with approval the example of Alexander Severus, who had court flatterers beheaded.[52] Evelyn, likewise, insists that Charles is above flattery.[53] What makes these disclaimers convincing are

50. Evelyn, p. 9. Similarly, Milton writes: "It is then not the people alone on whom such obedience is enjoined, but kings as well, who are in no way above the law." Milton, *A Defence of the People of England*, Wolfe, IV, i, 383.

51. Pliny, sec. 2.

52. Erasmus, *Panegyricus*, LeClerc, IV, 534A.

53. Evelyn, p. 10.

the alternative motives that the orations themselves suggest, motives perceived, moreover, by Renaissance commentators. The Warwick recorder of 1572, we should recall, views panegyric as a didactic oration, designed to
"put [princes] in mynde of their office and government."[54]
Thomas Farnaby, on the other hand, sees panegyric as
propaganda, designed to "exhort the nation to joy, obedience, and concord."[55] White Kennet expresses both of
these purposes in his preface to Pliny's panegyric: instruction aimed at the king and propaganda aimed at the
people.[56]

In panegyric, then, we are dealing not only with two
themes but with two audiences as well. The theme of
restoration, elaborated in a ceremonial way, serves the
function of popular propaganda. By celebrating the current monarch in relation to a historical pattern that is
made to seem inevitable or providential, the orator solicits
the obedience of the people. The theme of limitation, on
the other hand, is directed toward the king. Often elaborated in the context of a *topos* on royal education, the
function of this theme is to instruct or to advise, or even
to warn the king that he is not a law unto himself. These
two motives—propaganda and instruction—are expressly
avowed by Erasmus in his epistolary discussion of panegyric. On the one hand: "even when a sovereign is not
the best of men, those over whom he rules should think
the best of him." On the other: "For there is no such
efficacious mode of making a prince better, as that of

54. *The Progresses and Public Processions of Queen Elizabeth*,
ed. John Nichols, 3 vols. (London, 1823), I, 311.
55. Farnaby, p. 13.
56. Kennet, "Preface." See above, chap. 1, "Critical Definition."

setting before him, under the guise of praise, the example of a good sovereign, provided you so attribute virtues and deny vices, as to persuade him to the former and deter him from the latter."[57]

To translate Erasmus's observations into rhetorical terms, we can say that panegyric is a hybrid kind of oratory, at once demonstrative (laudatory) and deliberative (advisory). There is, moreover, support for this formulation in the rhetoric books. Noting that the distinctions among the three kinds of oratory are not rigid, Aristotle goes on to explain: "Deliberative and demonstrative eloquence have one point of agreement. They may be converted easily into each other. That which, in deliberation, has been given as counsel, may, by a slight verbal change, be employed as a topic of praise."[58] Enlarging this "point of agreement" with particular reference to panegyric, Quintilian writes: "Will any one deny the title of *epideictic* [i.e., demonstrative] to *panegyric*? But yet *panegyrics* are advisory in form and frequently discuss the interests of Greece."[59] Even the Dionysius rhetoric provides brief acknowledgment of the advisory as well as the laudatory aspect of this kind of oration. In this author's ideal panegyric, section 4 (discussion of the contests being held) would recommend to the audience (which includes the king) education for both body and soul, gymnastic for the one and music for the

57. Erasmus, "Epistle 177" and "Epistle 176," *The Epistles of Erasmus*, trans. Francis Morgan Nichols, 3 vols. (London, 1901), I, 367, 364.

58. Aristotle, *Rhetoric*, book 1, chap. 9.

59. Quintilian, *Institutio Oratoria*, book 3, chap. 4, *Quintilian*, trans. H. E. Butler, Loeb Classical Library, 4 vols. (Cambridge, Mass., 1963), I, 395.

other.[60] Although Renaissance rhetoricians place panegyric in the demonstrative category without much hesitation, they too offer a good reason for considering the
panegyric also as deliberative. They frequently distinguish the three branches of oratory according to the temporal relationship between the orator and his subject.
That is, judicial oratory concerns the past, demonstrative
the present, and deliberative the future. Insofar as panegyric concentrates on the future, it should be classed as
deliberative.

In sum, the theme of restoration, which celebrates the
present moment as a turning point in national history,
defines panegyric as demonstrative oratory. The theme
of limitation, which focuses the king's attention on his
political future, defines panegyric as deliberative oratory.
It is, in fact, both.

Panegyric cannot, however, entirely escape the common censure of "flattery" by claiming other motives. The
very defensiveness of many Renaissance commentaries
is a sufficient indication that there is some truth to the
charges brought against this kind of oratory. Erasmus,
for example, is especially touchy on this subject, and in
his letters feels obliged to argue the issue of flattery not
only with his contemporaries but also with such thinkers
as Socrates and Saint Augustine. "Another difficulty was
this, that the simplicity of my character, to speak hon-
estly, somewhat shrank from this kind of writing, to
which that sentence of Socrates seems alone, or mainly,
to apply, when he says that Rhetoric is one of three parts
flattery. And yet this kind of ours [*i.e.*, panegyric] is not

60. The *"Dionysius Rhetoric,"* chap. 1.

so much praise as admonition . . ."[61] These typical
reservations can be placed in perspective by considering
more carefully the function of the *laus regis* as it is derived from Pliny.

Pliny praises Trajan by idealizing him according to
the emperor's assumed title, *optimus princeps*. The oration is nominally about Trajan, of course, but the real
basis of the *laus regis* is Pliny's own conception of the
perfect prince.[62] Thus, in the tradition that stems from
this address, orators are primarily concerned not with the
deeds and achievements of actual men, but rather with
the portrayal of the ideal monarch. Erasmus acknowledges
this conception of the *laus regis* when he writes: "Lastly
these orations are also written for posterity, and for the
world; and in this view it is of little importance, in whose
person the example of a good sovereign is put before the
public, provided it is so skillfully done, that the intelligent
may see the effect was not to deceive but to admonish."[63]
Evelyn confirms this conception when he actually addresses Charles, "O best Idea of Princes . . ."[64] Charles,
like Trajan and Philip before him, is the temporary em-
bodiment of an inherited ideal. The flattery involved in
panegyric is the initial assumption that a particular monarch is to be identified with this ideal. Once this assumption is granted, however, it becomes evident that the
speech is only incidentally a matter of flattery, for the
real subject of panegyric is the *optimus princeps*, or the
"best of Kings."

61. Erasmus, "Epistle 176."
62. This point has been made by Born, "The Perfect Prince According to the Latin Panegyrists."
63. Erasmus, "Epistle 177."
64. Evelyn, p. 14.

In the *laus regis,* moreover, the demonstrative and deliberative purposes of panegyric coincide. The portrayal of the perfect prince functions both as popular propaganda and as royal instruction. But to see more clearly how the themes of restoration and limitation are reconciled in the figure of the king, we need to consider first the linguistic texture of panegyric and especially the recurrent patterns of imagery. For this we can focus on the derivative tradition of verse panegyric, beginning with the poetry of Claudius Claudianus.

POETRY

Deriving his topics directly from the tradition of panegyrical oratory, Claudian embellishes the themes of restoration and limitation with images and allusions that recur in the verse panegyrics of the Renaissance. To isolate the more influential metaphoric patterns, we can concentrate on the restoration theme as it is expressed in the *Panegyricus De Sexto Consulatu Honorii Augusti* and the limitation theme as it is elaborated in the *Panegyricus De Quarto Consulatu Honorii Augusti.*[65]

Claudian's last panegyric, on the sixth consulship of Honorius, was recited not at Milan like the earlier panegyrics to the emperor, but rather at Rome.[66] Claudian

65. Although it is more convenient for purposes of illustration to discuss the two themes by reference to different poems, it should be emphasized that the themes of restoration and limitation are important in both panegyrics.

66. For a biographical and historical discussion of Claudian's panegyrics, see Alan Cameron, *Claudian: Poetry and Propaganda at the Court of Honorius* (Oxford, 1970). This is by far the best study available on Claudian. For a specific discussion of Claudian's

seizes upon this circumstance to celebrate not only the restoration of past Roman glories but also the return of the emperor to the imperial city. The poet embellishes the idea of restoration by defining an arrested cyclical pattern of history in natural, mythological, and historical metaphors. The return of the emperor brings, for example, revival of the laurels on the Palatine hill, laurels which are then cut to grace Roman standards for the parades in honor of the occasion.[67] These ceremonies serve the additional purpose of celebrating the recent Roman "victory" over the rebellious Alaric, whose impiety is established by allusions to Phaethon and the Titans.[68] Honorius himself is celebrated by comparison with figures from Roman history: he is Trajan returning after the Dacian campaign and Marcus Aurelius returning after his war against the Marcomanni.[69] These images of nature, myth, and history are combined to express the restoration of ancient Roman majesty, proclaimed in the opening lines of the poem.

---

relationship to the oratorical tradition of panegyric, see L. B. Struthers, "The Rhetorical Structure of the Encomia of Claudius Claudian," *Harvard Studies in Classical Philology*, XXX (1919), 49–87. For a more general but more useful consideration of this problem, see O. B. Hardison, Jr., *The Enduring Monument: A Study of the Idea of Praise in Renaissance Theory and Practice* (Chapel Hill, N.C., 1962), pp. 24–36, and E. R. Curtius, *European Literature and the Latin Middle Ages*, trans. Willard R. Trask (New York, 1953), pp. 154–166, 174–182. In the background of all of these studies lies Theodore C. Burgess's *Epideictic Literature* (Chicago, 1902).

67. Claudian, *Panegyricus De Sexto Consulatu Honorii Augusti*, lines 35–38, *Claudian*, trans. Maurice Platnauer, 2 vols. (Cambridge, Mass., and London, 1922), II, 76.

68. Claudian, *VI Cons.*, 178ff.

69. Claudian, *VI Cons.*, 311ff.

> *Aurea Fortunae Reduci si templa priores*
> *ob reditum vovere ducum, non dignius umquam*
> *haec dea pro meritis amplas sibi posceret aedes,*
> *quam sua cum pariter trabeis reparatur et urbi*
> *maiestas . . . (1–5)*

If our ancestors vowed temples to "Home-bringing Fortune" in honour of the return of their generals, never would this goddess more worthily claim for her services a noble temple than when their proper majesty is restored alike to the consulship and to Rome.

This pattern of restored majesty does, moreover, function as propaganda. The comparison between Alaric and Phaethon makes this especially clear. Aimed at anyone who would support or imitate Alaric, Claudian's allusion to Phaethon is carefully explained by the river god Eridanus, who is personified for just this rhetorical purpose.

> *nec te meus, improbe, saltem*
> *terruit exemplo Phaëthon, qui fulmina praeceps*
> *in nostris efflavit aquis, dum flammea caeli*
> *flectere terrenis meditatur frena lacertis*
> *mortalique diem sperat diffundere vultu?*
> *crede mihi, simili bacchatur crimine, quisquis*
> *adspirat Romae spoliis aut Solis habenis. (186–192)*

If none other, was not my Phaëthon a warning to thee, Phaëthon fall'n from heaven to quench his flames in my waters, what time he sought with mortal hand to hold the fiery reins of the sky and hoped to spread day's brilliance from a mortal countenance? 'Tis the same mad crime, I tell thee, whosoever aspires to spoil Rome or drive the sun's chariot.

Phaethon should have been a warning to Alaric, and Alaric himself now becomes a warning to anyone else who might be tempted to disobey the monarch. Crimes against the state become crimes against nature. What is restored in this poem is not just Roman majesty, but the very order of the universe, which had been temporarily upset by the madness of the Phaethon figure, Alaric.

The complementary theme of limitation Claudian expresses most vigorously in his panegyric on the fourth consulship of Honorius.

In commune iubes si quid censesque tenendum, / primus iussa subi: tunc observantior aequi / fit populus nec ferre negat, cum viderit ipsum / auctorem parere sibi.[70]

If thou make any law or establish any custom for the general good, be the first to submit thyself thereto; then does a people show more regard for justice nor refuse submission when it has seen their author obedient to his own laws.

The concept of limitation by law, which recalls the injunctions of Pliny and anticipates those of Evelyn, is elaborated in familiar metaphors. The sun image, for example, is here developed by reference to Phoebus rather than to Phaethon.

> *nonne vides, operum quod se pulcherrimus ipse*
> *mundus amore liget, nec vi conexa per aevum*
> *conspirent elementa sibi? quod limite Phoebus*
> *contentus medio, contentus litore pontus*
> *et, qui perpetuo terras ambitque vehitque,*
> *nec premat incumbens oneri nec cesserit aër?* (284–289)

Seest thou not how the fair frame of the very universe binds itself together by love, and how the elements, not united by violence, are for ever at harmony among themselves? Dost thou not mark how that Phoebus is content not to outstep the limits of his path, nor the sea those of his kingdom, and how the air, which in its eternal embrace encircles and upholds the world, presses not upon us with too heavy a weight nor yet yields to the burden which itself sustains?

70. Claudian, *IV Cons.*, lines 296–299, Platnauer, I, 308.

The ideal of natural order and harmony can be preserved only if each of the natural elements stays within its own set boundaries. This includes the sun and, by analogy, the emperor, to whom these lines are directly addressed. To emphasize the theme of limitation, Claudian later alludes to the unhappy fates of Julius Caesar and Tarquinius Superbus.

Romani, qui cuncta diu rexere, regendi, / qui nec Tarquinii fastus nec iura tulere / Caesaris (309–311).

Thou must govern Romans who have long governed the world, Romans who brooked not Tarquin's pride nor Caesar's tyranny.

If, in effect, the emperor does not respect the limits of the law, he will eventually be checked by the popular will. Once again the panegyrist evokes an image of assassination.

The purpose of the limitation theme is, however, not to threaten but to instruct the emperor.[71] The central

71. Cameron argues that this part of the speech would not have been taken seriously by either Claudian or his audience. Although it is easy to be cynical about the fourth century, Cameron's suggestion that Honorius may have even fallen asleep during the panegyric seems to me gratuitously negative. I have taken the instructions of Theodosius to Honorius seriously here because my interest is in the later influence of the panegyric. During the Renaissance, Claudian's advice to the emperor was taken very seriously indeed. Perhaps the most perceptive observation on this panegyric is still Edward Gibbon's: "The lessons of Theodosius, or rather Claudian (iv Cons. Honor. 214–418) might compose a fine institution for the future prince of a great and free nation. It was far above Honorius and his degenerate subjects." Edward Gibbon, *The Decline and Fall of the Roman Empire*, chap. 19 (386–398 A.D.), fn. 62, Modern Library Edition, 3 vols. (New York, n.d.), II, 90. For further discussion, see Cameron, p. 381.

third of the poem, from which the above passages have
been extracted, is devoted entirely to the education of Honorius. Claudian sets forth his instructions to the emperor
by creating a flashback in which the emperor's father,
Theodosius, is imagined to be educating his son in the
arts of government. In the course of this speech the father
gives his son models of conduct. Chief among these is,
predictably, Trajan.

> *victura feretur*
> *gloria Traiani, non tam quod Tigride victo*
> *nostra triumphati fuerint provincia Parthi,*
> *alta quod invectus fractis Capitolia Dacis,*
> *quam patriae quod mitis erat.* (315–319)

The fame of Trajan will never die, not so much because,
thanks to his victories on the Tigris, conquered Parthia became
a Roman province, not because he brake the might of Dacia
and led their chiefs in triumph up the slope of the Capitol,
but because he was kindly to his country.

By minimizing Trajan's military success and emphasizing
instead his kindness toward the people, Claudian suggests
his conception of the *optimus princeps* and provides a
model which Honorius must follow:

ne desine tales, / nate, sequi (319–320).

Fail not to make such as he thine example, my son.

By modeling his conduct on the kindness of Trajan, the
emperor will win the love of his people:

non extorquebis amari; /hoc alterna fides, hoc simplex gratia
donat (282–283).

Love thou canst not extort; it is the gift of mutual faith and
honest good will.

Claudian's panegyrics thus illustrate the truth of Aristotle's observation that "by a slight verbal change" the demonstrative can be converted into the deliberative. The same natural, mythological, and historical images that define the demonstrative theme of restoration can be modified to develop the deliberative theme of limitation. The combined significance of these two themes in the panegyrics of Claudian is perhaps captured in the last citation above. The demonstrative function of these poems is to secure the faith of the people in their ruler, whereas the deliberative function is to secure the faith of the ruler in the people. The ultimate purpose is to reconcile emperor and subjects, to achieve mutual trust, or *alterna fides*. Nor does this purpose die with Claudian. As we shall see, English poets of the Renaissance like Samuel Daniel and Ben Jonson borrow segments from Claudian's panegyrics to help reconcile the English monarchs and the English people.

But Daniel and Jonson did not have to look all the way back to Claudian for models of verse panegyric. The neo-Latin poetry of the sixteenth century supplies important examples of the genre written by the humanists. To the published version of his *Panegyricus*, Erasmus added a poem of about one hundred lines. Although labeled a *Gratulatorium Carmen*, Erasmus writes that the poem is "of the same texture" as the panegyric, but "of an impromptu kind."[72] Five years later Thomas More followed suit with a *Carmen Gratulatorium* honoring the coronation of Henry VIII. Although it is no doubt true that roughly similar poems had been written on English soil in earlier times, More's poem can be taken to mark the

72. Erasmus, "Epistle 177."

beginning of the panegyrical tradition in England that leads finally to Dryden. Whereas the coronation of Henry VIII's father had been celebrated in doggerel Latin by the Augustinian friar Bernardus Andreas, his daughter Elizabeth was greeted in remarkably fine neo-Latin verse by the humanist Walter Haddon. In 1603, Daniel diverted this neo-Latin tradition into English with his "panegyrike congratulatorie," thereby uniting the classical and neo-Latin names for the genre.

A full century before Daniel's poem appeared, Erasmus celebrated the return of Archduke Philip by shaping natural metaphors into a pattern of diurnal and seasonal change. The whole poem is organized around a contrast between absence and return, winter and spring, night and day. The recent past is darkness, winter, night, in contrast to the light, spring, day of the present. In this metaphoric elaboration of the restoration theme, the king becomes the sun.

> *Sic simul auricomus se condidit aequore Titan*
> *Mox perit haec nitidi facies pulcherrima mundi,*
> *Pigra quies subit et nigrantibus horrida pennis*
> *Nox operit mortique simillimus omnia torpor;*
> *Rursum ubi purpureis aurora revecta quadrigis*
> *Rorantes tenero detexit lumine terras,*
> *Cuique repente sua species redit atque renasci*
> *Cuncta putes blandoque magis iuvenescere vultu.*[73]

In this way as soon as the golden-haired Titan had hidden himself in the sea, then this extremely beautiful appearance of the splendid universe disappears, a sluggish stillness comes

73. Erasmus, *Illustrissimo principi Philippo feliciter in patriam redeunti gratulatorium carmen Erasmi sub persona patriae*, lines 32–39, *The Poems of Desiderius Erasmus*, ed. C. Reedijk (Leiden, 1956), p. 273.

up, and frightful night on black wings and a numbness very much like death cover everything; but again when Aurora is borne back on her bright, rosy-colored chariot and with her gentle light has disclosed the dew-covered earth, each thing suddenly regains its unique appearance, and you would think that everything is being reborn and becoming still younger because of the charming countenance of Aurora.

If light thus returns with the king, so too does the spring.

> *Quum procul hinc aberas squalebant omnia luctu,*
> *Mox ut saluus ades renitescunt omnia cultu.*
> *Sic ubi tristis hyems aquilonibus asperat auras*
> *Nuda senescit humus, moerent sine floribus horti,*
> *Torpescunt amnes, languet sine frondibus arbos,*
> *Stat sine fruge seges, marcent sine gramine campi;*
> *Rursus ubi zephyris tepidum spirantibus anni*
> *Leta iuventa redit, gemmantur floribus horti,*
> *Effugiunt amnes, revirescit frondibus arbos,*
> *Fruge nitent segetes, hilarescunt gramine campi.* (22–31)

When you were far away from here, everything was in a state of neglect due to grief; then as soon as you are here safe and sound, everything glows again with care and cultivation. Thus when bitter winter makes the breezes harsh with north winds, the bare ground lies wasted and spent with age, gardens are in mourning without flowers, rivers become sluggish, trees are lifeless without their leaves, the grainfield lies barren of its crop, the plains dry up without grass; again when spring returns with west winds blowing warmly, gardens are studded with flower buds like jewels, rivers are free to flow, trees become green and alive again with foliage, grain fields flourish in their crop, the plains delight in their grass.

Natural change symbolizes political and institutional change, as the return of the king is transformed into an event of universal significance. This is not just a new day or new year, but a new age.

The natural imagery of the poem underlines the larger significance of the occasion by asking us to view the king as a mythic figure, as a vegetation deity. The emphasis on seasonal rejuvenation and returning light even suggests a parallel with the Christian celebration of Easter. The imagery in this poem to Philip is, in fact, comparable to that in Erasmus' poem on Christ's triumphant harrowing of Hell and His joyous return. Here too we find the revival of nature.

Florida plaudit humus, fundat sua munera tellus,
Squallorem excutiat, blandis se floribus ornet.

. . . .

Terris haec celebranda dies, nova gaudia terris
Christus agit superis nondum gustata vel ipsis.[74]

The flowering ground applauds; the earth pours forth its gifts, shakes off its squalor, and decks itself in charming blossoms. . . . This is a day which should be celebrated by the earth; Christ brings new joy to the world—joy not yet savored by even the heavens above.

The *celebranda dies* of this poem seems very similar to the *semper memoranda dies* that is the occasion for the verse panegyric to Philip. Although Erasmus does not explicitly compare Philip to Christ, his imagery does suggest the possibility of elaborating the restoration theme by allusion to the resurrection. More importantly, Erasmus adds a potential Christian dimension to the classical figure of the *optimus princeps*.

Although Thomas More develops his *Carmen Gratulatorium* of 1509 according to the *prius . . . nunc . . .*

74. Erasmus, *Carmen heroicum de solemnitate paschali atque de tryumphali Christi resurgentis pompa et descensu eius ad inferos*, lines 11–12, 27–28, Reedijk, p. 191.

pattern elaborated by Erasmus, his poem is designed for immediate, practical application by the new king. In this poem the dark past is not just the night or the winter; it is also, emphatically, the reign of Henry VII. The contrast between the two kings, like that between the emperors Domitian and Trajan in Pliny's panegyric, is expressed by contrasting past and present conditions in the state.

> *Nobilitas, vulgi iamdudum obnoxia faeci,*
>   *Nobilitas, nimium nomen inane diu,*
> *Nunc caput attolit, nunc tali rege triumphat,*
>   *Et merito causas unde triumphat habet.*
> *Mercator variis deterritus ante tributis,*
>   *Nunc maris insuetas puppe resulcat aquas.*
> *Leges invalidae prius, imo nocere coactae,*
>   *Nunc vires gaudent obtinuisse suas.*
> *Congaudent omnes pariter pariterque rependunt*
>   *Omnes venturo damna priora bono.*[75]

The nobility, long since at the mercy of the dregs of the population, the nobility, whose title has been too long without meaning, now lifts its head, now rejoices in such a king, and has proper reason for rejoicing. The merchant, heretofore deterred by numerous taxes, now once again plows seas grown unfamiliar. Laws, heretofore powerless—yes, even laws put to unjust ends—now happily have regained their proper authority. All are equally happy. All compare their earlier losses with the advantages to come.

75. Thomas More, *In Suscepti Diadematis Diem Henrici Octavi, Illustrissimi Ac Faustissimi Britanniarum Regis Ac Catherinae Reginae Eius Felicissimae, Thomae Mori Londoniensis Carmen Gratulatorium*, lines 19–26, *The Latin Epigrams of Thomas More*, ed. and trans. Leicester Bradner and Charles Arthur Lynch (Chicago, 1953), pp. 16–17. All translations from this poem are by Leicester Bradner and Charles Arthur Lynch.

Thus "exhorting to virtue under pretext of praise," More goes on to recommend harsh laws against informers, light mercantile taxes, and employment at court of educated men. Very much in the specific manner of Theodosius's speech to Honorius, More carefully instructs the new king. The twist in this poem, however, is that the king's father is not his instructor, but rather his model of how not to rule.

This broad limitation on the king's power—"don't rule as your father ruled"—is later spelled out against the background of potential civil war. More asks, in effect, for a guarantee that the king will not use troops to terrorize the people.

> *Nominibus populus multis obnoxius omnis*
> *Regi erat: hoc unum pertimuitque malum.*
> *At rex, hinc metui quum posset, posset et inde*
> *Congerere immensas, si voluisset, opes.*
> *Omnibus ignovit: securos reddidit omnes,*
> *Sollicitique malum substulit omne metus.* (114–119)

The whole people used to be, on many counts, exposed to danger from the king; this in particular they feared. A king, since he could thus inspire fear, could also, if he wished, accumulate untold wealth. Our prince [Henry VIII] ignored this opportunity in every case, freed them all from care, and entirely removed the evil practice which caused their anxious fears.

By condemning former kings who inspired popular fear, More indirectly defines the *optimus princeps* as a man of peace. Significantly, too, he locates the source of the king's power not in the sword, but in the love of his subjects.

> *Ergo alios populi reges timuere, sed istum,*
> *Per quem nunc nihil est quod timeatur, amant.*

> *Hostibus O princeps multum metuende superbis,*
>   *O populo princeps non metuende tuo,*
> *Illi te metuunt: nos te veneramur, amamus.*
>   *Illis noster erit, cur metuaris, amor.*
> *Sic te securum demptoque satellite tutum*
>   *Undique praestabunt hinc amor, inde timor.* (120–127)

And so it is that subjects have always feared kings; but this king, who has banished fear, his subjects love. O Prince, terror to your proud enemies but not to your own people, it is your enemies who fear you: we revere and love you. Our love for you will prove the reason for their fear. And thus it is that, in the absence of sycophants, your subject's love and your enemies' fear will hedge you round in peace and safety.

Although the parallel with Claudian's panegyric on Honorius's fourth consulship is quite evident, More emphasizes the idea of contingency: the power of the king is not only limited by, but is contingent on, the love of his people. To establish this important principle, More eschews the elaborate image patterns of Erasmus's poem to Philip and relies instead on direct, hortatory praise.

The demonstrative, or ceremonial, emphasis of Erasmus's verse panegyric to Philip and the deliberative, or political, emphasis of More's address to Henry are very successfully combined in Walter Haddon's poem on the coronation of Queen Elizabeth. Haddon begins quite conventionally by concentrating on the significance of the occasion, adapting natural imagery to the purpose of ceremony.

> *Anglia, tolle caput, saevis iactata procellis,*
>   *Exagitata malis Anglia tolle caput.*
> *Aurea virgo venit, roseo venerabilis ore,*
>   *Plena deo, princeps Elisabetha venit.*
> *Quaque venit, festos circumfert undique ludos,*
>   *Undique, qua graditur, gaudia laeta ciet,*

> *Stella salutaris salve, praesentia serva,*
>   *Splendeat ex radiis terra Britanna tuis.*
> *Formosum sydus, patriam caligine mersam,*
>   *Admota propius luce levato nova.*
> *Frigidus horribili Boreas terrore strepebat,*
>   *Atque diu terras aspera laesit hyems.*
> *Nunc Zephyrus mollis iucundas commovet auras,*
>   *Anglia vere novo nunc recreata viret.*[76]

England, lift up your head, though you have been tossed about by savage tempests; though you have been harrassed with troubles, England, lift up your head. The golden maiden is coming, revered with rosy countenance, filled with God, princess Elizabeth is coming. Wherever she comes, she spreads festivities around in all directions; everywhere she goes, she is the cause of joy and happiness. Hail, star of salvation, preserve what we have at present; let Britain shine forth from your rays of light. Beautiful star, with new light brought nearer, bring relief to the country sunk in darkness. The cold north wind shrieked with dreadful terror, and for a long time bitter winter ravaged the lands. Now the gentle west wind stirs up pleasant breezes; England now flourishes, refreshed with a new springtime.

The repeated *nunc*, as in earlier Latin panegyrics, marks a decisive break with the immediate past and thus an occasion for celebration and festive games. The recent history of storms, evils, disturbances, now gives way to a new age inaugurated by Elizabeth and defined by Christian and classical myth. Elizabeth comes as a figure of the Virgin Mary, *plena deo*, metaphorically pregnant with God. The star imagery which follows not only confirms the discreet allusion to the nativity, but also brings into

76. Walter Haddon, *In auspicatissimum serenissimae Reginae Elisabethae regimen*, lines 1–14, *The Poetry of Walter Haddon*, ed. Charles J. Lees (The Hague, 1967), p. 169.

focus the classical *virgo* enshrined as a constellation, namely Astraea.[77] Although thus created as a mythic figure, the queen still needs political advice.

> *Consiliis rectis attentam praebeat aurem,*
> *Et ferat oppressis, quando rogatur, opem.*
> *Fulminet in vitiis, et corda rebellia frangat,*
> *Supplicibus parcat, quos meliora movent.*
> *In domini iusto maneat cultuque, metuque,*
> *Sit similis princeps Elisabetha sui.* (31–36)

May she offer an attentive ear to upright counsels and, when asked, bring help to the oppressed. May she strike like thunder and lightning in the midst of vices and crush rebellious hearts. May she spare suppliants whom better things motivate. May she abide by the just worship and fear of the Lord; may princess Elizabeth be true to herself.

By urging her to crush rebellion and to relieve the oppressed, Haddon makes his contribution to the syncretic figure of the perfect prince.

What distinguishes this poem, however, is the harmony that Haddon expresses between metaphor and fact, ceremony and advice. The coronation of Elizabeth represents, above all, the union of ideal and actual, as the divine becomes human. Specifically, her accession represents the institution of the new law (spiritual) and the abandonment of the old law (carnal).

> *Exeat ex regno libertas impia carnis,*
> *Spiritus est liber, res placitura deo.* (45–46)

Let wicked license of the flesh leave the kingdom; the spirit is free—that is what will please God.

77. For discussion of Elizabeth and Astraea, see Frances A. Yates, "Queen Elizabeth as Astraea," *Journal of the Warburg and Courtauld Institutes,* x (1947), 27–82.

Given this spiritual conception of the state, sanctioned by God, the monarch is idealized as a figure who must crush rebellion, thus showing divine justice, but who must also relieve the oppressed, thus showing divine mercy. The analogy between the monarch and God, with its implied corollary that political rebellion is a form of impiety or sin, is a staple assumption of many later panegyrists. As we shall see, however, the tide of events during the seventeenth century ultimately makes the unity achieved by Haddon impossible for later poets to attain.

But before turning to Stuart panegyric, we can now consider more precisely the significance of the *laus regis*. Although each of the neo-Latin verse panegyrics mentioned here includes praise of the monarch, More's poem deserves particular attention because there is solid evidence that this panegyric continued to be read with pleasure over a century after it was written. At least, in 1622 Henry Peacham describes More as "sometime Lord Chancellor of *England*, a man of most rich and pleasant invention: his verse fluent, nothing harsh, constrained or obscure," and goes on to approve specifically his *Carmen Gratulatorium*: "What can be more loftie then his gratulatorie verse to King *Henrie* upon his Coronation day . . ."[78] More's praise of Henry is indeed "loftie," but it takes a conventional form inherited from the oratorical tradition of panegyric. This traditional

78. Henry Peacham, "Of Poetrie," from *The Compleat Gentleman*, in *Critical Essays of the Seventeenth Century*, ed. J. E. Spingarn, 3 vols. (Oxford, 1908), I, 130. Peacham also praises Claudian as "an excellent and sweete Poet," although he objects to "the meanness of his subject." Spingarn, I, 128.

form involves a union of qualities designated as *augustus* with those described as *amabilis.*[79]

> *Ter spectare iuvat: quid ni hunc spectare iuvaret,*
> *Quo natura nihil finxit amabilius?*
> *Mille inter comites excelsior omnibus extat,*
> *Et dignum augusto corpore robur habet.* (50–53)

Three times they delight to see him—and why not? This king who is amiable as any creature in the realm of nature. Among a thousand noble companions he stands out taller than any. And he has strength worthy of his regal person.

Strong and yet gentle, Henry even combines masculine and feminine principles.

> *Illa quidem facies alacri veneranda vigore*
> *Esse potest tenerae virginis, esse viri.* (60–61)

In fact, that face, admirable for its animated strength, could belong to either a young girl or a man.

In effect, More finds in Henry a symbol of comprehension and unity. He symbolizes national reconciliation not only as the surviving beneficiary of the Wars of the Roses, but also as a figure who can contain a balance of opposites within himself. He is both *augustus* and *amabilis;* he is the perfect prince, or rather he becomes perfect in More's poem, the purpose of which is not to celebrate the actual but to inaugurate the ideal.

This same purpose lies behind other poems on this occasion, including one by the churchman Andreas Ammonius. After presenting the new king as a union of Mars

79. See Erasmus, *Panegyricus*, LeClerc, IV, 523–524, and especially the following passage: "quam sic augustam esse voluerunt, ut nihil tamen amabilius, sic rursus amabilem, ut nihil augustius."

and Minerva, Ammonius idealizes him by allusion to history, mythology, and the Bible. Punning on the title "Henricus Octavius," Ammonius brings Caesar Augustus into the poem accompanied by Astraea and perhaps also Moses, as England is now seen to flow with milk and honey.

> *Neglectasque diu terras Astraea revisat,*
> *Et profugas artes cogat abire malas.*
> *Cernis ut incipiant fluvii candescere lacte,*
> *Arboribusque fluant roscida mella cavis.*
> *Aurea, si nescis, rediens Octavius orbi*
> *Saecula restituit.*[80]

Astraea again visits long-neglected lands and compels evil devices to leave as exiles. You notice that rivers begin to gleam white with milk, and honey dripping like drops of dew flows from hollow trees. In case you are unaware of it, a returning Octavius has restored the age of gold to the world.

Ammonius concludes his poem by expanding the parallel between England and Rome.

> *Sit melior Nerva, Augusto felicior ipso,*
> *Robore Traianum praestat et imperio.* (101–102)

May he be better than Nerva, more fortunate than Augustus himself, and surpass Trajan in strength and power.

What we have here is a poetic rendering of the three sources of praise defined in the rhetoric books: fortune (Augustus), body (Trajan), and character (Nerva). It all adds up to *imperium*.

The purpose of the *laus regis* is to unite individual

80. Andreas Ammonius, *Elegia De Obitu Regis Henrici VII Et Felici Successione Henrici Octavi*, lines 94–99, *Andreae Ammonii Carmina Omnia*, ed. Clemente Pizzi (Florence, 1958), p. 17.

and institution. Through praise the panegyrist elevates a man into a king, thereby publicly acknowledging his royal power, his *imperium*. But this power, acknowledged by praise, is also limited by praise. The man must possess the virtues demanded by the institution, as More explains to Henry.

> *Enervare bonas immensa licentia mentes*
> *Idque etiam in magnis assolet ingeniis.*
> *At quamvis erat ante pius, mores tamen illi*
> *Imperium dignos attulit imperio.* (84–87)

Unlimited power has a tendency to weaken good minds, and that even in the case of very gifted men. But howsoever dutiful he was before, his crown has brought our prince a character which deserves to rule . . .

Here More praises Henry not for what he is, but for what he must be, and the essence of this ideal is expressed by the concept of *pietas*. Power is thus qualified by piety.

Implicit in this broad moral norm are love and duty toward the divine, and conscientiousness, affection, and loyalty in dealings with other men. In panegyric, however, piety also assumes a special, public meaning. When Claudian advises Honorius, "Sis pius in primis . . . ," and Walter Haddon advises Elizabeth, "Sit pia . . . ," the panegyrist defines the obligations of the prince to his people.[81] This significance of the word in traditional panegyric is most clearly revealed in Claudian's last poem to Honorius. Exploring the son's role as avenger of the father, Claudian considers Orestes, then Augustus, and finally Honorius. In his reference to Augustus, the poet makes a fine distinction between true and false piety:

81. Claudian, *IV Cons.*, 276; Haddon, *In auspicatissimum*, 27.

> *pavit Iuleos inviso sanguine manes*
> *Augustus, sed falsa pii praeconia sumpsit*
> *in luctum patriae civili strage parentans . . .*[82]

Augustus sated the shade of Caesar with his enemies' blood, but he made a false advertisement of piety when, to the grief of his fatherland, he offered the blood of citizens to his father's ghost.

Although usually the prime example of the pious ruler, Augustus here becomes an emblem of false piety because he placed personal duty to his (adopted) father above his duty to his subjects. Contrasting this example of false piety with the true piety of Honorius, Claudian implicitly gives two levels of meaning to the term, one private and one public. The piety of a ruler is above duty to the father; it is rather duty to the fatherland. In panegyric, piety is a public virtue that means, above all, preservation and protection of the commonweal.

The ideal of *pietas* thus defines and limits the monarch's *imperium* by restricting him from any action that would endanger the public safety. If the demonstrative rhetoric of panegyric acknowledges the monarch's power, the deliberative rhetoric qualifies that power by emphasizing the public moral virtue of piety. It should not, therefore, seem surprising that when English poets of the seventeenth century attempt to adopt panegyric as a "branch of epic," they turn repeatedly to the example of the pious Aeneas.

82. Claudian, *VI Cons.*, 116–118.

3: English Verse Panegyric, 1603–1660

THE HISTORY of English verse panegyric begins with the Stuart succession. The traditional themes of restoration and limitation are first translated from the Latin by Samuel Daniel and Ben Jonson, whose panegyrics to James I provide model topics for a host of lesser poets anxious to celebrate, but also to restrict, the early Stuart monarchy. Thus established as a useful kind of poetry during the reigns of the first two Stuarts, panegyric is given a new significance and a new popularity by the poets of the mid-century, most notably by Abraham Cowley and Edmund Waller. Cowley transforms the oratorical conventions of panegyric by assimilating them to his conception of the Pindaric ode. Waller, on the other hand, transforms panegyric into a "branch of epic," making the king an epic hero. While these poets were raising panegyric to a place of considerable importance in neo-classical poetics, Andrew Marvell was challenging the very premises of the genre. Although Marvell's Cromwell poems do not belong to the tradition of panegyric, they do illuminate both the weaknesses and strengths of the genre. Dryden's Restoration panegyrics respond directly to the tradition established by Daniel and Jonson and to the transformation effected by Cowley and Waller, indirectly to the challenge posed by Marvell.

TRADITION

In his "panegyrike" on the accession of James I, Samuel Daniel declares 1603 to be a year of "Restauration" and identifies James with the restored ideals. "Religion comes with thee, peace, righteousnesse, / Judgement and justice . . ."[1] To develop the traditional pattern of *prius . . . nunc . . .* , Daniel turns predictably, although not very felicitously, to the seasonal cycle. "What a returne of comfort dost thou bring / Now at this fresh returning of our bloud, / Thus meeting with the opening of the Spring, / To make our spirits likewise to imbud" (129–132). By alluding to the "fresh returning of our bloud," Daniel reminds the people of the Stuart king's descent from the first Tudor and thus certifies James's right to the throne. Later in the poem Daniel is more explicit on this point.

> *The broken frame of this disjoynted State,*
> *Being by the blisse of thy great Grandfather*

1. Samuel Daniel, *A Panegyrike Congratulatorie Delivered to the Kings most excellent majesty, at Burleigh-Harrington in Rutlandshire,* lines 554, 27–28, *The Complete Works in Verse and Prose of Samuel Daniel,* ed. Alexander B. Grosart, 5 vols. (New York, 1963), I, 166, 144. This edition was originally published under the same title in 1885. The revival of interest in seventeenth-century political poetry has not included much discussion of panegyric as a genre or of Daniel's *Panegyrike* as a model. However, see Ruth Nevo, *The Dial of Virtue,* especially pp. 10–17, 27–30, 138ff. Although I am not always in agreement with this study, I have found it useful and am indebted to it.

> Henry *the seventh, restor'd to an estate*
> *More sound than ever, and more stedfaster,*
> *Owes all it hath to him, and in that rate*
> *Stands bond to thee that art his successer:*
> *For without him it had not beene begunne,*
> *And without thee we had beene now undone.* (321–328)

The natural and historical metaphors of restoration function as acknowledgments of the king's power. Specifically, this theme is aimed at those "vile disnatur'd Vipers" (102) who oppose the Stuart succession. Condemning any "impious workings" (101) that would "embroile the State" (103), Daniel develops the restoration theme as propaganda on behalf of the new king.

Like Daniel, Ben Jonson insists on popular obedience to the monarch. Instead of elaborating the conventional imagery of restoration, however, Jonson achieves his purpose by idealizing his public audience.

> *Some cry from tops of houses; thinking noise*
> *The fittest herald to proclaime true joyes:*
> *Others on ground runne gazing by his side,*
> *All, as unwearied, as unsatisfied:*
> *And every windore griev'd it could not move*
> *Along with him, and the same trouble prove.*[2]

A version of what can be called the "processional *topos*," this passage has several parallels in the neo-Latin poetry of the preceding century, most obviously in More's panegyric to Henry VIII.

2. Ben Jonson, *A Panegyre, on The Happie Entrance of James Our Soveraigne, To His first high Session of Parliament in this his Kingdome, the 19. of March, 1603,* lines 41–46, *Ben Jonson,* ed. C. H. Herford and Percy and Evelyn Simpson, 11 vols. (Oxford, 1941), VII, 114.

> *Quacunque ingreditur studio conferta videndi*
> *Vix sinit angustam turba patere viam.*
> *Opplenturque domus, et pondere tecta laborant.*
> *Tollitur affectu clamor ubique novo.*
> *Nec semel est vidisse satis. Loca plurima mutant,*
> *Si qua rursus eum parte videre queant.*[3]

Wherever he goes, the dense crowd in their desire to look upon him leaves hardly a narrow lane for his passage. The houses are filled to overflowing, the rooftops strain to support the weight of spectators. On all sides there arises a shout of new good will. Nor are the people satisfied to see the king just once; they change their vantage points time and time again in the hope that, from one place or another, they may see him again.

The idea of universal acclaim for the monarch, common to both poems, had been given more exaggerated and yet more precise treatment in Erasmus's poem to Philip of Burgundy.

> *Ecce canunt reducem populusque patresque Philippum,*
> *Clamat io reducem laeta undique turba Philippum,*
> *Responsant reducem vocalia tecta Philippum,*
> *Nec fallax ista est iteratae vocis imago:*
> *Saxa enim reducem sentiscunt muta Philippum*
> *Et recinunt reducem minime iam muta Philippum.*[4]

Behold, the people and the lords sing of Philip returned. From all around a joyful crowd shouts a cry of triumph for Philip returned. Rooftops endowed with voices answer in response to the song of Philip returned, and that is no deceitful echo

3. Thomas More, *Carmen Gratulatorium*, lines 43–48, *The Latin Epigrams of Thomas More*, ed. and trans. Leicester Bradner and Charles Arthur Lynch (Chicago, 1953), p. 17.

4. Erasmus, *Gratulatorium Carmen*, lines 16–21, *The Poems of Desiderius Erasmus*, ed. C. Reedijk (Leiden, 1956), p. 273.

either; the mute rocks in fact perceive that Philip is returned and—not at all silent now—resound with the song for Philip returned.

While the incantatory repetitions here express the central idea of restoration, the phrase *populusque patresque* directs attention to the public audience itself. By uniting upper and lower classes, *patres* and *populus,* in celebration of the monarch, Erasmus gives the general idea of universal acclaim the particular force of national reconciliation. In this attempt he had been preceded by Claudian, who develops the same *topos* in his panegyric on Honorius's third consulship.

> *Quanti tum iuvenes, quantae sprevere pudorem*
> *spectandi studio matres, puerisque severi*
> *certavere senes, cum tu genitoris amico*
> *exceptus gremio mediam veherere per urbem*
> *velaretque pios communis laurea currus!*[5]

How many youths, how many matrons set modesty aside in eagerness to behold thee! Austere greybeards struggle with boys for places whence to see thee in the tender embraces of thy sire, borne through the midst of Rome on a triumphal chariot decked but with the shade of a simple laurel branch.

The public audience of the poem is thus idealized in terms of symbolically reconciled groups: old and young, men and women, as well as upper and lower classes. This idea can, moreover, be traced to Pliny's processional *topos,* which begins:

5. Claudian, *Panegyricus De Tertio Consulatu Honorii Augusti,* lines 126–130, *Claudian,* trans. Maurice Platnauer, Loeb Classical Library, 2 vols. (Cambridge, Mass. and London, 1963), pp. 278–280.

Ergo non aetas quemquam non valetudo, non sexus retardavit, quo minus oculos insolito spectaculo impleret. Te parvuli noscere, ostentare iuvenes, mirari senes . . . [6]

Thus neither age, health nor sex held your subjects back from feasting their eyes on this unexpected sight: small children learned who you were, young people pointed you out, old men admired . . .

The processional *topos*, which provides a particularly clear demonstration of the continuity of panegyrical topics, expresses the idea of national reconciliation.

This idea is given formulaic statement by Thomas More in 1509:

Conveniunt igitur simul aetas, sexus, et ordo . . . [7]

The people gather together, every age, both sexes, and all ranks.

Jonson repeats the formula a century later. "No age, nor sex, so weake, or strongly dull, / That did not beare a part in this consent / Of hearts, and voices" (58–60). By uniting to witness the royal procession, the people express their joyful "consent," and implicitly their obedi-

6. Pliny, *Panegyricus*, sec. 22, *Pliny, Letters and Panegyricus*, trans. Betty Radice, Loeb Classical Library, 2 vols. (Cambridge, Mass., and London, 1969), II, 370.

7. More, *Carmen Gratulatorium*, 39. See for comparison, Andreas Ammonius, *Elegia De Obitu Regis Henrici VII Et Felici Successione Henrici Octavi*, lines 37–38: "Hic plebem proceresque sibi iuvenesque senesque / Vinciet, humani delicium generis . . ." *Andreae Ammonii Carmina Omnia*, ed. Clemente Pizzi (Florence, 1958), p. 17. This *topos* is discussed by Ernst Robert Curtius, *European Literature and the Latin Middle Ages*, trans. Willard R. Trask (New York, 1953), p. 160: "One of the oddest flowers of rhetorical style appears in the assurance that every age and sex celebrates so-and-so—as if there were as many sexes as ages. 'Omnis sexus et aetas' becomes a standard formula."

ence, to the new king. In Jonson's *Panegyre*, then, the demonstrative function of traditional panegyric is preserved in the processional *topos*.

Popular obedience, however, is contingent on the future conduct of the king. To guarantee that the king will deserve obedience, Jonson calls on the goddess Themis (daughter of heaven and earth) to instruct James in his duties. Her instructions, although comparatively brief and narrated in the third person, parallel the speech of Theodosius in Claudian's panegyric on the fourth consulship of Honorius. For example, Themis argues that the king must not base public policy on private vice.

> *That they, by Heaven, are plac'd upon his throne,*
> *To rule like Heaven; and have no more, their owne,*
> *As they are men, then men. That all they doe,*
> *Though hid at home, abroad is search'd into:*
> *And, being once found out, discover'd lies*
> *Unto as many envies, there, as eyes.*
> *That princes, since they know it is their fate,*
> *Oft-times, to have the secrets of their state*
> *Betraid to fame, should take more care, and feare*
> *In publique acts what face and forme they beare.* (79–88)

Although Jonson might have garnered such unexceptionable sentiments from other writers, the most probable source is Claudian.

> *Hoc te praeterea crebro sermone monebo,*
> *ut te totius medio telluris in ore*
> *vivere cognoscas, cunctis tua gentibus esse*
> *facta palam nec posse dari regalibus usquam*
> *secretum vitiis; nam lux altissima fati*
> *occultum nihil esse sinit, latebrasque per omnes*
> *intrat et abstrusos explorat fama recessus.*[8]

8. Claudian, *IV Cons.*, lines 269–275, Platnauer, I, 306.

Of this too I cannot warn thee too often: remember that thou livest in the sight of the whole world, to all peoples are thy deeds known; the vices of monarchs cannot anywhere remain hid. The splendour of their lofty station allows nought to be concealed; fame penetrates every hiding-place and discovers the inmost secrets of the heart.

Moreover, just as Theodosius closes his speech by giving Honorius a list of historical exempla, Themis concludes by warning James not to imitate his great-uncle, Henry VIII.

> *Where acts gave licence to impetuous lust*
> *To bury churches, in forgotten dust,*
> *And with their ruines raise the panders bowers:*
> *When, publique justice borrow'd all her powers*
> *From private chambers; that could then create*
> *Lawes, judges, counsellors, yea prince, and state.* (101–106)

Henry's reign thus becomes the prime historical example of private desire obscuring the public interest. It is to prevent a recurrence that Jonson instructs James.

One passage of instruction in this poem calls for particular attention. Themis stresses the argument that James must rule, not by force, but by example: "That kings, by their example, more doe sway / Then by their power; and men doe more obay / When they are led, then when they are compell'd" (125–127). These lines are also paraphrased from Claudian's panegyric on Honorius's fourth consulship:

> *componitur orbis*
> *regis ad exemplum, nec sic inflectere sensus*
> *humanos edicta valent quam vita regentis.* (299–301)

The world shapes itself after its ruler's pattern, nor can edicts sway men's minds so much as their monarch's life . . .

This particular adaptation of Claudian has special significance because James himself had quoted the same passage in *Basilikon Doron*: "teach your people by your example; for people are naturallie inclined to counterfaite (like apes) their Princes maners, according to the notable saying of *Plato* expressed by the poet, '. . . *componitur orbis regis ad exemplum, nec sic inflectere sensus humanos edicta valent quam vita regentis.*' "⁹ Jonson's instruction of James thus incorporates James's advice to his son, Prince Henry. In effect, Jonson catechizes the king according to the king's own principles as they had been announced in his treatise on royal education.

Jonson may well have borrowed this ingenious technique from Daniel, who vigorously attempts to restrict James's rule by reference to the ideals affirmed in *Basilikon Doron*. First, Daniel calls the king's attention to the book.

> *It is the greatest glory upon earth*
> *To be a King, but yet much more to give*
> *The institution with the happy birth*
> *Unto a King, and teach him how to live:*
> *We have, by thee, far more then thine owne worth,*
> *That doth encourage, strengthen and relieve*
> *Our hopes in the succession of thy blood,*
> *That like to thee, they likewise will be good.* (161–168)

Then, in subsequent stanzas, the poet adopts a variation on the Erasmian device of "exhorting to virtue under pretext of praise," instructing the king through a series of complimentary allusions to the king's book. The best ex-

9. King James VI, *Basilikon Doron*, book 2, *The Basilicon Doron of King James VI*, ed. James Craigie, 2 vols. (Edinburgh and London, 1944), I, 53.

ample of the congruence between panegyrical convention
and the king's treatise concerns the problem of flattery.
In poetry, as in oratory, it had become conventional for
the panegyrist to condemn flattery and, usually in the
same breath, to urge the monarch to accept good advice.[10]
Daniel (in language reminiscent of Walter Haddon's
"Consiliis rectis attentam praebeat aurem . . .") urges
the king to choose "counsels that lie right" (181). Daniel's technique of admonition, however, is simply to assume that James will choose good advisers. "We find the
good shall dwell within thy Court; / Plaine zeale and
truth, free from base flatterings" (178–179). Daniel's
confidence is justified by a passage in *Basilikon Doron*
where James had admonished his son on this very topic:
"Choose then for all these offices, men of knowne wisdom,
honestie, and good conscience; well, practised in the
points of the crafte, that ye ordaine them for; and free of
all factions and partialities: but speciallie free of that
filthy vice of Flattery, the pest of all princes . . ."[11] More
specifically than Jonson, Daniel has taken the king's
avowed ideals and turned them into obligations, thereby
circumscribing the king's future conduct.

To emphasize the theme of limitation, Daniel treats
Basilikon Doron as a contractual agreement.

> *We have an everlasting evidence*
> *Under thy hand, that now we need not dread*

10. The anti-flattery *topos* is often developed to secure the
orator's right to advise the prince. First condemning any prince
who countenances flattery, the orator points out that the perfect
prince listens carefully to his advisers. The current prince cannot,
therefore, condemn the advice offered in the panegyric without re-
linquishing his claim to perfection.

11. James VI, *Basilikon Doron*, book 2, Craigie, I, 115.

> *Thou wilt be otherwise in thy designes*
> *Then there thou art in those judiciall lines.* (157–160)

Signed by the king, "those judiciall lines" have the force of law.

> *We have an earnest, that doth even tie*
> *Thy Scepter to thy word, and binds thy Crowne*
> *(That els no band can binde) to ratifie*
> *What thy religious hand hath there set downe,*
> *Wherein thy all commanding Soveraigntie*
> *Stands subject to thy Pen . . .* (169–174)

In each clause of this contract with the people, power ("Scepter," "Crowne," "Soveraigntie") is limited ("tie," "binds," "Stands subject to") by the word ("thy word," "What thy religious hand hath there set down," "thy Pen"). Because Daniel's panegyric incorporates specific allusions to the king's "word," the poem itself functions as a check on royal power.

Daniel concretely illustrates the theme of limitation by appropriating similes and images from the Latin tradition. The restrained exercise of political power is, in fact, summarized in a river simile lifted with little alteration from Claudian's *Panegyricus Dictus Manlio Theodoro Consuli.* Claudian had written:

> *lene fluit Nilus, sed cunctis amnibus extat*
> *utilior nullo confessus murmure vires;*
>
> . . . .
>
> *torrentes inmane fremant lassisque minentur*
> *pontibus et volvant spumoso vertice silvas:*
> *pax maiora decet; peragit tranquilla potestas,*
> *quod violenta nequit, mandataque fortius urget*
> *imperiosa quies.*[12]

12. Claudian, *Panegyricus Dictus Manlio Theodoro Consuli,* lines 232–233, 237–241, Platnauer, I, 345–356.

Gently flows the Nile, yet it is more beneficent than all rivers for all that no sound reveals its power. . . . Let torrents roar horribly, threaten weary bridges, and sweep down forests in their foaming whirl; 'tis repose befits the greater; quiet authority accomplishes what violence cannot, and that mandate compels more which comes from a commanding calm.

In Daniel's English the concept of *tranquilla potestas* is literally translated as "calme power."

> *Thus mightie rivers quietly doe glide,*
> *And doe not by their rage their powers professe,*
> *But by their mightie workings, when in pride*
> *Small* Torrents *roar more lowd, and work much lesse:*
> *Peace, greatnesse best becomes: calme power doth guide*
> *With a farre more imperious statelinesse,*
> *Then all the swords of violence can doe,*
> *And easier gaines those ends she tends unto.* (249–256)

The "greatnesse" of the king, expressed through peace rather than violence, depends on cooperation from the other audience of the poem, the people. "The pedestall whereon thy greatnesse stands, / Is built of all our hearts, and all our hands" (583–584). These final lines echo More's sentiments in the closing of his panegyric to Henry.

> *Anglia thure feras, sacrumque potentius omni*
> *Thure, bonas mentes innocuasque manus.* (185–186)

England, I hope you will bring incense and an offering even more effective, good hearts and innocent hands.

The restriction on the king's power over the people, coupled with the people's promise of obedience to the king, completes the pattern of mutual responsibility which Claudian had called *alterna fides*.

Daniel and Jonson, by adopting the conventions of Latin panegyric, provide a traditional basis for the development of the genre in English. But during the early Stuart period this development proceeds within a rather narrow compass. Beginning in 1617, it became customary for Scottish poets to celebrate the return of the Stuart kings to Scotland and for English poets to answer with panegyrics on the king's return from the north. Primarily (but not exclusively) an exercise for university poets, whole volumes of panegyrics came out of Oxford, Cambridge, and Edinburgh in 1617, 1633, and 1641, bearing such titles as *Rex Redux* and *Solis Britannici Perigaeum*. The minor poets represented in these volumes establish the most characteristic occasion for English panegyric, the return of the king, and thus anticipate the great outpouring of panegyrical poetry in 1660, when (according to George Granville) "Our King return'd, and banisht Peace restor'd, / The Muse ran Mad to see her exil'd Lord."[13]

The most influential of these early "return poems" is William Drummond's *Forth Feasting*, written in 1617 to celebrate James I's visit to his native Scotland. The poem, which reads like an anthology of panegyrical topics, is entirely traditional.

> *That Murder, Rapine, Lust, are fled to Hell,*
> *And in their Roomes with us the* Graces *dwell,*
> *That* Honour *more than* Riches *Men respect,*
> *That* Worthinesse *than Gold doth more effect,*
> *That* Pietie, *unmasked showes her Face,*
> *That* Innocencie *keepes with* Power *her Place,*

13. George Granville, *An Essay upon Unnatural flights in Poetry*, lines 75–76, *Critical Essays of the Seventeenth Century*, ed. J. E. Spingarn, 3 vols. (Oxford, 1908), III, 294. Written in 1701, Granville's implied indictment of panegyric suggests the emerging eighteenth-century view of the genre.

> *That long-exil'd* Astrea *leaves the Heaven,*
> *And turneth right her Sword, her Weights holds even,*
> *That the* Saturnian *World is come againe,*
> *Are wish'd Effects of Thy most happie Raigne.*[14]

The first lines of this typical excerpt invoke a common-place of Latin panegyric, the exile of the vices. Claudian, for classical example, had developed this *topos* in the *Panegyricus De Tertio Consulatu Honorii Augusti.*

> *luget Avarities Stygiis innexa catenis*
> *cumque suo demens expellitur Ambitus auro.*
> *non dominantur opes nec corrumpentia sensus*
> *dona valent: emitur sola virtute potestas.*[15]

Avarice is left to weep in Stygian chains, mad Ambition and his gold banished afar. Wealth does not hold sway; sense-corrupting gifts are of no avail; virtue alone can purchase power.

Clearly, however, Drummond's immediate source is the English panegyric of his friend Ben Jonson, who specifically exiles "*Murder, Rapine, Lust,*" lest they "infect the Crowne."[16] Drummond's ensuing conjunction of "*Pietie*" and "*Power,*" his allusion to the return of Astraea, and his celebration of the renewed Saturnian age, all reflect a thorough acquaintance with the tradition of the genre.

Elsewhere in the poem, moreover, Drummond expresses the ceremonial theme of restoration by allusion to the vegetation myth, referring specifically to the story of Proserpina, and crediting national regeneration to the

14. William Drummond, *Forth Feasting. A Panegyricke to the Kings most excellent Majesty,* lines 255–264, *The Poetical Works of William Drummond of Hawthornden,* ed. L. E. Kastner, 2 vols. (Manchester, 1913), I, 149.

15. Claudian, *III Cons.,* 185–188.

16. Jonson, *A Panegyre,* 12, 17.

return of the king. "Let Mother Earth now deckt with Flowres bee seene, / And sweet-breath'd *Zephyres* curle the Medowes greene" (33–34). Drummond is equally conventional, if less detailed, in adopting the theme of limitation. His couplet, "If *Brutus* knew the Blisse Thy Rule doth give, / Even *Brutus* joye would under Thee to live" (297–298), is a rather clumsy translation of Claudian's "nunc Brutus amaret / vivere sub regno"[17] [Now would Brutus love to live under a king]. Thus celebrated and restrained, James emerges as the *optimus princeps,* who commands not by force, but by "Example." "[By] Example more than anie Law, / This People fierce Thou didst to Goodnesse draw" (181–182).

The influence of Drummond's copiously traditional poem is readily apparent in the university anthologies published in 1633. Armed with Drummond's topics, students at Edinburgh greeted Charles I in familiar strains. David Primrose, who begins by simply plagiarizing the *Forth Feasting,* later acknowledges his debt to Drummond: "Feast fertile *Forth,* feast as thou didst before, / Whiles Heavens-blest James was seen upon our shore."[18] William Douglas shows slightly more imagination by changing the locale of the celebration. Instead of the *Forth Feasting,* Douglas gives us *Grampius Gratulation To his high and mightie Monarch King Charles.* Both of these poems, however, reveal the passage of time since 1617; both emphasize Scottish concerns and take a hard line with respect to any changes Charles may have been

17. Claudian, *Manlio Theodoro,* 163–164.
18. David Primrose, *Scotland's Welcome to Her dread Soveraigne K. Charles,* lines 25–26, E I Σ O Δ I A *Edinensium in Caroli Regis, Musarum Tutani, ingressu in Scotiam* (Edinburgh, 1633).

contemplating. With respect to religion, for example: "For by thy zeale Gods true religion stands / Unchang'd within my well reformed lands."[19] With respect to law as well: "Myne ancient lawes in full integritie, / By thyne indulgence are preserv'd to mee."[20] The tone of these passages recalls lines Daniel had delivered to Charles's father in 1603.

> *We shall continue and remaine all one,*
> *In Law, in Justice, and in Magistrate;*
> *Thou wilt not alter the foundation*
> *Thy Ancestors have laid of this Estate,*
> *Nor grieve thy Land with innovation . . .* (233–237)

Conceived as welcome addresses to a returning king, the Scottish panegyrics of 1633, like Daniel's English panegyric of thirty years earlier, carefully establish the conditional terms of welcome. The theme of limitation thus complements the more obvious theme of restoration.

When the king arrived once again in England, Oxford poets answered their Scottish rivals in equally conventional verse. Jasper Maine's version of the processional *topos* typifies the verse in this collection: "Then all the heapes of people you did meete, / Making the high-way as you past, a streete; / Whilst every sexe and age to you pressed, / And left their Townes, for that time wildernesse."[21] The one poem in this volume that rises above the others is by William Cartwright, who celebrates the power, or "Presence," of the king, limited by the traditional ideal of piety.

19. Primrose, *Scotland's Welcome*, 183–184.
20. Primrose, *Scotland's Welcome*, 195–196.
21. Jasper Maine, *Upon the Kings return from Scotland*, lines 11–14, *Solis Britannici Perigaeum Sive Itinerantis Caroli Auspicatissima Periodus* (Oxford, 1633).

> *Your pious Reign secur'd your Throne, your Life*
> *Was guard unto your Scepter: no rude strife,*
> *No violence there disturb'd the Pompe, unlesse*
> *Their eager Love, and Loyalty did presse*
> *To see and know, whiles lawful Majesty*
> *Spread forth its Presence, and its Piety.*[22]

The "Love" and "Loyalty" of the people combined with the "Presence" and "Piety" of the king create once again the pattern of mutual responsibility, thus extending the English tradition of verse panegyric established a generation earlier by Daniel and Jonson.

TRANSFORMATION

Charles I made another trip to Scotland in 1641. On his return to England he was celebrated in new volumes of student verse, and among those contributing to the Cambridge anthology was the young Abraham Cowley. Written more than ten years before his first imitation of Pindar, Cowley's return poem of 1641 is a brief, conventional panegyric. The poet seizes the occasion ("our joyful *Holiday*") to celebrate this *optimus princeps* (the "best of *Kings*") for restoring the blessings of peace.[23] Two decades later, now a mature and famous poet, Cowley revived these themes in his poem on the return of Charles II. But this later poem is cast in the form of a Pindaric ode. By this transformation of the genre Cowley

22. William Cartwright, *To the King*, lines 27–32, *Solis Britannici Perigaeum*.

23. Abraham Cowley, *On his Majesties Return out of Scotland*, lines 16, 61, *The English Writings of Abraham Cowley*, ed. A. R. Waller (Cambridge, 1905), pp. 22–24. Unless specified otherwise, all citations from Cowley's poems are repeated from this edition.

exercised a significant influence over Dryden and other poets of the later Stuart period, including (after 1688) Jonathan Swift.

To appreciate the importance of Cowley in the tradition of panegyric, we need to consider as a preliminary the place of Pindar himself. Although Pindar is often called a "panegyrical" poet, his odes differ in significant ways from the panegyrics written on the Roman model of Pliny.[24] First, Pindar celebrates an individual, whereas Pliny and his followers celebrate an institution. Second, Pindar has no apparent theory of history, in contrast to the Latin panegyrists, whose persistent ceremonial theme is restoration. Third, Pindar pays almost no attention to the public at large, whereas the Latin panegyrist speaks both to and for that public.[25] Because Pindar's occasional lyrics were inspired or commissioned to celebrate real human achievement, victory in the festival games, the poet glorifies this individual by comparing him with mythic heroes. Personal glory thus stands out against the background of history, providing the hero with a kind of immortality, but it does not change history. Pindar's odes do not proclaim the renewal of the golden age, nor do they attempt to ensure political stability, either through instruction of the monarch or through propaganda aimed at the people.

In effect, the function of praise changes as we move

24. Modern criticism of panegyric, what little exists, has generally failed to make this kind of distinction. See Warren L. Chernaik, *The Poetry of Limitation: A Study of Edmund Waller* (New Haven and London, 1968), p. 117.

25. For Pindar's audience, see C. M. Bowra, *Pindar* (Oxford, 1964), pp. 100–101.

from the Greek ode to the Latin oration. The purpose of Pindar's praise is to immortalize a man, whereas the purpose of Pliny's praise is to bridge the gap between the nature of the man and the demands of the institution. Thus, Pindar's odes celebrate personal glory and power, limited only by the jealousy of the gods, whereas Pliny's panegyric celebrates the glory and power of a monarch, limited by his obligations to the people. This functional difference is reflected in the choice of laudatory analogies. The highest honor bestowed by Pindar is a comparison with Hercules. In the tradition of Roman panegyric, on the other hand, the ideal figures are not Herculean heroes but great rulers, above all Trajan and Augustus. By reviving Pindar and attempting to reconcile the Greek ode and the Roman oration, Cowley aims at a reconciliation of heroic and monarchical ideals.

Between his welcome to Charles I in 1641 and his welcome to Charles II in 1660, Cowley wrote Pindaric odes on a range of subjects and occasions. Some of these odes, although far removed from Pindar, anticipate Cowley's panegyric on the Restoration. *Brutus*, for example, and *The 34. Chapter of the Prophet Isaiah*, both seem to reflect contemporary events.[26] If not precise political allegories, these odes at least touch on themes that are relevant to the condition of interregnum England. Even more relevant is Cowley's other Pindaric paraphrase of the Bible, *The Plagues of Egypt*. Based on several chapters of *Exodus*, this poem describes the liberation of the

26. For a discussion of the possible political significance of Cowley's Pindarics, see Arthur A. Nethercot, *Abraham Cowley, The Muse's Hannibal* (London, 1931), p. 155ff.

Hebrew people from Egyptian captivity with Moses as
hero. And yet the moral of the poem is suggestively derived from *Genesis*.

> *Is this thy* Brav'ery Man, *is this thy* Pride?
> Rebel *to* God, *and* Slave *to all beside!*
> Captiv'ed *by everything! and onely* Free
>   *To fly from thine* own Libertie!
> *All* Creatures *the* Creator *said* Were Thine;
> *No* Creature *but might since, say,* Man is Mine!
> *In black* Egyptian Slavery *we lie;*
> *And sweat and toil in the vile Drudgerie*
>   *Of* Tyrant Sin . . . [27]

The incessant language of politics, *"Rebel," "Slave,"*
"Libertie," "Tyrant," creates at least suspicion that Cowley had more than the Bible in mind when he thus developed rebellion as a metaphor to define the nature of
the plague. In another of the interregnum odes, *To Dr.
Scarborough,* Cowley reverses tenor and vehicle, making
plague a metaphor for rebellion. "How long, alas! has
our mad *Nation* been / Of *Epidemick War* the *Tragick
Scene* . . ."[28] These odes provide the immediate literary
background for the *Ode Upon His Majesties Restoration
and Return.*

Here Cowley picks up where he had left off at the end
of *The Plagues of Egypt,* placing the Stuart exiles in the
role of the chosen people. "How through a *rough Red sea*
they had been led, / By *Wonders* guarded, and by *Wonders* fed."[29] Ignoring the fine points of the Biblical story,
Cowley extends the parallel until Charles is conducted

27. Cowley, *The Plagues of Egypt*, 1–9.

28. Cowley, *To Dr. Scarborough*, 1–2.

29. Cowley, *Ode Upon His Majesties Restoration and Return*,
158–159.

into the *"promis'd Land"* (169). Cast in the role of national redeemer, Charles himself can be compared with Cowley's Dr. Scarborough, a remarkably successful physician: "thy *Patients* seem to be / Restor'ed not to *Health* onely, but *Virginitie.*"[30] In the Restoration ode Charles provides the same health care for the plagued body of the state. He restores the nation to *"Innocence."*

> *Thou mad'st of that fair* Month *thy choice,*
>   *In which* Heaven, Air, *and* Sea, *and* Earth,
> *And all that's in them all does* smile, *and does* rejoyce.
> *'Twas a right* Season, *and the very* Ground
> *Ought with a face of* Paradise *to be found,*
>   *Then when we were to entertain*
> Felicity *and* Innocence *again.* (29–35)

Cowley here unites the historical rhythm of panegyric, expressed in the traditional imagery of the seasons, with Biblical myth, thus transforming restoration into redemption. Recent events assume for Cowley the pattern of the fortunate fall.

The role of Satan in this scheme of history belongs to Oliver Cromwell, who is described as "that great *Serpent*" (67). A military leader become monarch (of sorts), Cromwell is here seen as the characteristic villain of panegyric, the usurper who would upset the natural order of the state, like Maximus or Alaric. As the monarch is traditionally the sun, Cowley adapts a series of contrasting astronomical metaphors for the usurper; the *"Imposter Cromwell"* (209) is an *"Ignis Fatuus"* (207) and a comet, while "that *Falling-star* his *Son*" (210) provides an obvious link between the astronomical and mythological imagery of the poem. The dark night of the interregnum

30. Cowley, *To Dr. Scarborough,* 47–48.

is relieved only by false lights which fade out with the royal dawn. The poem's seasonal imagery is thus complemented by an imaginative adaptation of the conventional diurnal metaphor of panegyric.

But Cowley goes one step beyond convention and blesses the immediate past—the winter, the night, the rebellion—for it is only by such contrast that the present joy of Restoration can be significant.[31] "We welcome both, and with improv'd delight / Bless the *preceding Winter* and the *Night*" (229–230). The fall is fortunate because it brings redemption. In this Christian context, the Restoration of Charles II becomes the resurrection of Charles I.

> *He who had seen him in his* Clowd *so bright:*
> *He who had seen the double* Pair
> *Of* Brothers *heavenly good, and* Sisters *heavenly fair,*
> *Might have perceiv'd (me thinks) with ease,*
> *(But* wicked men *see only what they please)*
> *That God had no intent t'extinguish quite*
> *The* pious King's eclipsed Right. (145–151)

Conversely, the suffering of Charles I has been shared by his son.

> *As a choise* Medal *for* Heaven's Treasury
> God *did* stamp *first upon one side of* Thee
> *The* Image *of his* suffering Humanity:
> *On th' other side, turn'd now to sight, does shine*
> *The* glorious Image *of his* Power Divine. (270–274)

The ideal king, who combines the piety of Charles I with the power of Charles II, thus embodies the two aspects of

31. Robert Hinman has not only recognized the pattern of *felix culpa* in the ode, he has also suggested comparisons with *Paradise Lost*. Robert Hinman, *Abraham Cowley's World of Order* (Cambridge, Mass., 1960), pp. 217–226.

Christian divinity, humility and authority. In this poem the traditional *optimus princeps* is transformed into the divine redeemer.

Transformation of the king into a Christian hero does not, however, represent a major innovation. Not only does Cowley preserve the traditional terms, power and piety, he also adopts the traditional imagery of the sun and the seasons. As we have already seen in connection with Erasmus and Walter Haddon, the possibilities of panegyric as redemptive ritual were simply waiting to be rigorously exploited. William Drummond, for example, had recognized this possibility in his celebration of James I: "O *Vertues* Patterne, Glorie of our Times, / Sent of past Dayes to expiate the Crimes . . ."[32] Cowley's emphasis on the Christian heroism of the king, although given greater prominence here by the context of the fortunate fall, is nothing very new.

The potential for a far more radical transformation of the genre lies in Cowley's attempt to make Charles into a classical hero. Given the Pindaric form of the poem we might expect Cowley to compare Charles with Hercules. Cowley was surely aware of the important place of Hercules in Pindar's lyrics, as he had translated the first Nemean and second Olympic odes, both of which include celebration of this hero. Indeed, in Cowley's version of Nemean 1, four of the poem's nine stanzas are devoted to celebration of Hercules, and Cowley makes a special point of comparing his subject, Chromius, with this model of heroism. As he observes in his notes to the poem: "*Pindar*, according to his manner, leaves the Reader to find as he can, the connexion between *Chromius* and the story of

32. Drummond, *Forth Feasting*, 285–286.

Hercules, which it seem'd to me necessary to make a little more perspicuous."[33] Cowley not only perceived, but also reinforced the heroic analogy. But in his original Pindaric *Ode Upon His Majesties Restoration and Return,* Cowley—significantly—does not compare Charles with Hercules. Instead we find:

> *So when the wisest* Poets *seek*
> *In all their liveliest colours to set forth*
>   *A* Picture *of* Heroick *worth,*
>   *(The* Pious Trojan, *or the* Prudent Greek)
> *They chuse some* comely Prince *of* heavenly Birth . . .
>   (275–279)

Prudence, one of the cardinal virtues that the subject of a demonstrative oration should possess, and piety, the essential virtue in panegyric, are here recommended by allusion to classical epic. The goal of this prudent and pious hero is, moreover, restoration.

> *He does long* troubles *and long* wars *sustain,*
>   *E're he his* fatal Birth-right *gain.*
>   *With no less* time *or* labour *can*
>   Destiny build *up such a* Man,
>   *Who's with sufficient virtue fill'd*
>   His *ruin'd* Country *to* rebuild. (292–297)

The achievement of Odysseus and Aeneas, in Cowley's interpretation, is the acquisition, not of power, but of the virtues necessary for the proper exercise of power. What the hero attains is only his right by birth; what he has learned through suffering is how to perform the duty that accompanies that right. In effect, the normative fig-

33. Cowley, note to stanza 6 of *The First Nemean Ode of Pindar,* Waller, p. 177.

ures drawn from classical epic function as substitutes for the conventional allusions to historical kings and emperors. Human heroism is subordinated to the traditional ideals of panegyric.

Cowley's adaptation of Pindaric to panegyric thus appears to be formal without finally being functional. Only the surface of the poem is changed; underneath Cowley's apparent debt to Pindar, the tradition of Latin panegyric survives essentially unchanged. But this conclusion needs to be qualified in one significant respect. If Cowley implicitly admits that the heroic figure of Hercules is inappropriate to panegyric, he does not make the same admission with respect to Pindar's antiheroes. In contrast to the *"pious Trojan"* and the *"Prudent Greek,"* Cowley points to the Titans: "(No proud *Gigantick son* of *Earth*, / Who strives t' usurp the *god's forbidden seat*)" (280–281). The story of the Titans, as we have seen in Claudian's poem on Honorius's sixth consulship, is for the panegyrist a conventional emblem of impiety and rebellion. But the Titans are also the type of all Pindar's antiheroes, those who by arrogance or pride offend the gods. Cowley's parenthetical allusion suggests, for example, Pindar's description of Bellerephon in the seventh Isthmian ode. "But, if any man lifteth up his eyes to things afar, he is too short to attain the brass-paved floor of heaven; for the winged Pegasus threw Bellerephon his rider, who would fain have gone to the homes of heaven and the goodly company of Zeus."[34] Here, then, is a very real point of similarity between Pindaric and pane-

34. Pindar, Isthmian 7, lines 45–48, trans. Sir John Sandys, Loeb Classical Library (Cambridge, Mass., and London), p. 495.

gyric. Pindar's vivid portrayals of impiety can be adapted
to serve one of the traditional functions of panegyric,
propaganda on behalf of the established order.

Toward the end of his Restoration ode, Cowley includes a tribute to General Monck.

> *Thou worthiest Person of the* Brittish Story,
>   (*Though 'tis not* small *the* Brittish glory)
> *Did I not know my* humble Verse *must be*
> *But ill-proportion'd to the* Heighth *of* Thee,
>   Thou, *and the* World *should see*
> *How much my* Muse, *the* Foe *of* Flattery,
> *Do's make* true Praise *her* Labour *and* Design;
> *An* Iliad *or an* Aeneid *should be* Thine. (412–419)

Expanding the antiflattery *topos*, Cowley proposes Monck
as the subject of an English epic. The measure of "*true
Praise*" here becomes the epic poem, specifically the *Iliad*
and the *Aeneid*. In effect, Cowley defines a direction in
panegyrical poetry already taken by his contemporary,
Edmund Waller.

Waller was obviously conversant with the traditional
themes and topics of panegyric, which are given felicitous
if unremarkable expression in his own poem on the Restoration. The familiar ceremonial pattern of *prius . . .
nunc . . .* , so appropriate to both the genre and the
occasion, is here presented in the traditional vocabulary
of panegyric. "Faith, law, and piety, (that banished
train!) / Justice and truth, with you return again."[35]

35. Edmund Waller, *To The King, Upon His Majesty's Happy
Return*, lines 109–110, *The Poems of Edmund Waller*, ed. George
Thorn-Drury (New York, 1968), p. 167. Unless specified otherwise
all citations from Waller's poems will be repeated from this
edition, originally published under the same title in two volumes
in 1905.

The instructional theme of limitation is also conventionally developed.

> *While to yourself severe, to others kind,*
> *With power unbounded, and a will confined,*
> *Of this vast empire you possess the care,*
> *The softer part falls to the people's share.*
> *Safety, and equal government, are things*
> *Which subjects make as happy as their kings.* (103–108)

Although it should be noticed in passing that Waller does not attempt to restrict the "power" of the monarchy, but only the "will" of the individual king, he does reaffirm the king's obligation to his people. The rest of the poem is equally traditional.

In other poems on other occasions, however, Waller effects a major transformation of the genre by combining three innovations: (1) emphasis on action instead of ceremony, (2) celebration of the king as hero rather than as monarch, and (3) insistence on facts even at the expense of ideals. In his poem to Roscommon, Waller sums up this artistic purpose as "Praise of great acts."

> *The Muses' friend, unto himself severe,*
> *With silent pity looks on all that err;*
> *But where a brave, a public action shines,*
> *That he rewards with his immortal lines.*
> *Whether it be in council or in fight,*
> *His country's honour is his chief delight;*
> *Praise of great acts he scatters as a seed,*
> *Which may the like in coming ages breed.*[36]

36. Waller, *Upon The Earl Of Roscommon's Translation Of Horace,* 29–36. This passage is cited and discussed in similar terms by Chernaik, pp. 133–134. My own discussion of Waller's panegyrics has benefited significantly from chapter 3 of Professor Chernaik's book and from his earlier article, "Waller's *Panegyric to My Lord Protector* and the Poetry of Praise," *SEL,* IV (1964), 109–124.

Measured against the tradition of panegyric, this concept of praise reveals a relaxation of the courtly and occasional determinants of the genre, and no commitment at all to its oratorical mode. Measured against the epic theory of emulation, on the other hand, this concept of praise differs in but one significant respect: the hero of the poem is a contemporary. By abandoning ceremony in favor of action, by celebrating modern heroism, Waller forges a strong new link between public poetry and actual fact.

In order to celebrate the events of his own time, Waller recreates them in the light provided by Homer, Vergil, and Tasso. This aspect of Waller's public poetry was noticed toward the end of the seventeenth century by Thomas Rymer. In the context of a brief discussion of *To The King On His Navy*, Rymer cites the last couplet of the poem ("To thee, his chosen, more indulgent, he / Dares trust such power with so much piety") and then comments: "Here is both *Homer* and *Virgil*; the *fortis Achilles*, and the *pius Aeneas*, in the person he Compliments . . ."[37] Although Rymer's suggestion is not quite complete, it is true to the spirit of Waller's public poetry. This particular couplet is expanded in Waller's poem *Of The Queen*.

> *None might the mother of Achilles be,*
> *But the fair pearl and glory of the sea;*
> *The man to whom great Maro gives such fame,*

37. Thomas Rymer, *A Short View of Tragedy*, in *The Critical Works of Thomas Rymer*, ed. Curt A. Zimansky (New Haven, 1956), p. 127. Rymer's comment is cited by Elijah Fenton, ed., *The Works of Edmund Waller, Esq.* (London, 1729), p. x, by Chernaik, pp. 146–147, and by Nevo, p. 24.

> *From the high bed of heavenly Venus came;*
> *And our next Charles, whom all the stars design*
> *Like wonders to accomplish, springs from thine.*[38]

Here, indirectly, the prince unites in himself Achilles and Aeneas. Waller is known to have been fond of Chapman's Homer, and he frequently alludes to the heroes of the *Iliad* in his public poems. In the early poem on the king's response to Buckingham's death, for example, Charles plays Achilles to Buckingham's Patroclus.[39] But the more important influence on Waller is Vergil. Allusions to the *Aeneid*, scattered throughout his poetry, are as likely to be encountered in addresses to court ladies as in poems to their husbands.

> *Who from our flaming Troy, with a bold hand,*
> *Snatched her fair charge, the Princess, like a brand?*
> *A brand! preserved to warm some prince's heart,*
> *And make whole kingdoms take her brother's part.*
> *So Venus, from prevailing Greeks, did shroud*
> *The hope of Rome, and save him in a cloud.*[40]

In these lines from *To My Lady Morton*, for example, the English civil war becomes the Trojan war, as Waller sees the facts of seventeenth-century English history in the mirror of the *Aeneid*.

Vergil's importance to Waller is perhaps equaled by that of Tasso. Since Waller's day it has become a critical commonplace to discuss his poetry by reference to Fairfax's translation of the *Gerusalemme Liberata*. Samuel

---

38. Waller, *Of The Queen*, 65–70.

39. Waller, *Of His Majesty's Receiving The News Of The Duke Of Buckingham's Death*, 9–16.

40. Waller, *To My Lady Morton, On New Year's Day, 1650*, 17–22.

Johnson even devotes the last several pages of his *Life of Waller* to an extract from Fairfax, in order that by "knowing the state in which Waller found our poetry, the reader may judge how much he improved it."[41] But this influence extends beyond prosody and conditioned Waller's concept of heroism as well. The great heroic combat for Waller is driving the Turks from Europe. He alludes to this heroic mission repeatedly in his poems. In *To The Queen Mother Of France, Upon Her Landing*, for example:

> *Would those commanders of mankind obey*
> *Their honoured parent, all pretences lay*
> *Down at your royal feet, compose their jars,*
> *And on the growing Turk discharge these wars,*
> *The Christian knights that sacred tomb should wrest*
> *From Pagan hands, and triumph o'er the East:*
> *Our England's Prince, and Gallia's Dauphin, might*
> *Like young Rinaldo and Tancredo fight;*
> *In single combat by their swords again*
> *The proud Argantes and fierce Soldan slain;*
> *Again might we their valiant deeds recite,*
> *And with your Tuscan Muse exalt the fight.*[42]

Here Waller enlarges on Tasso's own plea voiced in the first book of the poem and translated by Fairfax: "You must from realms and seas the Turks forth drive, / As Godfrey chased them from Judah's land."[43] Waller, then,

41. Samuel Johnson, *Life of Waller*, in *Lives of the English Poets*, ed. G. B. Hill, 3 vols. (Oxford, 1905), I, 296. For a modern discussion of Waller and Fairfax, see Alexander Ward Allison, *Toward an Augustan Poetic: Edmund Waller's "Reform of English Poetry"* (Lexington, Ky., 1962), especially pp. 35–42.

42. Waller, *To The Queen-Mother Of France, Upon Her Landing*, 19–30.

43. Torquato Tasso, *Jerusalem Delivered*, book 1, stanza 5,

would be the English Tasso, although in another poem he defers to his friend Thomas Higgons.

> *If, listening to your charms, we could our jars*
> *Compose, and on the Turk discharge these wars,*
> *Our British arms the sacred tomb might wrest*
> *From Pagan hands, and triumph o'er the East,*
> *And then you might our own high deeds recite*
> *And with great Tasso celebrate the fight.*[44]

Military victory over the Turks is the ideal "action" for Waller's heroic praise.[45] Waller's transformation of panegyric thus begins with his re-creation of the *optimus princeps* on the model of the epic hero.

The traditional panegyrist, although he may occasionally allude to the classical epics, limits the monarch in a way that specifically denies him the usual means of heroism, the sword. According to Daniel, for instance, the monarch's power is based on "example and respect," which means that he can rule the state "without a sword."[46] Drummond of Hawthornden is even more emphatic on this point.

> *Let Others boast of Blood and Spoyles of Foes,*
> *Fierce Rapines, Murders, Iliads of Woes,*
>
> .   .   .   .
>
> *Thou a true Victor art, sent from above*
> *What Others straine by Force to gaine by Love . . .*
>
> (229–230, 239–240)

---

trans. Edward Fairfax, Centaur Classics Edition (Carbondale, Ill., 1962), p. 4.

44. Waller, *To His Worthy Friend, Sir Thos. Higgons, Upon The Translation Of "The Venetian Triumph,"* 17–22.

45. The term "heroic praise" I have borrowed from the title of Chernaik's third chapter.

46. Daniel, *A Panegyrike Congratulatorie*, 225–226.

Drummond here excludes conquest and military heroism
from the province of panegyric, and specifically excludes
the epic heroism of the *Iliad*. Even in Cowley's Restoration panegyric, with its several allusions to epic, the king
is not a military hero.

> *The* King *and* Truth *have greatest* strength,
> *When they their sacred force unite,*
>   *And twine into one* Right,
> *No frantick* Common-wealths *or* Tyrannies,
>   *No* Cheats, *and* Perjuries, *and* Lies,
>   *No* Nets *of humane* Policies;
> *No stores of* Arms *or* Gold *(though you could joyn*
> *Those of* Peru *to the great* London Mine)
> *No* Towns, *no* Fleets *by Sea, or* Troops *by Land,*
> *No deeply entrencht* Islands *can withstand,*
>   *Or any small resistance bring*
> *Against the* naked Truth, *and the* unarmed King. (191–202)

The king's power has nothing to do with the sword; because his power is "sacred," he can go "unarmed."

On the other hand, the villains of panegyric—from
Alaric and Maximus to Cromwell—actively use physical
force. Cowley identifies this source of power with Satan.

> *Vain men! who thought the Divine Power to find*
> *In the fierce* Thunder *and the violent* Wind:
>   *God came not till the storm was past,*
> *In the* still voice *of* Peace *he came at last.*
> *The cruel business of* Destruction,
> *May by the* Claws *of the great* Fiend *be done.*
> *Here, here we see th'* Almighty's hand *indeed*
> *Both by the* Beauty *of the* Work, *we see't, and by the* Speed.
>   (137–144)

The rigorous distinction between the two sources of
power, between the divine monarch and the infernal

usurper, between love and force, between peace and war, is fundamental to the genre. It is, in fact, the traditional basis for the panegyrist's definition of political stability. To quote Drummond once again:

> *They many feare who are of many fear'd,*
> *And Kingdomes got by Wrongs by Wrongs are tear'd,*
> *Such Thrones as Blood doth raise Blood throweth downe,*
> *No Guard so sure as Love unto a Crowne.*[47]

Traditional panegyric is a ceremonial confirmation of an institution that exists rightfully, lawfully, and by divine will; it is not an instrument for the validation of personal power seized by force, no matter how heroic. To praise the monarch for personal heroism is potentially to subvert the monarchy as an institution. At least, to celebrate the monarch as hero is to place individual over institution, "cause" over "laws" (to use Dryden's terms), and this is exactly what the panegyrist seeks to prevent. In short, to celebrate the monarch as military hero would be to invite the possibility of celebrating a military hero as monarch. And this brings us back to Edmund Waller, who confronted precisely this situation in his panegyric to Cromwell.

About thirty years before Cromwell's rise to power, Waller had begun his career by praising Charles I. Although his first poem, titled *Of The Danger His Majesty (Being Prince) Escaped In The Road At Saint Andrews,* is not very successful, it does illustrate Waller's characteris-

47. Drummond, *Forth Feasting,* 243–246. Compare Erasmus, *Panegyricus,* in *Opera Omnia,* ed. J. LeClerc, 10 vols. (Hildesheim, 1962), IV, 524: "Ne id quidem referam, tametsi memorabile, quod cum plerisque necesse sit, imperium sibi multa caede ac sanguine asserere, ferro tueri, periculo ac scelere propagare . . ."

tic approach to panegyric. The occasion for this poem, the return of the monarch, offered a perfect opportunity for the young poet to show his skill by embellishing the conventional topics.[48] But instead of concentrating on the significance of this restoration or extracting the educational value of the foreign journey, Waller celebrates the action of crossing the seas. As the poet describes this voyage, Charles emerges as a hero braver than Aeneas.

> *Great Maro could no greater tempest feign,*
> *When the loud winds usurping on the main*
> *For angry Juno, laboured to destroy*
> *The hated relics of confounded Troy;*
> *His bold Aeneas, on like billows tossed*
> *In a tall ship, and all his country lost,*
> *Dissolves with fear . . .*
>
> . . . .
>
> *. . . our hero, set*
> *In a small shallop, Fortune in his debt,*
> *So near a hope of crowns and sceptres, more*
> *Than ever Priam, when he flourished, wore;*
> *His loins yet full of ungot princes, all*
> *His glory in the bud, lets nothing fall*
> *That argues fear . . .* [49]

Although the narrative has Charles at the center, the action is given over entirely to the waves and winds. Charles himself neither acts nor suffers. The poem is ineffective as narrative because Charles is not free, is not human. It is ineffective as ceremony, on the other hand, because of its epic pretensions.

48. It is true that the events described in the poem occurred before Charles became king, but this is not sufficient to account for the unconventional nature of Waller's celebration.

49. Waller, *Of The Danger His Majesty (Being Prince) Escaped In The Road At Saint Andrews*, 85–91, 93–99.

The problems of the poem are compounded by another aspect of Waller's approach: romance. The poet asks us to believe that his hero, although fearless in the face of the storm, is worried about communicating his love to his future wife. This romantic theme is prepared for by the interpolated story of Edward IV, Warwick, and the Lady Bona, sung by Arion as a preface to the main action of the poem. In Arion's song we find the conflict between love and honor. Affairs of state are balanced against affairs of love, with a decided tilt toward the latter. In the process, the monarch becomes not the "best of kings" but the "best of English hearts."

> *Of the Fourth Edward was his noble song,*
> *Fierce, goodly, valiant, beautiful, and young;*
> *He rent the crown from vanquished Henry's head,*
> *Raised the White Rose, and trampled on the Red;*
> *Till love, triumphing o'er the victor's pride,*
> *Brought Mars and Warwick to the conquered side;*
>
> . . . .
>
> *Ah! spare your swords, where beauty is to blame;*
> *Love gave the affront, and must repair the same;*
> *When France shall boast of her, whose conquering eyes*
> *Have made the best of English hearts their prize;*
> *Have power to alter the decrees of Fate,*
> *And change again the counsels of our state.* (13–18, 25–30)

The Wars of the Roses thus serve a quite different function here from that seen in Daniel's panegyric of two decades earlier. In fact, the last lines cited here evoke precisely that situation feared by More, Daniel, and especially Jonson: public good sacrificed to private desire. But this traditional consideration does not disturb Waller, who makes Arion's theme his own.

Throughout Waller's political poetry we find an emphasis on women and romance that is entirely alien to the tradition of panegyric. In the panegyrics of Claudian, Erasmus, More, and Daniel, praise of the queen-consort is dynastic and public. The two virtues consistently attributed to female royalty in these poems are the obvious ones of chastity and fecundity. Because the queen is perceived as a national asset, she has no private or romantic dimension. In More's poem, for example, the marriage of Henry and Katherine functions as an emblem of the larger marriage between king and people. The queen, as chaste mother of future monarchs, will ensure the continuity of the harmonious relationship between the crown and the public. In Waller's political poetry, however, there is a persistent romantic theme derived ultimately from *Aeneid IV*. The conflict between romantic love and public duty (or piety) is most explicitly defined in *To The Queen*.

> *The royal youth pursuing the report*
> *Of beauty, found it in the Gallic court;*
> *There public care with private passion fought*
> *A doubtful combat in his noble thought* . . . [50]

A few lines later Buckingham appears as Achates, thus making Charles once again Aeneas. This "doubtful combat," so characteristic of Vergilian epic, is nevertheless new to panegyric.

Waller's desire to idealize contemporary events as episodes of heroic romance is complemented by a desire to reach beyond the traditional goal of national reconciliation to the goal of conquest. Waller's imperialism,

50. Waller, *To The Queen, Occasioned Upon Sight Of Her Majesty's Picture*, 43–46.

readily apparent in such poems as *Of A War With Spain,
And A Fight At Sea* and *Instructions To A Painter,* is
ideally expressed in a series of three poems written toward the very end of the poet's life. All three poems were
written in response to Christian victories over the Turks
in Central Europe during the 1680's, and in all three
Waller links contemporary history with the epic ideal
derived from Tasso. In each poem, moreover, the current English king, Charles II in *Of The Invasion And
Defeat Of The Turks, In The Year 1683,* and James II
in *A Presage Of The Ruin Of The Turkish Empire* and
*To His Majesty . . . Occasioned By The Taking Of Buda,
1686,* is given credit for the international Christian unity
that has made defeat of the Turks possible and is cast as
the leader who will finally drive them from Europe.

> *What angel shall descend to reconcile
> The Christian states, and end their guilty toil?
> A prince more fit from heaven we cannot ask
> Than Britain's king, for such a glorious task . . .* [51]

Charles here assumes the role of Godfrey in Tasso's
Christian epic, a role that Waller readily transfers to
James after 1685.

> *A prince more fit for such a glorious task,
> Than England's king, from Heaven we cannot ask;
> He, great and good! proportioned to the work,
> Their ill-drawn swords shall turn against the Turk.* [52]

In these three poems, Waller creates an ideal of conquest
based on Tasso that has little recognizable connection

51. Waller, *Of The Invasion And Defeat Of The Turks, In The
Year 1683,* 45–48.
52. Waller, *A Presage Of The Ruin Of The Turkish Empire,*
9–12.

with the traditional themes and topics of English panegyric. In his attempt to attach current events to an epic
ideal, Waller abandons the purpose of traditional panegyric: to persuade a dual audience, the prince and the
people, to act in a way that will produce political stability.
Waller, the most factual of English panegyrists, is also
the most impractical.

Although neither the poem on the king's escape nor
these poems on the Turks can be considered successful,
on other occasions Waller was a very effective panegyrical poet. The perfect occasion for "heroic panegyric"
came with the rise of Oliver Cromwell. Whereas in the
early poem on Charles I and in the later poems on Charles
II and James II Waller is trying to make a hero out of a
king, in *A Panegyric To My Lord Protector* he is trying
to make a king out of a hero. It was a task perfectly suited
to Waller's conception of the genre.

The rhetorical strategy of Waller's poem is succinctly
revealed in a couplet that occurs about one-third the way
through the poem. "Here the Third Edward, and the Black
Prince, too, / France-conquering Henry flourished, and
now you . . ."[53] The significance of this comparison
emerges very clearly when we place Waller's lines next
to a passage from Drummond's *Forth Feasting*.

> *Of* Henries, Edwards, *famous for their Fights,*
> *Their Neighbour Conquests, Orders new of Knights,*
> *Shall by this Princes Name be past as farre*
> *As Meteors are by the* Idalian *Starre.* (315–318)

53. Waller, *A Panegyric To My Lord Protector, Of The Present
Greatness, And Joint Interest Of His Highness, And This Nation*,
68–69.

The point of Drummond's comparison is that the pacific James surpasses those kings whose fame rests on "their Fights." Drummond's poem thus represents the conventional attitude of panegyric, the celebration of peace. Waller, on the other hand, attempts to reconcile conquest and rule, heroic and monarchical ideals. The comparisons with Henry V, Edward III, and the Black Prince (who incidentally was to be one of the proposed subjects of Dryden's unwritten epic), are perfect vehicles for this reconciliation. There are two elements in the comparison, heroism and kingship; Waller's rhetoric asks us to grant the second because we have already conceded the first.

Cromwell's military heroism is emphasized by the subsequent comparison with Alexander the Great, whom Erasmus (in his prose *Panegyricus*) had roundly condemned for inflicting war, tumult, and terror on the world.[54] Waller also denigrates Alexander, but from a radically different point of view. Waller belittles Alexander's conquests by comparing them with Cromwell's. Whereas the Macedonian had defeated the "unwarlike" Persians and Medes, Cromwell conquered the Scots.

> *A race unconquered, by their clime made bold,*
> *The Caledonians, armed with want and cold,*
> *Have, by a fate indulgent to your fame,*
> *Been from all ages kept for you to tame.* (81–84)

In writing these lines, Waller departs from another longstanding tradition. Daniel, Drummond, Cowley, and numerous collegiate poets had proclaimed the peaceful union of Scotland and England. Perhaps Daniel is the

54. Erasmus, *Panegyricus*, LeClerc, IV, 521F.

most typical: "What heretofore could never yet be wrought / By all the swords of pow'r, by bloud, by fire, / By ruine and distruction; here is brought / To passe with peace, with love, with joy, desire" (17–21). Waller's divergence from this tradition is characteristic of his state poetry. On the one hand, he simply follows the facts. Cromwell did win victories over the Scots. On the other, he celebrates these facts by analogy with the heroic past. A more conventional panegyrist would have glossed over such heroics, minimized them, left them out altogether in preference for the theme of peace, or—more likely—not written the poem at all. Cowley, for example, had emphatically declared in his juvenile panegyric to Charles I: "The gain of *Civil Wars* will not allow / *Bay* to the *Conquerors Brow.*"[55] But for Waller this is Cromwell's claim to military glory, and the poet regrets only that his hero cannot be honored in epic. "Had you, some ages past, this race of glory / Run, with amazement we should read your story; / But living virtue, all achievements past, / Meets envy still, to grapple with at last" (145–148). Waller thus acknowledges the critical dictum, set down in English by Davenant, that living heroes are unsuitable for epic poems because they inspire envy. As Waller cannot write an epic about Cromwell, he writes a panegyric instead.

The purpose of the poem is to transform the heroic Cromwell into an ideal king. This purpose is announced in the opening lines, where Cromwell is introduced as both *augustus* and *amabilis*: "While with a strong and yet a gentle hand, / You bridle faction, and our hearts command" (1–2). The immediate source of this couplet,

55. Cowley, *On his Majesties Return out of Scotland,* 25–26.

moreover, is Jonson's catechism of James I. "He knew, that those, who would, with love, command, / Must with a tender (yet a steadfast) hand / Sustaine the reynes . . ."[56] By allusion to the didactic theme of a highly traditional panegyric, Waller declares his intention of dressing Cromwell in royal robes. The first step toward fulfillment of this intention is to establish Cromwell's credentials as peacemaker.

> *Your never-failing sword made war to cease;*
> *And now you heal us with the arts of peace;*
> *Our minds with bounty and with awe engage,*
> *Invite affection, and restrain our rage.* (109–112)

Peace finally supersedes war in the poem and Cromwell performs the crucial, and traditionally monarchical, function of guaranteeing order. But the ruler himself must exercise restraint and be merciful to the conquered.

> *Less pleasure take brave minds in battles won,*
> *Than in restoring such as are undone;*
> *Tigers have courage, and the rugged bear,*
> *But man alone can, whom he conquers, spare.* (113–116)

Here, not only do we have the theme of limitation, but also the theme of restoration, which Waller develops quite conventionally. "Your drooping country, torn with civil hate, / Restored by you, is made a glorious state" (13–14). In this context Cromwell becomes not Alexander, but Augustus.

> *As the vexed world, to find repose, at last*
> *Itself into Augustus' arms did cast;*
> *So England now does, with like toil oppressed,*
> *Her weary head upon your bosom rest.* (169–172)

56. Jonson, *A Panegyre*, 121–123.

Cromwell the hero thus emerges as Cromwell the ideal monarch.

The source of Cromwell's power, moreover, is divine.

> *When fate, or error, had our age misled,*
> *And o'er these nations such confusion spread,*
> *The only cure, which could from Heaven come down,*
> *Was so much power and clemency in one!* (121–124)

The phrase "power and clemency" appears as "power and piety" in the quarto text of the poem, which is the text used in Elijah Fenton's edition and the text Johnson had in mind when he wrote: "It is not possible to read, without some contempt and indignation, poems of the same author, ascribing the highest degree of *power and piety* to Charles the First, then transferring the same *power and piety* to Oliver Cromwell; now inviting Oliver to take the Crown, and then congratulating Charles the Second on his recovered right."[57] But it is evident that Johnson has missed Waller's point, which is not to praise an individual man, but rather to create the image of a perfect ruler. Waller's ideal is simply consistent. By transferring the "power and piety" of Charles I to Oliver Cromwell, Waller places Cromwell within a tradition that includes earlier kings and emperors as well. Thomas More, we can recall, had written to Henry VIII in the same terms.

> *At quamvis erat ante pius, mores tamen illi*
> *Imperium dignos attulit imperio.*[58]

But howsoever dutiful he was before, his crown has brought our prince a character which deserves to rule.

57. Johnson, *Life of Waller*, Hill, I, 270–271.
58. More, *Carmen Gratulatorium*, 85–86.

Claudian had likewise addressed Honorius.

> *tantaque se rudibus pietas ostendit in annis,*
> *sic aetas animo cessit, quererentur ut omnes*
> *imperium tibi sero datum.*[59]

And so did thy virtue show in earliest years, so did thy soul
out-range thy youth that all complained that to thee empire
was granted late.

In each of these poems, evidence of duty (*pietas*) qualifies
the ruler for power (*imperium*). Waller thus carefully
brings his hero into line with a persistent ideal of monarchy.

But Waller does more than just adopt the conventions
of panegyric. He also shows how epic allusions can serve
the functions of panegyric.

> *Above the waves as Neptune showed his face,*
> *To chide the winds, and save the Trojan race,*
> *So has your Highness, raised above the rest,*
> *Storms of ambition, tossing us, repressed.* (9–12)

The first couplet of this citation is transposed from Fairfax's Tasso: "Above the waves as Neptune lift his eyes /
To chide the winds, that Trojan ships oppress'd . . ."[60]
Waller's allusion through Tasso to the *Aeneid* is then
shaped into a simile illustrating one of the duties of the
monarch: to restrain the ambitious. This duty, as it is
presented in traditional panegyric, is complemented by
another obligation: to relieve the oppressed. Drummond,
for example, specifically links these two duties in his
panegyric to James: "To know the Weight, the Atlas of a

59. Claudian, *III Cons.*, 85–87.
60. Tasso, Book III, stanza 52. The allusion has been recognized
by Thorn-Drury, p. 324.

Crowne, / To spare the Humble, Prowdlings pester down"
(163–164). Walter Haddon expresses essentially the same
idea, although he pointedly refers to rebellion rather than
mere ambition.

> *Fulminet in vitiis, et corda rebellia frangat,*
> *Supplicibus parcat, quos meliora movent.*[61]

May she strike like thunder and lightning in the midst of
vices and crush rebellious hearts. May she spare suppliants
whom better things motivate.

Here, however, panegyric and epic are in fact congruent,
as precisely this same conjunction of duties is found in
Aeneid VI, where Anchises speaks to Aeneas. "Remember thou, O Roman, to rule the nations with thy sway—
these shall be thine arts—to crown Peace with Law, to
spare the humbled, and to tame in war the proud."[62]
Waller, then, is following both Vergil and the tradition of
panegyric when he completes his statement of the monarch's duties: "Hitherto the oppressed shall henceforth
resort, / Justice to crave, and succour, at your court"
(29–30). As in the case of Cowley's union of panegyric
and Pindaric, so in Waller's fusion of panegyric and epic,
we must finally recognize the generic similarity. Vergil's
definition of piety can be adapted to serve as instruction
to the monarch.

Waller's panegyric to Cromwell is a skillful merging
of the two genres, designed to effect a reconciliation between Cromwell as hero and Cromwell as monarch. This

61. Walter Haddon, *In auspicatissimum*, 33–34, *The Poetry of
Walter Haddon*, ed. Charles J. Lees (The Hague, 1967), p. 170.

62. Vergil, *Aeneid*, book 6, lines 851–853, *Virgil*, trans. H. Rush-
ton Fairclough, Loeb Classical Library, 2 vols. (Cambridge, Mass.,
and London, 1969), I, 567.

reconciliation is especially evident in the poem's conclusion.

> *Then let the Muses, with such notes as these,*
> *Instruct us what belongs unto our peace;*
> *Your battles they hereafter shall indite,*
> *And draw the image of our Mars in fight;*
>
> *Tell of towns stormed, of armies overrun,*
> *And mighty kingdoms by your conduct won;*
> *How, while you thundered, clouds of dust did choke*
> *Contending troops, and seas lay hid in smoke.*
>
> *Illustrious acts high raptures do infuse,*
> *And every conqueror creates a muse.*
> *Here, in low strains, your milder deeds we sing;*
> *But there, my lord; we'll bays and olive bring*
>
> *To crown your head; while you in triumph ride*
> *O'er vanquished nations, and the sea beside;*
> *While all your neighbor-princes unto you,*
> *Like Joseph's sheaves, pay reverence, and bow.* (173–188)

Clearly we have in this poem two different incarnations of the man, the conqueror and the king. Line 183 ("Here, in low strains, your milder deeds we sing") stands out by contrast to the acknowledgment of heroic exploits around it, and also expresses Waller's own idea of the poem's purpose. And yet, there is an implied regret that he had been so restrained, that he could not celebrate Cromwell in true epic fashion. In the final lines of the poem it is, strictly speaking, the crown of the victor, the bays and (appropriately) the olive, not the golden crown of kingship, that Cromwell wears. Nevertheless, the striking and unusual enjambment across the last stanza division emphasizes the act of coronation itself. Because, moreover, heroic and monarchical ideals, epic and panegyrical allu-

sions, are so carefully intertwined in the poem, it is difficult to dissociate the crown of bays from the crown of
gold. Perhaps we should not even try, for Waller's next
important poem, *Of A War With Spain, And A Fight
At Sea*, confirms the reconciliation of heroic and monarchical in the figure of Cromwell.

> *His conquering head has no more room for bays;*
> *Then let it be as the glad nation prays;*
> *Let the rich ore forthwith be melted down,*
> *And the state fixed by making him a crown;*
> *With ermine clad, and purple, let him hold*
> *A royal sceptre, made of Spanish gold.*[63]

In the poems of Waller, as in those of Cowley, traditional panegyric is ennobled. The conventional themes
and topics of the genre emerge in a more elevated and, on
occasion, a more pretentious style. When panegyric was
anglicized from the Latin at the turn of the century, it
had no status as a poetic genre; it does not appear, for example, in the lists of poetic "kinds" that are so common
in Renaissance literary criticism. Panegyric, still considered a kind of oratory, appears instead among the categories listed in the rhetoric books. Cowley and Waller
lift the genre out of the rhetoric books and give it an
important place in neoclassical poetics by assimilating it
to the Pindaric ode and the epic. By thus linking panegyric with two very respectable genres, they not only
popularize panegyric, they also demonstrate very real
points of similarity between panegyric and these major
literary traditions. Cowley's contrast between the monarch and the Titans, although a conventional topic of
panegyric, is given renewed vitality and authority by the

63. Waller, *Of A War With Spain, And A Fight At Sea*, 105–110.

suggestion of Pindar. Likewise Waller's conjunction of "power and piety," also a convention of the genre, is given broader significance by specific allusion to Vergil. By disciplining Pindaric and epic to the purposes of panegyric, Cowley and Waller redirect and reinvigorate the tradition established in England by poets like Thomas More and Ben Jonson.

CHALLENGE

The essential, defining characteristic of traditional panegyric, even as transformed by Cowley and Waller, is the reconciliation of actual and ideal. The demonstrative theme of restoration creates a vision of an ideal world, a golden age, whereas the deliberative theme of limitation concerns the actual world of political realities, including even the iron-age possibility of assassination. The panegyrist's problem is to bridge the gap between these two worlds without acknowledging that such a gap exists. To achieve this the orator or poet expresses power through ceremony and simultaneously adapts ceremony to express the limits of power. This union of ceremonial and political purpose is at once the greatest weakness and greatest strength of the genre: greatest weakness because the ideal is not actual, greatest strength because men, at least in the seventeenth century, persistently hoped that someday it would be. Both the weakness and strength of the genre are illuminated by Andrew Marvell's poems to Cromwell.

The difficulty of reconciling the two worlds of panegyric is, however, evident long before the 1650's. In Claudian's panegyrics to Honorius, the latent dualism of the genre is personified by the pairs of figures celebrated. The emperor Honorius is always praised in tandem with a military hero, either Theodosius or Stilicho. In the first of the Honorius panegyrics, for example, the restoration of order is achieved by the combined efforts of Theodosius and Honorius.

> *Pugnastis uterque:*
> *tu fatis genitorque manu . . .* [64]

Both fought for us—thou with thy happy influence, thy father with his strong right arm.

Honorius rules by divine influence, Theodosius by virtue of military force. By linking son and father, Claudian effectively unites ceremony and power. But Claudian does not always achieve this union so easily or successfully. In his final panegyric to Honorius, the effort of reconciliation even leads him to the brink of absurdity.

> *nunc quoque praesidium Latio non deesset Olympi,*
> *deficeret si nostra manus; sed providus aether*
> *noluit humano titulos auferre labori,*
> *ne tibi iam, princeps, soceri sudore paratam,*
> *quam meruit virtus, ambirent fulmina laurum.*[65]

Today, also, assuredly Heaven's favour would not be wanting to Latium should our own hand fail, but a beneficent providence has shown itself unwilling to rob human endeavor of its honor or to let the lightning win the well merited crown of laurel which the efforts of thy father-in-law Stilicho, have secured for thy brows.

Here the divine influence is portrayed as a back-up army, prepared to intervene on behalf of Rome should the human power of Stilicho fail. This semiludicrous union of

64. Claudian, *III Cons.*, 88–89.
65. Claudian, *VI Cons.*, 351–355.

divine and human on a contingency basis reveals the inherent difficulty of reconciling the ceremonial and political directions of the poem.

The obvious source of unity in panegyric is the figure of the monarch himself, who traditionally has both a ceremonial and a political role in the state. Even in Claudian, where the two roles are divided between Honorius and Stilicho, there is an effort made to bind the two figures together. In the above passage, for example, Claudian emphasizes the familial tie between Honorius and Stilicho and concludes by observing that the victories of the general are laurel for the emperor. In the Renaissance, ceremony and power, ideal and actual, divine and human, are commonly united in a single figure. Erasmus praises Philip as a vegetation deity and yet implicitly criticizes him as a man for abandoning his subjects. More urges Henry to adopt specific new policies, but also praises him by comparison with the sun. Both Erasmus and More, however, seek less to unite actual and ideal than to avoid inadvertently suggesting discrepancies between them. Thus, Erasmus emphasizes ceremony and minimizes the problems of power, while More concentrates on current political issues at the expense of celebration. Walter Haddon, although he follows the example of his neo-Latin predecessors, combines the two dimensions of panegyric without apparent hesitation. In his poem to Elizabeth, the two worlds of panegyric are perfectly merged: actual is ideal, reality is ritual, Elizabeth is Astraea. Here the bridge between actual and ideal is the balanced and controlled development of conventional metaphors, which serve to unite the current ruler with the *optimus princeps.*

English panegyrists of the early Stuart monarchy at-

tempt to preserve this sense of union between ceremony
and power by anglicizing the topics and metaphors of
Latin panegyric. The natural, mythological, and historical
metaphors of the Renaissance humanists reappear in the
English panegyrics of Daniel, Jonson, and their followers, who use them to unite the twin themes of restoration
and limitation. It is precisely this characteristic union that
Marvell challenges in *An Horatian Ode upon Cromwel's
Return from Ireland*.[66] By isolating ceremony and power,
he denies the essential premise of traditional panegyric.
Whereas Claudian had strenuously tried to unite Honorius and Stilicho, the emperor and the general, Marvell
sharply contrasts the ceremonial Charles and the military
Cromwell. Whereas Walter Haddon had revealed a world
in which power is derived from God, Marvell shows us a
world where power is derived from men. Although the
poem expresses a deep sense of loss in the disjunction of
ritual and reality, Marvell concludes with a very clear-
eyed view of Cromwell's governance.

> *But thou the Wars and Fortunes Son*
> *March indefatigably on;*
>   *And for the last effect*
>   *Still keep the Sword erect:*
> *Besides the force it has to fright*
> *The Spirits of the shady Night,*
>   *The same* Arts *that did* gain
>   *A* Pow'r *must it* maintain.[67]

66. Although this poem has been a battleground of modern
criticism and has been studied in a variety of contexts, it remains
a difficult poem to interpret satisfactorily. I do not pretend here to
anything like a complete reading of the poem, but I do wish to
show where the poem stands in relationship to the tradition of
panegyric.

67. Andrew Marvell, *An Horatian Ode upon Cromwel's Return*

In this new order, power is attended and expressed not by ceremony but by the sword.

The conventional metaphors, designed to unite power and ceremony, are here developed to express the gulf between them. In traditional panegyric, for example, it is not uncommon to find the monarch as player. In Claudian's panegyric on Honorius's fourth consulship, the emperor participates in ceremonial war games.

> *Cum vectaris equo simulacraque Martia ludis,*
> *quis mollis sinuare fugas, quis tendere contum*
> *acrior aut subitos melior flexisse recursus?*[68]

When mounted on thy horse thou playst the mimicry of war, who is quicker smoothly to wheel in flight, who to hurl the spear, or more skillful to sweep around in swift return?

After the Restoration we find the same kind of king-player in Waller's poem *On St. James's Park.*

> *Here, a well-polished Mall gives us the joy*
> *To see our Prince his matchless force employ;*
> *His manly posture, and his graceful mien,*
> *Vigour and youth, in all his motions seen;*
> *His shape so lovely, and his limbs so strong,*
> *Confirm our hopes we shall obey him long.*
> *No sooner has he touched the flying ball,*
> *But 'tis already more than half the Mall;*
> *And such a fury from his arm has got,*
> *As from a smoking culverin 'twere shot.*[69]

---

from Ireland, lines 113–120, *The Poems and Letters of Andrew Marvell*, ed. H. M. Margoliouth, 2d ed., 2 vols. (Oxford, 1967), I, 90. All citations from Marvell's poems are taken from this edition.

68. Claudian, *IV Cons.*, 539–541.

69. Waller, *On St. James's Park, As Lately Improved By His Majesty*, 57–66.

In both Claudian and Waller the player image functions as a ceremonial, metaphoric expression of monarchical power. It provides a way of celebrating the king's authority without making his rule dependent on force. Marvell's version of the player-king analogy, in contrast, expresses the weakness of the king.

> *That thence the* Royal Actor *born*
> *The* Tragick Scaffold *might adorn:*
> *While round the armed Bands*
> *Did clap their bloody hands.* (53–56)

Although Marvell's analogy has the additional associations of the tragic stage, it strikingly defines the poem's thematic divorce of power from ceremony. Charles exists only in the ceremonial world of the play, where his is the role of king. Power resides in the real world represented by the audience of "armed Bands." Finally, we perceive that Marvell's metaphor is not a metaphor at all, but a fact. Charles is literally an actor; he has all the trappings of kingship; what he does not have is power.

A decade later the panegyrical poets who celebrate the Restoration of Charles II attempt to reunite the two separate worlds of *An Horatian Ode*. Even before the Restoration, however, Marvell himself acknowledges the enduring strength of traditional panegyric in *The First Anniversary Of the Government under O. C.* That strength lies in the continuing desire to believe that power is, must be, consistent with some ideal order that can be expressed through ceremony. *The First Anniversary* is evidence that the inherent weakness of panegyric, relentlessly demonstrated in *An Horatian Ode*, is also its greatest strength.

In reuniting ceremony and power, Marvell adopts many of the images and allusions conventional to panegyric. He also introduces comparisons which, if not common-places of panegyric, nevertheless have a royalist heri-tage.[70] The best example of such a simile is the comparison of Cromwell with Amphion. Waller had developed the same simile with reference to Charles I in *Upon His Maj-esty's Repairing Of Paul's*.

> *He, like Amphion, makes those quarries leap*
> *Into fair figures from a confused heap;*
> *For in his art of regiment is found*
> *A power like that of harmony in sound.*[71]

Waller's lines anticipate the opening of Marvell's simile.

> *So when* Amphion *did the Lute command,*
> *Which the God gave him, with his gentle hand,*
> *The rougher Stones, unto his Measures hew'd,*
> *Dans'd up in order from the Quarreys rude;*
> *This took a Lower, that an Higher place,*
> *As he the Treble alter'd, or the Base:*
> *No Note he struck, but a new Story lay'd,*
> *And the great Work ascended while he play'd.*[72]

Clearly, Waller and Marvell share not only a common political and poetical vocabulary, but also a common ideal of harmony and order.[73]

70. For a discussion of the royalist imagery, see Harold E. Toliver, *Marvell's Ironic Vision* (New Haven and London, 1965), pp. 193–202.

71. Waller, *Upon His Majesty's Repairing Of Paul's*, 11–15. For a valuable discussion of this poem, see Brendan O Hehir, *Expans'd Hieroglyphicks: A Study of Sir John Denham's Coopers Hill With a Critical Edition of the Poem* (Berkeley and Los Angeles, 1969), Appendix B.

72. Marvell, *The First Anniversary Of the Government under O. C.*, 49–55.

73. After 1688, when the political poetry of the period was

At this point of maximum similarity, however, there remains a significant difference. Waller's Amphion is rebuilding an old structure. "The King built all, but Charles the western end" (54). The man Charles extends the work of earlier kings, as Waller carefully unites individual and institutional. Indeed, any idea of a new edifice is specifically rejected in the poem. "Ambition rather would affect the fame / Of some new structure, to have borne her name" (27–28). It is, on the other hand, precisely a "new structure" that Marvell's Amphion does build, and this structure is not a kingdom, but a commonwealth. "The Commonwealth then first together came, / And each one enter'd in the willing Frame" (75–76). Whereas Waller praises the work of Charles in light of a long tradition, Marvell celebrates the achievement of Cromwell in contrast to that same tradition. In short, Waller celebrates an institution; Marvell celebrates a man. If Marvell returns to the vocabulary and imagery of panegyric, he does not return to the institution of monarchy.[74]

In the first forty-eight lines of *The First Anniversary*, which lead to the Amphion simile, Marvell develops a contrast between the man Cromwell and the institution of monarchy. In this passage Marvell applies the tradi-

collected in several volumes under the title *Poems on Affairs of State*, Marvell's poem was sometimes attributed to Waller. See, for example, *Poems on Affairs of State*, 4 vols. (London, 1716), IV, x.

74. Although I have found John Wallace's discussion of the poem stimulating and helpful, I cannot agree with his conclusions. See John Wallace, *Destiny His Choice: The Loyalism of Andrew Marvell* (Cambridge, 1968), pp. 106–144.

tional image of the sun to Cromwell, but at the same time denies the application of this image to kings. "*Cromwell alone*" (7) is sunlike, whereas "heavy Monarchs" (15) are compared to the lethargic and malignant Saturn, on account of (what Marvell later calls) their "Regal Sloth" (122).

> *Their earthy Projects under ground they lay,*
> *More slow and brittle then the* China *clay:*
> *Well may they strive to leave them to their Son,*
> *For one Thing never was by one King don.* (19–22)

The last couplet of this citation tells us how to read the earlier reference to "heavy Monarchs." As the succession of the crown from father to son is the basis of royal authority, the whole passage must refer to monarchy as an institution. "Heavy" describes that institution; it does not discriminate among its various representatives. In effect, Marvell separates Cromwell from earlier kings, thus rejecting the example of Waller's *Panegyric*.

Instead of institutional restoration, *The First Anniversary* celebrates the personal restoration of Cromwell by allusion to the coaching accident. Cromwell, "returning yet alive / Does with himself all that is good revive" (323–324). The effect of this episode is to identify the nation's immediate future with this individual man, who is not a king and yet is more than a king. "For to be *Cromwell* was a greater thing / Then ought below, or yet above a King" (225–226). But Marvell does not ask the people to accept Cromwell as a ruler *sui generis*.[75]

75. The basis of Cromwell's authority as defined by Marvell has been a topic of debate in recent years. See Joseph A. Mazzeo,

Though not a king, Cromwell is like the *optimus princeps* as that figure is defined in traditional panegyric.

> *Hence oft I think, if in some happy Hour*
> *High Grace should meet in one with highest Pow'r,*
> *And then a seasonable People still*
> *Should bend to his, as he to Heavens will,*
> *What we might hope, what wonderful Effect*
> *From such a wish'd Conjuncture might reflect.*
> *Sure, the mysterious Work, where none withstand,*
> *Would forthwith finish under such a Hand:*
> *Fore-shortned Time its useless Course would stay,*
> *And soon precipitate the latest Day.*
> *But a thick Cloud about that Morning lyes,*
> *And intercepts the Beams of Mortal eyes,*
> *That 'tis the most which we determine can,*
> *If these the Times, then this must be the Man.* (131–144)

The union of power and grace, of human and divine, of actual and ideal, although hypothetical, represents a return to the tradition of panegyric. This reconciliation, moreover, suggests the panegyrical theme of limited sovereignty. Specifically, it recalls the "glory and grace" that Daniel had found in James I and the "power and piety" that Waller had discovered in Charles I and later in Cromwell himself.[76]

"Cromwell as Davidic King," *Reason and the Imagination: Studies in the History of Ideas, 1600–1800* ed. Joseph A. Mazzeo (New York and London, 1962), pp. 29–55; Steven N. Zwicker, *Dryden's Political Poetry: The Typology of King and Nation* (Providence, 1972), pp. 53–55; John Wallace, "Andrew Marvell and Cromwell's Kingship: 'The First Anniversary,'" *ELH*, XXX, no. 3 (September 1963), 209–232.

76. See Daniel, *A Panegyrike Congratulatorie*, 81, and Waller, *To The King On His Navy*, 32, and *A Panegyric To My Lord Protector*, 124.

In subsequent passages Marvell defines Cromwell's limited power in even more obvious ways.

> *'Tis not a Freedome, that where All command;*
> *Nor Tyranny, where One does them withstand:*
> *But who of both the Bounders knows to lay*
> *Him as their Father must the State obey.*
> *Thou, and thine House, like* Noah's *Eight did rest,*
> *Left by the Wars Flood on the Mountains crest:*
> *And the large Vale lay subject to thy Will,*
> *Which thou but as an Husbandman wouldst Till:*
> *And only didst for others plant the Vine*
> *Of Liberty, not drunken with its Wine.* (279–288)

The agricultural imagery, the Biblical allusion, the patriarchal idea, are all commonplaces that will be seen again in Dryden. What these images combine to express is the "Bounders" of power. But it is important to recognize that these boundaries are set by Cromwell himself. Everything in the poem finally hinges on the nature of this man; his legitimacy is derived from his actual conduct. In effect, Marvell argues: in his first year of "highest Pow'r" Cromwell has demonstrated that he is in fact what "heavy Monarchs" had only claimed to be, the *optimus princeps*. The contrast between the man Cromwell and the institution of monarchy is achieved by transferring to Cromwell the traditional ideals of monarchy without the crown. It is in this sense that he is both more and less than a king.

> *He seems a King by long Succession born,*
> *And yet the same to be a King does scorn.*
> *Abroad a King he seems, and something more,*
> *At Home a Subject on the equal Floor.* (387–390)

This fine distinction, preserved throughout *The First Anniversary*, places the poem just outside the tradition of panegyric. At the same time, however, *The First Anniversary* reveals the essential durability of the tradition and anticipates the reunion of ceremony and power celebrated by the panegyrists of the Restoration.

4: Dryden's Oratory, 1660-1688

THE HERITAGE of panegyric is of central importance to a consideration of Dryden's public poetry. This relatively minor genre provides the background for understanding the progress of Dryden's career and the framework for judging individual poems. To demonstrate the various ways in which Dryden's poetry embodies the themes, topics, and values of panegyric, the discussion of his poems is divided into two parts. The present chapter will focus on the tradition of panegyric: Dryden's reassertion of the original, oratorical function of the genre. The next chapter will consider the transformation of panegyric: Dryden's accommodation of panegyrical oratory and heroic poetry.

To trace Dryden's career against the background of classical and Renaissance oratory is to recognize, first of all, the ambitious nature of his political poems. To influence power with poetry, Dryden stands between the prince and the people during a period that is bounded at both ends by revolution. Addressing the people on behalf of the prince, Dryden elaborates the theme of restoration, designed to secure popular obedience to the monarch. Addressing the prince on behalf of the people, Dryden emphasizes the theme of limitation, intended to assure restrained and orderly rule. Striving to maintain this poised rhetorical stance, Dryden attempts to reconcile the often-opposed interests of his dual audience. Dryden's special brand of oratory is, in effect, precisely that combination of the demonstrative and deliberative types that defines panegyric. By considering first the poems surrounding the Restoration, then the poems of the reign of James II, we can appreciate and admire Dryden's efforts to find a voice and an argument suitable for an address to both the prince and the people.

Although some steps have already been taken toward an accurate assessment of Dryden's oratory, this aspect of his work has never received the attention it deserves, partly (I think) because of our modern distrust of political oratory. In Mark Van Doren's groundbreaking study of the poetry, for example, the conception of Dryden as poet-orator is presented under the chapter heading "False Lights." After a very brief survey of the connection between oratory and poetry, Van Doren observes: "It was not until Dryden's time, when the inspiration of the Elizabethans had in a way given out, and the full body of modern classical doctrine was being received in its most systematic form from France, that eloquence came to feel completely at home in poetry." "Dryden," adds Van Doren, "was peculiarly fitted to lead the rhetorical grand march in English poetry."[1]

This negative approach to the subject persists, with

1. Mark Van Doren, *John Dryden: A Study of His Poetry* (Bloomington, Ind., 1946), pp. 46–47.

modifications, to the present day. K. G. Hamilton, for example, has qualified Van Doren's conclusion on the
grounds that Dryden himself would not have recognized
the distinction between poetic and rhetoric as a very
meaningful one.[2] This revised assumption leads Hamilton
to an analysis of the poetry that is more precise and detailed, but not essentially different from Van Doren's
approach of fifty years ago. Although useful in assessing
the style of Dryden's so-called "poetry of statement,"
this approach through rhetorical *amplificatio* misses the
obvious. As an orator Dryden has an audience, a voice,
and an argument, as well as an appropriate style. Because
Dryden defines his role in society as that of public speaker, his poetry should be read in light of the public functions it was intended to serve.

This direction has been pointed out by two of Dryden's
most persuasive critics. In the introductory chapter to his
book *Alexander Pope: The Poetry of Allusion*, Reuben
Brower writes: "Dryden did something else for his generation that Marvell and Milton, much less Cowley, could
not do: he reaffirmed the public role of the poet, the
Graeco-Roman conception of the poet as the voice of a
society."[3] Lillian Feder, in her important article on "John
Dryden's Use of Classical Rhetoric," agrees. She concludes that for Dryden, as for Cicero and Quintilian, the
art of oratory "is a public good, that a man speaking
to his fellows must use eloquence to lead them; in
other words, that formal speech is true and practical

2. K. G. Hamilton, *John Dryden and the Poetry of Statement*
(St. Lucia, Australia, 1967), pp. 125–126.
3. Reuben Brower, *Alexander Pope: The Poetry of Allusion*
(Oxford, 1959), p. 11.

speech . . ."[4] Considering Dryden's career chronological-
ly, we can explore this conception of the poet as public
speaker by reference to the specific oratorical model developed in chapter 2.

First, however, we can sharpen this conception of Dryden's career by taking a hint from James Sutherland. In
his pamphlet (originally a lecture) aptly titled *John Dryden: The Poet as Orator*, Sutherland briefly considers a
number of poems, concentrating on several of Dryden's
prologues and epilogues.[5] In these brief addresses to his
theater audience, Dryden's verse does quite obviously
function as oratory. Speaking through an actor, Dryden
(like other dramatists of the period) considers the condition of the stage, takes sides on various theatrical con-
troversies, and of course comments on his own plays. In
several of the prologues and epilogues, however, Dryden
uses the Restoration stage as a podium for comment on
current topics of broader public interest, including politics. During the Exclusion crisis in particular, Dryden
considers his theater audience as the representatives of the
whole English nation. Moreover, on some of these occasions, the "nation" was complemented by the actual presence of the king, thus creating in fact the dual audience
characteristic of panegyric.

One such occasion was a performance of John Banks's
The Unhappy Favourite, for which Dryden wrote the prologue. Here Dryden revives the myth of national innocence which we have already seen in Cowley's Restora-

4. Lillian Feder "John Dryden's Use of Classical Rhetoric,"
PMLA, LXIX (1954), 1259.

5. James Sutherland, *John Dryden: The Poet as Orator* (Glas-
gow, 1963).

tion panegyric and which we shall see again in Dryden's own coronation panegyric of 1661.

> *When first the Ark was Landed on the Shore,*
> *And Heaven had vow'd to curse the Ground no more,*
> *When Tops of Hills the Longing Patriark saw,*
> *And the new Scene of Earth began to draw;*
> *The Dove was sent to View the Waves Decrease,*
> *And first brought back to Man the Pledge of Peace . . .*[6]

After the purifying waters subside, "The Ark is open'd to dismiss the Train, / And People with a better Race the Plain" (11–12). But the new race succumb to the same temptations as the old, including the desire for innovation.[7] The alternative to this "Scene of Changes" (18) is a steady reliance on the monarch.

> *Our Land's an Eden, and the Main's our Fence,*
> *While we Preserve our State of Innocence;*
> *That lost, then Beasts their Brutal Force employ,*
> *And first their Lord, and then themselves destroy:*
> *What Civil Broils have cost we know too well,*
> *Oh let it be enough that once we fell,*
> *And every Heart conspire with every Tongue,*
> *Still to have such a King, and this King Long.* (27–34)

In this conclusion, Dryden emphasizes the close connection between his prologue and traditional panegyric by quoting the last line of Jonson's *Panegyre*. Jonson had

6. John Dryden, "Prologue to *The Unhappy Favourite*," lines 1–6, *The Poems of John Dryden*, ed. James Kinsley, 4 vols. (Oxford, 1958), I, 244. Hereafter in the notes Dryden's poems will be identified only by title and line numbers. All citations are from the Kinsley edition.

7. For an excellent discussion of Dryden's prologues and epilogues, including commentary on the political theme of innovation, see Arthur W. Hoffman, *John Dryden's Imagery* (Gainesville, Fla., 1962), pp. 20–54.

concluded his poem with the following couplet: "*Yet, let blest* Brittaine *aske (without your wrong) / Still to have such a king, and this king long.*"[8]

A second example of a prologue which functions as a panegyric is that written "To His *Royal Highness* Upon His first appearance at the *Duke's Theatre* since his Return from *Scotland.*" Addressed to James, who had passed part of his Exclusion-crisis exile in Scotland, this prologue is an evident extension of the tradition of return poems discussed in the previous chapter. The seasonal and diurnal imagery appropriate to the theme of restoration provides the background for Dryden's attempt to reconcile his two audiences. This purpose Dryden expresses unequivocally.

> *Yet, late Repentance may, perhaps, be true;*
> *Kings can forgive if Rebels can but sue:*
> *A Tyrant's Pow'r in rigour is exprest:*
> *The Father yearns in the true Prince's Breast.*[9]

Here both audiences are admonished, the people to repentance and the prince to forgiveness, thus defining the conditions of Dryden's welcome to the returning royalty. "O welcome to this much offending Land / The Prince that brings forgiveness in his hand" (36–37). Dryden then concludes by urging James to "relax the rights of Sov'-reign sway" (42). Thus combining the theme of limitation

8. Ben Jonson, *A Panegyre,* lines 161–162, *Ben Jonson,* ed. C. H. Herford and Percy and Evelyn Simpson, 11 vols. (Oxford, 1941), VII, 117. The quotation has previously been noticed by Steven N. Zwicker, "Dryden's Borrowing from Ben Jonson's 'Panegyre,'" *N & Q,* XV (1968), 105–106.

9. "To His *Royal Highness* Upon His first appearance at the *Duke's Theatre* since his Return from Scotland," 26–29, *Poems,* I, 262.

with the theme of restoration, Dryden completes the pattern of traditional panegyric.

The orator's stance revealed in these two prologues had been confidently assumed in the 1660's and was to be maintained only with great difficulty in the 1680's. But as the beginning of Dryden's career antedates the Restoration, we must consider first two poems written at a time when the oratorical stance characteristic of panegyric was not possible.

THE EARLY POEMS

It is often observed that Dryden's elegy *Upon the death of the Lord Hastings* has minimal political significance. Unlike other poets on this occasion, most notably John Denham, Dryden does not develop the idea that Hastings's death was caused by the execution of the king.[10] It is, however, true that Dryden elaborates the lament for Hastings in imagery that defines the state of English political institutions in 1649. The two major similes in the poem both involve the human body, always potentially an analogue for the body politic. The first simile describes the body in its healthy state as a perfect orb that contains the "Reg'lar Motions" of the soul.[11] The soul, shining through the body, "The whole Frame render'd was Celestial" (38). The possible political significance of this comparison is revealed by Dryden's later poetry. In

10. See Ruth Wallerstein, *Studies in Seventeenth-Century Poetic* (Madison, Wis., 1950), p. 132. See also Edward Niles Hooker and H. T. Swedenberg, eds., *The Works of John Dryden*, 7 vols. to date (Berkeley and Los Angeles, 1956–), I, 176. Hereafter this edition will be referred to as the California Dryden.

11. *Upon the death of the Lord Hastings*, 29, *Poems*, I, 1.

To My Lord Chancellor he refers to "The Nations soul (our Monarch) . . . ," and in *Absalom and Achitophel* he develops the architectural suggestion of the word "Frame" to define the nature of the state.[12] The second simile, the infamous smallpox conceit, describes the body in an advanced state of disease. As this comparison does not have traditional political associations, Dryden bluntly gives it special significance in connection with the recent rebellion.

> *Each little Pimple had a Tear in it,*
> *To wail the fault its rising did commit:*
> *Who, Rebel-like, with their own Lord at strife,*
> *Thus made an Insurrection 'gainst his Life.* (59–62)

Although the metaphors and similes in the poem are not sufficiently continuous to justify an allegorical reading of the poem, it is evident that the death of Hastings and the death of the king are at least sporadically analogous. Dryden does not suggest a causal link between the two events because he wishes to indicate instead their symbolic parallelism.

Other images in the poem, especially those consistent with the tradition of panegyric, establish the significance of the poem as a royal elegy. One couplet in particular evokes the death of Charles more effectively than the death of Hastings. "The Nations sin hath drawn that Veil, which shrouds / Our Day-spring in so sad benighting Clouds" (49–50). The conventional imagery of the couplet, especially the term "Day-spring," has evident

12. *To My Lord Chancellor. Presented on New-years-day,* 27, *Poems,* I, 29; *Absalom and Achitophel. A Poem,* especially 801–806, *Poems,* I, 237.

royalist associations, and the appearance of "benighting
Clouds" reveals the pattern of the elegy to be a reversal
of the restorative pattern found in panegyric.

Dryden extends the poem's latent analogy between private and public experience to the very end of the poem,
where he considers the plight of Hastings's "*Virgin-
Widow*" (93). Although the passage has a specific, factual basis in relation to Hastings, this topic also describes
the condition of a nation without a king. Marriage as an
emblem of the harmony between king and people, evident
for example in Thomas More's Latin poem to Henry VIII,
is explicitly developed by Dryden in *Astraea Redux*:
"While Our cross Stars deny'd us *Charles* his Bed /
Whom Our first Flames and Virgin Love did wed."[13] In
the Hastings elegy as in the later panegyric, the bride
can be seen as a symbol of the nation, in this case a nation
without a king. The trouble with these last lines, whether
read as elegiac consolation to a particular woman or as a
covert address to the nation as a whole, is that Dryden
has no real consolation or policy to offer. Nevertheless,
in the conclusion to this immature poem, Dryden metaphorically anticipates the rhetorical stance of his poem
on the death of Cromwell: direct address to the whole
English nation.

This poem, unlike the lament for Hastings, is not an
elegy, but rather a funeral oration in verse. The *Heroique
Stanza's* follows the pattern of a classical oration more
closely than any other poem of Dryden's. The poem can

13. *Astraea Redux*, 19–20, *Poems*, I, 16. For a discussion of
this image, see George Wasserman, "The Domestic Metaphor in
Astraea Redux," *ELN*, III (1965), 106–111.

be readily outlined according to the seven-fold arrange-
ment favored by the classical rhetoricians.

Exordium (stanzas 1–4)
Narratio (5–9)
Propositio (10)
Divisio (11–31)
   Part 1 (11–15)
                Part 1 (11–20)
   Part 2 (16–20) or
                Part 2 (21–31)
   Part 3 (21–31)
Confirmatio (32)
Refutatio (33–34)
Peroratio (35–37)

This poem is the purest and simplest example of Dryden's oratory.

The exordium establishes with precision both the occasion and the reason for the speech. Dryden identifies
himself with his audience ("our") and contrasts himself
to other speakers on this occasion, including both those
who have already spoken ("they whose muses have the
highest flown") and those who may yet speak ("And
claime a *Title* in him by their praise").[14] The first group,
who are revealed as personally self-serving, have been
premature and disrespectful, but provide no reason for
Dryden to speak out. It is rather the second group, those
who may yet praise Cromwell, who worry Dryden and

14. *Heroique Stanza's, Consecrated to the Glorious Memory of
his most Serene and Renowned Highnesse Oliver Late Lord Protector of this Commonwealth, etc. Written after the Celebration
of his Funerall*, 10–16, *Poems*, I, 7.

call forth his speech. Although the phrase "claime a *Title in him*" is not entirely clear, Dryden seems to refer to the possibility that Cromwell's career may be appropriated as fodder for various political arguments. That is, praise for Cromwell may be cast in terms that would advance or justify some political cause or another. It is to prevent this occurrence that Dryden will accept the duty of praising Cromwell in a way that will further "our interest" (13), the interest not of a faction or a cause, but of the nation as a whole. This is a very skillful opening because it not only captures the audience's attention and concern, but also consolidates their self-interest.

In the next five stanzas Dryden presents an abstract of his speech. Starting with a version of what has been called the "inexpressibility" *topos* ("How shall I then begin . . . "), he outlines his perspective on Cromwell's career. In this exposition, which provides the evaluative background for the proposition announced in stanza 10, the crucial terms are "Fame" (18) and "Fortune" (22). The perspective indicated by these terms is a human one; they describe Cromwell as he seemed to Dryden's audience. Although his innate greatness is a divine gift, Cromwell's public fame is determined by the fortune of war. Dryden expresses this good fortune and resultant fame by adapting the familiar sun image, an image which also forecasts the second phase of Cromwell's career. "And Warr's like mists that rise against the Sunne / Made him but greater seem, not greater grow" (23–24). Initially the "Sunne" in this couplet refers to Charles I, for the king is indeed the sun that the mists of civil war rose against. But the second line changes the identification and establishes Cromwell as the sun who seems greater

because of the "mists" of war. This substitution of
Cromwell for Charles initiates the shift in Dryden's exposition to consideration of Cromwell as ruler.

> *No borrow'd Bay's his* Temples *did adorne,*
> *But to our* Crown *he did fresh* Jewells *bring,*
> *Nor was his Vertue poyson'd soon as born*
> *With the too early thoughts of being King.* (25–28)

Gliding smoothly and swiftly over the difficult constitutional questions of a few years earlier, Dryden suggests
the transition from hero ("Bay's") to monarch ("Crown"),
while simultaneously praising Cromwell for not aspiring
"too early" to be king. It is not ambition but rather matu-
rity that characterizes Cromwell as ruler.

> *He, private, mark'd the faults of others sway,*
> *And set as* Sea-mark's *for himself to shun;*
> *Not like rash* Monarch's *who their youth betray*
> *By Acts their Age too late would wish undone.* (33–36)

In sum, Dryden views Cromwell as the favorite of fortune
and yet as a man prepared for the fortune that came
to him.

Dryden is now ready to give the audience his argument,
beginning with a clear, succinct proposition.

> *And yet* Dominion *was not his Designe,*
> *We owe that blessing not to him but Heaven,*
> *Which to faire Acts unsought rewards did joyn,*
> *Rewards that lesse to him than us were given.* (36–40)

This, in effect, is what the oration will prove. Derived
directly from the preceding exposition, this passage foreshadows the major lines of argument to be developed
later in the poem. First of all, Dryden discards the possibility that Cromwell was ambitious for himself; his

"faire" acts brought "unsought" rewards. Second, these rewards, like his dominion, are blessings not as much to him as to "us." The first point of the proposition is demonstrated in parts 1 (stanzas 11–15) and 2 (16–20) of the argument, where Dryden traces Cromwell's career first as warrior and then as ruler. The second point is shown in the longer third part (21–31), which is devoted to the blessings of Cromwell's rule. As these blessings are due primarily to the Protector's aggressive foreign policy, Dryden here draws on the imperialist theme of Waller's panegyric. Waller had written:

> *To dig for wealth we weary not our limbs;*
> *Gold, though the heaviest metal, hither swims;*
> *Ours is the harvest where the Indians mow;*
> *We plough the deep, and reap what others sow.*[15]

Dryden adopts this topic in the final stanza of his argument.

By his command we boldly crost the Line
And bravely fought where Southern Starrs *arise,*
We trac'd the farre-fetchd Gold unto the mine
And that which brib'd our fathers made our prize. (121–124)

Having thus demonstrated his proposition, Dryden offers a brief confirmation ("Such was our Prince . . . ") and proceeds to a refutation of those who believe that Cromwell was slipping at the time of his death.

> *Nor dy'd he when his ebbing Fame went lesse,*
> *But when fresh Lawrells courted him to live;*

15. Edmund Waller, *A Panegyric To My Lord Protector*, lines 61–64, *The Poems of Edmund Waller*, ed. George Thorn-Drury (New York, 1968), p. 140. The parallels between Waller's poem and Dryden's have been noted by Hooker and Swedenberg in the California Dryden, I, 191–192.

> *He seem'd but to prevent some new successe;*
> *As if above what triumphs Earth could give.* (129–132)

The reason for refuting this particular anti-Cromwell argument is quite evident in Dryden's peroration. Here he carefully leaves his audience with a final implication of the whole speech: Cromwell's benign power continues after his death. Far from slipping, his influence persists.

> *No Civill broyles have since his death arose,*
> *But* Faction *now by* Habit *does obey:*
> *And* Warrs *have that respect for his repose,*
> *As* Winds *for* Halcyons *when they breed at Sea.* (141–144)

Dryden's oration is a memorial to Cromwell's achievement designed to help preserve the peace of the realm. This penultimate stanza explains what Dryden meant back in stanza 4: "Yet 'tis our duty and our interest too / Such monuments as we can build to raise . . ." (13–14) Keeping alive Cromwell's memory as England's *"Protecting Genius"* (139) is in the best "interest" of domestic peace and is therefore the "duty" of a poet-orator like Dryden.

The final stanza of the poem looks backward to the other Cromwell poems of the 1650's.

> *His Ashes in a peacefull Urne shall rest,*
> *His Name a great example stands to show*
> *How strangely high endeavours may be blest,*
> *Where* Piety *and* valour *joyntly goe.* (145–148)

The union of valor and piety suggests Waller's idealization of Cromwell in terms of "power and piety" and, indirectly, Marvell's celebration of the Protector as the perfect union of power and grace. In comparison with these poems, however, Dryden's eulogy is perhaps more significant for what it does not achieve, or even attempt, than for what it does. The poem is politically neutral, as Dryden makes not the slightest effort to solve the problem of legitimacy that had challenged earlier poets of the Protectorate. This neutrality is not an accident. In the opening Dryden assures his audience that the very purpose of his oration is to further "our interest," and in the peroration he defines this interest as civil order undisturbed by faction. To take a strong position on the constitutional issues then being debated would be to identify himself with a faction, and this Dryden resolutely and wisely refuses to do. Indeed the strength of his argument, his credibility as a speaker, and therefore the success of his oration depend on his neutrality. In the *Heroique Stanza's*, Dryden was awaiting the outcome of events without attempting to influence them in the manner of Waller and Marvell.

By speaking for and to all the people ("we," "our," "us"), Dryden does, however, establish the characteristic voice of his later verse orations. But these later poems, from *Astraea Redux* to *Britannia Rediviva*, are far more complex than the eulogy of Cromwell, because after 1660 Dryden's audience includes the king as well as the people. The poem on Cromwell is a demonstrative oration, pure and relatively simple. The later poems, on the other hand, combine demonstrative with deliberative oratory. The twin themes of restoration and limitation, focused by the traditional terms "power" and "piety," are here balanced in ways that transcend the restricted, if orderly, design of the *Heroique Stanza's*.

The greater complexity of *Astraea Redux* is evident in A. E. Wallace Maurer's attempt to read the poem as an oration. Maurer observes: "The audience directly addressed is, of course, Charles II, but the total audience includes the English nation listening in the background."[16] Although this seems to me exactly right, the poem nevertheless resists Maurer's attempt to outline its oratorical structure because, unlike the *Heroique Stanza's*, *Astraea Redux* is not simply an oration. The first two-thirds of the poem (to line 249) is a heroic narrative reflecting Waller's transformation of panegyric, while the last third is an oration addressed to the monarch with "the English nation listening in the background." The combination of elements in the poem has been recognized by Earl Miner, who concludes that the poem lacks coherence because it is not "clearly defined as a panegyric, as a narrative of historical events, or as a picture of heroic endeavor."[17] I suggest that the poem should be defined as a heroic panegyric and that, in spite of its vigorous diversity and range of tones, the poem is coherent. The two basic parts of the poem are closely related, for the narrative of recent events is necessary to establish the appropriate *ethos* for the people's spokesman. In part 1 we find revealed the guilt of the people, the suffering of the king, and the renewed felicity of both people and king at the Restoration. Through this narrative Dryden identifies himself with the penitent nation by using the characteristic pronoun "our"; then in part 2 he directly addresses the king ("you") on their behalf.

By focusing attention in the first part of the poem on

16. A. E. Wallace Maurer, "The Structure of Dryden's *Astraea Redux*," *PLL*, II (1966), 18.

17. Earl Miner, *Dryden's Poetry* (Bloomington, Ind., and London, 1968), pp. 6–7.

"our" fate and "our" past, Dryden reasserts the inclusive
public voice of the *Heroique Stanza's*. Here, however,
Dryden also identifies the enemy of the public interest,
"they" who have presumed to destroy what is "ours."

> *Nor could our Nobles hope their bold Attempt*
> *Who ruin'd Crowns would Coronets exempt:*
> *For when by their designing Leaders taught*
> *To strike at Pow'r which for themselves they sought,*
> *The Vulgar gull'd into Rebellion, arm'd,*
> *Their blood to action by the Prize was warm'd.* (29–34)

This "Faction" (22) is characterized by its pursuit of un-
restricted power.

> *Blind as the* Cyclops, *and as wild as he,*
> *They own'd a lawless salvage Libertie,*
> *Like that our painted Ancestours so priz'd*
> *Ere Empires Arts their Breasts had Civiliz'd.* (45–48)

These two narrative passages focus the argument of
Dryden's concluding oration: the limitation of power by
law and the restoration of the civilizing "Arts" of empire.
In final preparation for the oration itself, however, Dryden discards the pronoun "they" and generously returns
to a now-penitent "our." "We by our suff'rings learn to
prize our bliss . . ." (210). By calling attention to the
guilty faction and then confirming the repentance of the
whole nation, Dryden creates the perfect voice for his
address to the king, a voice that is at once forgiving and
penitent. Developed in the narrative section of the poem,
then, is the oratorical stance of the poem's conclusion.
Dryden stands poised between the people, who must repent, and the king, who must forgive.

Midway through the oration, Dryden pauses to ask a

rhetorical question: "How shall I speak of that triumphant Day / When you renew'd the expiring Pomp of *May*" (284–285). Dryden here defines the ceremonial purpose of panegyric in terms that suggest the original function of the genre: to celebrate a festival occasion, or holiday. It is worth recalling that the word "day" (or the Latin equivalent) is a significant catchword of the genre, appearing in the first lines of panegyrics by Erasmus, More, and Daniel, and as the final word in the first stanza of Cowley's Restoration Pindaric. By posing the question in the conventional vocabulary of panegyric, Dryden implicitly acknowledges the conventional nature of his answer. Although the address to Charles does not fit the strict patterns of a classical oration, it does unite the traditional themes of panegyric. For purposes of discussion we can break the speech into three parts. The first, lines 250 to about 275, is deliberative in purpose, designed to instruct the king. The second, lines 276–291, is demonstrative in purpose, designed to ensure popular obedience to the prince. The third part, derived from the first two, is a prophecy of England's future under an ideal monarch who rules over ideal subjects. Dryden's conception of both ideals is focused by familiar topics and expressed in traditional language.

In the first part of his oration, Dryden concentrates on the obligations of the king.

> *But you, whose goodness your discent doth show,*
> *Your Heav'nly Parentage and earthly too;*
> *By that same mildness which your Fathers Crown*
> *Before did ravish, shall secure your own.*
> *Not ty'd to rules of Policy, you find*
> *Revenge less sweet then a forgiving mind.*

> *Thus when th' Almighty would to* Moses *give*
> *A sight of all he could behold and live;*
> *A voice before his entry did proclaim*
> Long-Suff'ring, Goodness, Mercy *in his Name.* (256–265)

Royal "goodness" is defined emphatically, if somewhat redundantly, as mildness, forgiveness, and mercy. Although Dryden does not use the conventional word "piety" here, his emphasis on mercy accomplishes the traditional purpose of restraining the monarch equally well. In fact, in traditional panegyric *pietas* and *clementia* are closely associated. In Claudian's *Panegyricus Dictus Manlio Theodoro Consuli,* for example, Astraea, personified to address the consul, specifically links these two qualities:

> *nonne vides, ut nostra soror Clementia tristes*
> *obtundat gladios fratresque amplexa serenos*
> *adsurgat Pietas . . .*[18]

Seest thou not how my sister Mercy blunts the cruel sword of war; how Piety rises to embrace the two noble brothers . . .

In Walter Haddon's neo-Latin panegyric to Elizabeth we find the same conjunction:

Sit pia, sit clemens . . ."[19]

May she be pious, may she be merciful . . .

Moreover, as we have seen, Edmund Waller changed the wording but not the essential meaning of his panegyric

18. Claudian, *Manlio Theodoro,* lines 166–168, *Claudian,* trans. Maurice Platnauer, Loeb Classical Library, 2 vols. (Cambridge, Mass., and London, 1963), I, 350.

19. Walter Haddon, *In auspicatissimum,* line 27, *The Poetry of Walter Haddon,* ed. Charles J. Lees (The Hague, 1967), p. 170.

to Cromwell when he revised "power and piety" to read "power and clemency."

Dryden not only defines royal "goodness" in a traditional way, he also expressly unites this ideal with the traditional theme of limitation.

> *Your Pow'r to Justice doth submit your Cause,*
> *Your Goodness only is above the Laws;*
> *Whose rigid letter while pronounc'd by you*
> *Is softer made.* (266–269)

The balanced phrasing, "Your Pow'r . . ." in the first line, "Your Goodness . . ." in the second, gives this couplet something of the same force as Marvell's "power and grace" and Waller's "power and piety" (or "clemency"). Dryden then supplements the moral limitation on royal power by emphasizing the more tangible but equally traditional restriction provided by the "Laws." As the editors of the California Dryden have observed, "The rigid letter that Dryden was thinking of may have been the hard '*g*' in the Latin *leges*."[20] This may well be true, as the literary source of these lines is probably Pliny's admonitory praise of Trajan:

Quod ego nunc primum audio, nunc primum disco, non est princeps super leges, sed leges super principem . . .[21]

There is a new turn of phrase which I hear and understand for the first time—not the prince is above the law but the law is above the prince . . .

20. The California Dryden, I, 232. For a stimulating discussion of this passage, see Alan Roper, *Dryden's Poetic Kingdoms* (London, 1965), pp. 68–70.

21. Pliny, *Panegyricus*, sec. 65, *Pliny, Letters and Panegyricus*, trans. Betty Radice, Loeb Classical Library, 2 vols. (Cambridge, Mass., and London, 1969), II, 474–476.

The king, submitting himself to the law, tempers that law with mercy toward the people.

Charles can afford to be merciful because the people have promised to forsake their former ways of rebellion.

> *And welcome now* (Great Monarch) *to your own;*
> *Behold th' approaching cliffes of* Albion;
> *It is no longer Motion cheats your view,*
> *As you meet it, the Land approacheth you.*
> *The Land returns, and in the white it wears*
> *The marks of penitence and sorrow bears.* (250–255)

In these opening lines of the oration, Dryden recapitulates the penitence and submission of the people delineated in the preceding narrative. The unusual and often-abused metaphor of the land returning to the king perfectly complements the more traditional celebration of the king's return to the land. This meeting in mid-channel symbolizes the compromise of the Restoration settlement and thus represents Dryden's version of Claudian's *alterna fides*. More specifically, it represents an imagistic rendering of a sentence from Pliny:

scis tibi ubique iurari, cum ipse iuraveris omnibus.[22]

[Y]ou can be sure that everywhere the oath is being taken for you, as you have taken it for us all.

The mutuality of the renewed contract between prince and people is expressed by the reciprocal obligations of mercy on the one hand and obedience on the other. After

22. Pliny, *Panegyricus*, sec. 68. In his translation of the panegyric dedicated to the Electress Sophia, George Smith rendered this passage emphatically: "You know that the Whole Empire hath taken Oaths of Allegiance to you, *as you have mutually taken your Coronation Oath to them*." George Smith, trans., *Pliny's Panegyrick Upon the Emperor Trajan*, 2d ed. (London, 1730), p. 135.

stressing royal mercy, therefore, Dryden emphasizes popular obedience.

The demonstrative part of Dryden's oration takes the conventional form of the processional *topos*.

> *Methinks I see those Crowds on* Dovers *Strand*
> *Who in their hast to welcome you to Land*
> *Choak'd up the Beach with their still growing store,*
> *And made a wilder Torrent on the shore.*
> *While spurr'd with eager thoughts of past delight*
> *Those who had seen you, court a second sight;*
> *Preventing still your steps, and making hast*
> *To meet you often where so e're you past.* (276–283)

Dryden's lines are very similar to those of Ben Jonson, whose version of this *topos,* as we have seen, is based on Latin and neo-Latin models. Jonson, too, had portrayed an insatiable crowd of admirers running alongside the king. The purpose of this *topos* is to demonstrate what Jonson had modestly called the "consent" of the people to the rule of the new king. Dryden goes further, closing his demonstration with an allusion to the king's birth star, which "Did once again its potent Fires renew / Guiding our eyes to find and worship you" (290–291). The obedience of the people to the resurrected king, when read in light of the preceding qualifications on the king's power, creates a conventional political ideal sanctioned by divine authority. Here "consent" becomes "worship." Dryden thus combines the deliberative and demonstrative themes of panegyric to assert the highest ideal of the genre: national reconciliation.

This reconciliation between the idealized prince and the idealized people makes possible the prophecy with which the speech concludes. Here too Dryden asserts generic convention. Classical and Renaissance panegyrics frequently close with some global allusion, hyperbolically confirming the potential of a united nation. Usually this hyperbole takes the form of the so-called "two-Indies *topos*."[23] Claudian captures the essential idea of this topic in the conclusion of his *Panegyricus De Tertio Consulatu Honorii Augusti*:

> *vobis Rubra dabunt pretiosas aequora conchas,*
> *Indus ebur, ramos Panchaia, vellera Seres.*[24]

To you the Red Sea shall give precious shells, India her ivory, Panchia perfumes, and China silks.

Dryden's version of the *topos*, however, reflects the more frankly imperialist tone of Waller's Cromwell panegyric. Waller had written:

> *Fame, swifter than your winged navy, flies*
> *Through every land that near the ocean lies*
> *Sounding your name, and telling dreadful news*
> *To all that piracy and rapine use.*[25]

23. This *topos* is discussed by Ernst Robert Curtius, *European Literature and the Latin Middle Ages,* trans. Willard R. Trask (New York, 1953), pp. 160–161.

24. Claudian, *III Cons.*, lines 209–211, Platnauer, I, 284.

25. Waller, *A Panegyric To My Lord Protector,* 33–36. For a good neo-Latin example of the *topos*, see Andreas Ammonius, *Elegia De Obitu Regis Henrici VII Et Felici Successione Henrici Octavi,* lines 41–46, *Andreae Ammonii Carmina Omnia,* ed. Clemente Pizzi (Florence, 1958):

> Quae regio est aut quam vastus perlabitur Indus
> Aut Tartessiaci litoris unda quatit
> Quaeve sub ardenti squallens male culta leone
> Quaeve trucis boreae flatibus, ora rigens,
> Hunc quae non cupiat Dominum, cui libera colla
> Festinet grato subdere sponte iugo?

In Dryden this becomes:

> *Their wealthy Trade from Pyrates Rapine free*
> *Our Merchants shall no more Advent'rers be:*
> *Nor in the farthest East those Dangers fear*
> *Which humble* Holland *must dissemble here.*
> *Spain to your Gift alone her* Indies *owes;*
> *For what the Pow'rful takes not he bestowes.* (304–309)

Charles's empire abroad "shall no Limits know" (298) precisely because his power at home is limited. This celebration of English sea power reflects not the power of the prince alone, but the "united Int'rest" (296) of prince and people together. The storm of faction and disunity gives way in this conclusion to national harmony and reconciliation.

> *And now times whiter Series is begun*
> *Which in soft Centuries shall smoothly run;*
> *Those Clouds that overcast your Morne shall fly*
> *Dispell'd to farthest corners of the sky.*[26]

26. *Astraea Redux*, 292–295. Dryden's editors have often commented on the Latinate significance of the word "whiter" in this passage. See, for example, the California Dryden, I, 233. To add to this general knowledge, it is worth pointing to the opening lines of the neo-Latin panegyrics by both Erasmus and More, where we find specific parallels for Dryden's line. Erasmus writes:"Semper memoranda dies plaudendaque semper / Quam niveo faciles ducunt mihi vellere Parcae." Erasmus, *Gratulatorium Carmen*, lines 1–2, *The Poems of Desiderius Erasmus*, ed. C. Reedijk (Leiden, 1956), p. 272. Similarly, More opens his poem, repeating the key adjective *niveus*: 'Si qua dies unquam, si quod fuit Anglia tempus / Gratia quo superis esset agenda tibi, / Haec est illa dies niveo signanda lapillo, / Laeta dies fastis annumeranda tuis." More, *Carmen Gratulatorium*, lines 1–4, *The Latin Epigrams of Thomas More*, ed. and trans. Leicester Bradner and Charles Arthur Lynch (Chicago, 1953), p. 16. The white pebble that is used to mark the day of celebration in More's poem parallels the white thread in Erasmus's and both anticipate "times whiter Series" in *Astraea Redux*.

After the euphoria of the Restoration had subsided, most poets were content to pass over the coronation of 1661 in silence. But Dryden took the opportunity to re-assert the themes and ideals of *Astraea Redux* in *To His Sacred Majesty*. This poem has not received nearly as much critical attention as *Astraea Redux* and generally has been seen as a rather pale reflection of the earlier poem, a briefer and less vigorous celebration of the king.[27] The difference in length and design of the two poems does, however, deserve explanation. *Astraea Redux* is a heroic narrative concluded by an oration; *To His Sacred Majesty* is simply an oration, although it is almost twice as long as the earlier address to Charles.

In the coronation poem Dryden assumes the *ethos* previously developed in the narrative section of *Astraea Redux* and extends the significance (as well as the length) of his earlier oration. There can be no doubt about the kind of oration this is, for Dryden subtitled the poem *A Panegyrick on His Coronation*. Moreover, by using such words as "pomp" (7, 34), "feasted" (36), "solemn" (7, 50), and "Nations" (35), he echoes Philemon Holland's classical definition of the term written almost sixty years earlier: "Feasts, games, faires, marts, pompes, shewes, or any such solemnities, performed or exhibited before the general assembly of a whole nation."[28] The "solem-nitie" celebrated here is, of course, the coronation of the king. Dryden develops the significance of this event so that his poem answers the interregnum challenge to

27. See the California Dryden, I, 234–241.
28. Philemon Holland, trans., *The Philosophie, commonlie called, The Morals Written By the Learned Philosopher Plutarch of Chaeronea* (London, 1603), Appendix.

panegyric. The coronation symbolizes the reunion of ceremony and power in the figure of the monarch. In *To His Sacred Majesty*, then, Dryden reasserts a political tradition by adapting a traditional form of oratory. It is his most conventional panegyric.

The reunion of ceremony and power is expressed by the double strand of allusion in the poem, the one Hebraic and the other Roman.[29] Dryden compares Charles to the Biblical patriarch Noah at the beginning of the poem and to the Roman emperor Julius Caesar at the end.[30] Within this framework of patriarchal and imperial ideals, and near the center of the poem, Dryden compares Charles first to David and then to Augustus.[31] The poem thus achieves a balance between ceremony and power that suggests further the reconciliation of church and state. It is the church that confers the crown on the king in a ceremony that recalls the anointment of David by Samuel.[32]

> *Next to the sacred Temple you are led,*
> *Where waites a Crown for your more sacred Head:*
> *How justly from the Church that Crown is due,*
> *Preserv'd from ruine and restor'd by you!*
>
> . . . .
>
> *Now while the sacred Oyl annoints your head,*
> *And fragrant scents, begun from you, are spread*
> *Through the large Dome, the peoples joyful sound*
> *Sent back, is still preserv'd in hallow'd ground . . .*
> (45–48, 59–62)

29. This point has been made very nicely by Joel Blair, "Dryden's Ceremonial Hero," *SEL*, IX (1969), 379–393.

30. *To His Sacred Majesty, A Panegyrick on His Coronation,* 1–4, 103–104, *Poems,* I, 24, 27.

31. *To His Sacred Majesty,* 59, 84.

32. See the California Dryden, I, 237.

Once the ceremony has been performed, however, the power of the king as supreme religious authority is asserted by reference not just to the established church but to the sects as well.

> *The jealous Sects that dare not trust their cause*
> *So farre from their own will as to the Laws,*
> *You for their Umpire and their Synod take,*
> *And their appeal alone to* Caesar *make.* (81–84)

The idea of national reconciliation is thus emphasized by the union of Biblical ceremony and political power.

The allusions also provide a clue to the overall structure of the oration. The Biblical allusions are clustered at the beginning of the poem, giving way in the end to the Roman. Although the poem is not rigidly divided, the movement is from ceremony to power, with a transition near the center where the two are harmonized by the coronation. In rhetorical terms, the first part of the poem is demonstrative, the second deliberative.

Dryden embellishes the demonstrative theme of restoration with solar and seasonal imagery, as well as with Biblical allusions. The comparison of the king to the sun is, of course, a standard topic of the genre.

> *Till your kind beams by their continu'd stay*
> *Had warm'd the ground, and call'd the Damps away.*
> *Such vapours while your pow'rfull influence dryes*
> *Then soonest vanish when they highest rise.* (13–16)

Although this is too conventional to suggest a particular source, we can point to the opening of Jonson's *Panegyre*, where the healthy influence of the king is equally obvious.

> *Againe, the glory of our Westerne world*
> *Unfolds himself: & from his eyes are hoorl'd*
> *(To day) a thousand radiant lights, that stream*
> *To every nooke and angle of his realme.*
> *His former rayes did onely cleare the skie;*
> *But these his searching beams are cast, to prie*
> *Into those darke and deepe concealed vaults,*
> *Where men commit blacke incest with their faults;*
> *And snore supinely in the stall of sin . . .*[33]

The warmth of the sun in Dryden serves the same function as the light of the sun in Jonson; Dryden's "damps" and "vapours" are a milder, metaphoric version of the sins alluded to by Jonson. In both poems the rising sun marks the occasion as a turning point in national history. For Dryden, moreover, this occasion signifies national regeneration, which he expresses in an elaborate seasonal metaphor.

> *Now our sad ruines are remov'd from sight,*
> *The Season too comes fraught with new delight;*
> *Time seems not now beneath his years to stoop*
> *Nor do his wings with sickly feathers droop:*
> *Soft western winds waft ore the gaudy spring*
> *And opend Scenes of flow'rs and blossoms bring*
> *To grace this happy day, while you appear*
> *Not King of us alone but of the year.* (25–32)

This seasonal imagery evokes a host of earlier poems, but in particular it recalls the neo-Latin verse of the sixteenth century. The third couplet of the passage, for example, is anticipated by Erasmus:

> *Rursus ubi zephyris tepidum spirantibus anni*
> *Leta iuventa redit, gemmantur floribus horti . . .*[34]

33. Jonson, *A Panegyre*, 3–11.
34. Erasmus, *Gratulatorium Carmen*, 28–29.

Again when spring returns with west winds blowing warmly,
gardens are studded with flower buds like jewels . . .

And by Walter Haddon:

> *Nunc Zephyrus mollis iucundas commovet auras,*
> *Anglia vere novo nunc recreata viret.*[35]

Now the gentle westwind stirs up pleasant breezes; England
now flourishes, refreshed with a new springtime.

Dryden extends the potential of this imagery by explicitly
referring to the king as a vegetation deity. The combination of seasonal, solar, and Biblical metaphors suggests
that the Restoration is like the resurrection.[36] Natural regeneration of the earth symbolizes spiritual regeneration
of the nation, all brought about by the Restoration of
the king.[37]

The political significance of regeneration is established
by reference, once again, to the processional *topos*, which
underscores the ceremonial theme of restoration and
emphasizes the unanimity of the people in celebration
of the king.

> *All eyes you draw, and with the eyes the heart,*
> *Of your own pomp your self the greatest part:*
> *Loud shouts the Nations happiness proclaim*
> *And Heav'n this day is feasted with your name.*
> *Your Cavalcade the fair Spectators view*
> *From their high standings, yet look up to you.* (33–38)

35. Haddon, *In auspicatissimum*, 13–14.

36. For an excellent discussion of the Biblical typology of this
poem and of *Astraea Redux*, see Steven N. Zwicker, *Dryden's Political Poetry: The Typology of King and Nation* (Providence, 1972),
pp. 61–77.

37. The importance of regeneration in Dryden's panegyrics has
been emphasized by Blair, p. 393.

Again Dryden may well have had in mind Ben Jonson:
"Upon his face all threw their covetous eyes, / As on a
wonder" (34–35). In both panegyrics all eyes are fastened
on the king, and in Dryden, characteristically, all eyes
are lifted up in the process. Charles, identified as the
optimus princeps or "best of Kings" (54), is divine.

> *We add not to your glory, but employ*
> *Our time like Angels in expressing joy.*
> *Nor is it duty or our hopes alone*
> *Create that joy, but full fruition . . . (67–70)*

The corollary to the divinity of the king, then, is the
angelic nature of the people. The comparison is normative, recalling the fallen angel status of Cromwell in
Cowley's Restoration ode and, more importantly, fore-
shadowing the metaphoric situation of Shaftesbury in
Absalom and Achitophel. In *To His Sacred Majesty*,
Dryden presents the ideal against which the impiety of
rebellion is to be measured. By quietly restoring the
people to their proper place in heaven, Dryden expresses
the nation's renewed obedience to the king.

In the last lines of the above citation, Dryden begins
to bring us back down to earth. Moving from the ideal
to the actual world, he suggests that popular obedience
is contingent on the "blessings" (71) expected from the
king. Here, in short, Dryden shifts to deliberative oratory
and begins to advise the king.

> *No promise can oblige a Prince so much*
> *Still to be good as long to have been such.*
> *A noble Emulation heats your breast,*
> *And your own fame now robbs you of your rest:*
> *Good actions still must be maintain'd with good,*
> *As bodies nourish'd with resembling food. (73–78)*

Although the conditions presented here are not specified beyond the vague "Good actions," the words "promise," "oblige," and "must" establish the contractual intent of the passage. In subsequent lines, moreover, Dryden does provide a specific pattern for "Emulation" by outlining the proper royal response to the nation's former crimes. "Among our crimes oblivion may be set, / But 'tis our Kings perfection to forget" (87–88). The desired end of this advice is peace, as Dryden makes clear by repeating the instructions of *Astraea Redux*.

> *Virtues unknown to these rough Northern climes*
> *From milder heav'ns you bring, without their crimes:*
> *Your calmnesse does no after storms provide,*
> *Nor seeming patience mortal anger hide.* (89–92)

As in the earlier poem, the royal virtues necessary for domestic tranquillity are mildness, calmness, and patience. The admonitory significance of these lines is revealed by the qualifying phrases—"no after storms provide," no "mortal anger hide." Dryden's concern here, as in the traditional deliberative oration, is for the future. His praise functions as advice.

As he moves toward the end of his address, Dryden extends this advice to encompass the virtues of a leader in foreign affairs as well as in domestic. By reference to Charles's interest in naval affairs and by allusion to his improvements at St. James's Park, Dryden urges the king to guarantee "our defence" (110). Slyly, he even points to a model for the conduct of foreign affairs: "So safe are all things which our King protects" (116). The reconciliation of King and Protector in Charles, which functions both as royal instruction and popular propa-

ganda, succinctly completes Dryden's reunion of ceremony and power.

The poem closes with a variation on the two-Indies
topos, designed to reiterate the importance of national
reconciliation.

> *From your lov'd Thames a blessing yet is due,*
> *Second alone to that it brought in you;*
> *A Queen, from whose chast womb, ordain'd by Fate,*
> *The souls of Kings unborn for bodies wait.*
> *It was your Love before made discord cease:*
> *Your love is destin'd to your Countries peace.*
> *Both Indies (Rivalls in your bed) provide*
> *With Gold or Jewels to adorn your Bride.* (117–124)

Here Dryden combines the East-West hyperbole with
the image of marriage to symbolize the harmony between
prince and people. In this he adheres to the tradition as
exemplified by Claudian and Thomas More. Claudian
had concluded his panegyric on the fourth consulship of
Honorius with a similar, if more extravagant, expression
of the idea.

> *quae tali devota toro, quae murice fulgens*
> *ibit in amplexus tanti regina mariti?*
> *quaenam tot divis veniet nurus, omnibus arvis*
> *et toto donanda mari? quantusque feretur*
> *idem per Zephyri metas Hymenaeus et Euri!* [38]

Who shall be consecrated to such a couch; who, glorious in
purple, shall pass, a queen, to the embraces of such a husband?
What bride shall come to be the daughter of so many gods,
dowered with every land and the whole sea? How gloriously
shall the nuptial song be borne at once to farthest East and
West.

38. Claudian, *IV Cons.*, lines 645–649, Platnauer, I, 334.

The tone of Dryden's version, however, is closer to the conclusion of More's panegyric to Henry.

> *Illa tibi felix populos hinc inde potentes*
>   *Non dissoluenda iunxit amicitia.*
> *Regibus orta quidem magnis, nihiloque minorum est*
>   *Regum, quam quibus est orta, futura parens.*
> *Hactenus una tui navem tenet ancora regni,*
>   *Una, sat illa quidem firma, sed una tamen.*
> *At regina tibi sexu foecunda virili*
>   *Undique firmatam perpetuamque dabit.*[39]

This blessed lady has joined to you in lasting alliance nations which are, in various places, powerful. She is descended from great kings, to be sure; and she will be the mother of kings as great as her ancestors. To this time one anchor has protected your ship of state—a strong one, yet only one. But your fruitful queen will present you with a male heir, a protection in unbroken line, who shall be supported on every side.

Dryden, more laconic than either of his predecessors, is also more emphatically admonitory.

> *Your Subjects, while you weigh the Nations fate,*
> *Suspend to both their doubtfull love or hate:*
> *Choose only, (Sir,) that so they may possesse*
> *With their own peace their Childrens happinesse.* (133–136)

In the last lines of the poem Dryden calls for the extension of the traditional ideals to the next generation. Like Claudian and More, Dryden would persuade prince and people to maintain their present harmony in the future.

Only one year into this future, however, Dryden himself had begun to shift the emphasis of his political oratory. In *Astraea Redux* and *To His Sacred Majesty*, he adopts panegyrical conventions to idealize and to re-

39. More, *Carmen Gratulatorium*, 173–180.

strict the king. In *Astraea Redux* he summarizes his position in one neat couplet, discussed above but worth
repeating. "Your Pow'r to Justice doth submit your
Cause, / Your Goodness only is above the Laws" (266–
267). In *To His Sacred Majesty* he expresses the same
idea in a couplet which brings together the patriarchal
and imperial threads of the poem. "But you that are a
Soveraign Prince, allay / Imperial pow'r with your
paternal sway" (95–96). The limitation on the king's
power, suggested here by allusion to the ideals of law
and fatherhood, is further defined in both poems by a
virtue variously expressed as "mercy," "mildness," or
"goodness." In Dryden's next poem, *To My Lord Chancellor* of 1662, he takes a fresh look at this royal ideal.

> *Heav'n would your Royal Master should exceed*
> *Most in that Vertue which we most did need,*
> *And his mild Father (who too late did find*
> *All mercy vain but what with pow'r was joyn'd,)*
> *His fatal goodnesse left to fitter times,*
> *Not to increase but to absolve our Crimes . . .*[40]

Here Dryden repeats his warning against power without
mercy, but in the process he takes a longer look at the
other side of the problem: mercy without power. The
parenthesis indicates that mercy, or piety, or mildness,
or goodness, can qualify power only where power exists.
This passage, while urging mildness, parenthetically
warns that mildness by itself is politically meaningless.

In these early panegyrics Dryden does not shy away
from the fact of power. The question is rather how and
by whom power should be exercised. In *To My Lord
Chancellor* this question is succinctly answered.

40. *To My Lord Chancellor*, 55–60.

> *By you he fits those Subjects to obey,*
> *As Heavens Eternal Monarch does convey*
> *His pow'r unseen, and man to his designs,*
> *By his bright Ministers the Stars, inclines.* (83–86)

Power qualified by mercy belongs to Charles and is administered by the Lord Chancellor, thereby securing the obedience of the people. Clearly, however, this obedience can be guaranteed only if royal power is retained and asserted. *To My Lord Chancellor* thus points toward Dryden's later political poetry.

THE LATER POEMS

In *Absalom and Achitophel* Dryden expands, illustrates, and universalizes the themes of the early panegyrics. In this allegory of English politics, Charles is portrayed as a king who rules according to the ideals set forth in the poems of the 1660's. In rebelling against him, the people perversely rebel against the perfect prince and, in effect, violate the contract signed in *Astraea Redux* and reaffirmed in *To His Sacred Majesty*. The normative values of *Absalom and Achitophel* are consistently defined through echoes of the earlier poems.

> *My Father Governs with unquestion'd Right;*
> *The Faiths Defender, and Mankinds Delight:*
> *Good, Gracious, Just, observant of the Laws;*
> *And Heav'n by Wonders has Espous'd his Cause.*
> *Whom has he Wrong'd in all his Peaceful Reign?*
> *Who sues for Justice to his Throne in Vain?*
> *What Millions has he Pardon'd of his Foes,*
> *Whom Just Revenge did to his Wrath expose?*
> *Mild, Easy, Humble, Studious of our Good;*

> *Enclin'd to Mercy, and averse from Blood.*
> *If Mildness Ill with Stubborn* Israel *Suite,*
> *His Crime is God's beloved Attribute.*[41]

Because the "Stubborn" people resist the traditional ideals of law and justice, because, moreover, they rebel against the king's very "Mildness," Charles is compelled to reconsider his own virtues. In his decisive oration, the king elaborates the parenthetical warning of *To My Lord Chancellor* and thereby avoids the fate of "his mild Father (who too late did find / All mercy vain but what with pow'r was joyn'd,) . . ."

> *Thus long have I, by native mercy sway'd,*
> *My wrongs dissembl'd, my revenge delay'd:*
> *So willing to forgive th' Offending Age,*
> *So much the Father did the King asswage.*
> *But now so far my Clemency they slight,*
> *Th' Offenders question my Forgiving Right.*
> *That one was made for many, they contend:*
> *But 'tis to Rule, for that's a Monarch's End.* (939–946)

Whereas in *Astraea Redux* and *To His Sacred Majesty* Dryden had emphasized the limits of royal power, in *Absalom and Achitophel* he explores the limits of the king's mercy. "How ill my Fear they by my Mercy scan, / Beware the Fury of a Patient Man" (1004–1005).

In his oration the king not only polishes his ideal image by righting the balance between power and mercy, but he also reflects ironically on the nature of the ideal subject. "My Pious Subjects for my Safety pray, / Which to Secure they take my Power away" (983–984). The phrase "power and piety," traditionally voiced to restrain the king, is here adapted by the king himself as a re-

41. *Absalom and Achitophel,* 317–328.

straint on the people. The "Pious Subjects" referred to include, for example, the representative Puritan zealot Slingsby Bethel: "The City, to reward his pious Hate / Against his Master, chose him Magistrate" (593–594). More importantly, however, the irony is directed against Shaftesbury, who invokes the traditional royal virtue to incite rebellion against the monarchy: "Urge now your Piety" (419) is his advice to Monmouth. This inherited ideal, significantly enriched in this poem by the thematic context of religious and filial duty, is first perverted by the people and then re-established by the king. In effect, the monarch converts the traditional language of panegyric to achieve his own goal: restoration of those ideal "pious times" with which the poem begins. The speech succeeds, and in the final lines Dryden implicitly identifies the "pious times" of *Absalom and Achitophel* with "time's whiter Series" predicted in *Astraea Redux*.

> *Henceforth a Series of new time began,*
> *The mighty Years in long Procession ran:*
> *Once more the Godlike David was Restor'd,*
> *And willing Nations knew their Lawfull Lord.* (1028–1031)

By adapting the vocabulary and values of panegyric for this royal speech, Dryden forecasts a shift in the balance of his rhetorical stance. From 1660 to 1688 he attempts to maintain his position between the prince and the people, but in the early poems he is closer to the people, whereas in the later poems he is closer to the prince. And yet there is more involved in the later panegyrics than a movement toward the monarchy. The verse orations of the reign of James II are more complicated, more variable, and more resistant to precise for-

mulation, whether in terms of structure or type, than
either *Astraea Redux* or *To His Sacred Majesty*. In both
Threnodia Augustalis and *Britannia Rediviva* Dryden
shifts his ground uncomfortably, speaking sometimes
for the people to the king, sometimes for the king to the
people, but oftentimes throwing up his hands and addressing God in prayer for the nation. More important
than the apparent movement toward the prince is a
movement from an assured oratorical stance in 1660 to
a very shaky one in 1688. This shift indicates not only
Dryden's disillusionment with post-Restoration politics,
but also his reassessment of his own role as poet-orator.

The problematic nature of *Threnodia Augustalis* can
be dealt with only partially in terms of oratory. Nevertheless, the perspective suggested by reading the poem
as an oration on the accession of James II does comple-
ment and illuminate the more customary view of the
poem as an elegy on the death of Charles. The dual
occasion of death and accession had, of course, challenged earlier poets. The two basic techniques of hand-
ling the problem are apparent in the poems written in
1509. Thomas More's panegyric to Henry VIII disposes
of the previous king by making him the villain of the
piece. Condemning the policies of Henry VII, More celebrates the restoration of his own ideals in the person of
Henry VIII. The churchman Andreas Ammonius, whose
poem is titled *Elegia De Obitu Regis Henrici VII Et Felici
Successione Henrici Octavi*, adopts an alternative strategy, taking the new king first as the elegiac consolation
for the loss of the old, and only afterward as the ideal
monarch. In *Threnodia Augustalis* Dryden is closer to
Ammonius than to More. Still, the problem of coping

with two kings in one poem is new to Dryden and adds a degree of complexity not found in the panegyrics of the 1660's.

As Charles is dead and James is living, we might reasonably expect Dryden to address James, while considering Charles in a narrative, reflective, or purely elegiac manner. But instead it is Charles whom Dryden addresses in the apostrophe of stanza 10.

> *For all those Joys thy Restauration brought,*
> *For all the Miracles it wrought,*
> *For all the healing Balm thy Mercy pour'd*
> *Into the Nations bleeding Wound,*
> *And Care that after kept it sound,*
> *For numerous Blessings yearly shour'd,*
> *And Property with Plenty crown'd;*
> *For Freedom, still maintain'd alive,*
> *Freedom which in no other Land will thrive,*
> *Freedom an* English *Subject's sole Prerogative,*
> *Without whose Charms ev'n Peace wou'd be*
> *But a dull quiet Slavery . . .* [42]

Here Dryden praises Charles for having realized the ideals set forth in the early panegyrics. The "mercy" recommended in *Astraea Redux* appears in retrospect as the king's outstanding quality; it is one of the "blessings" that Dryden, in *To His Sacred Majesty*, had led the nation to expect from Charles. However, the last lines of this passage, with the severe emphasis on "Freedom," suggest that Dryden is thinking of the future as well as the past. The function of Dryden's eulogy of Charles is, in part, to educate James.

That one purpose of the poem is the instruction of the

42. *Threnodia Augustalis, A Funeral-Pindarique Poem Sacred to the Happy Memory of King Charles II*, 292–303, *Poems*, I, 450.

new king is suggested from the very beginning. In stanzas 2 and 3 Dryden uses the adjective "pious" three times to describe James. Because the piety of the new king must be demonstrated before he inherits the royal power, Dryden portrays James as the "Pious Duke" (71) and the "Pious Brother" (36 and 93). Indeed James first rejects the allure of "Approaching Greatness" which "met him with her Charms / Of Pow'r" (56–57), turning instead to pray for the life of his brother, an action that expresses the appropriate sense of duty. The deathbed scene further develops the educational theme, as Dryden concentrates on the significance of the royal inheritance. "He took and prest that ever loyal hand, / Which cou'd in Peace secure his Reign, / Which cou'd in wars his Pow'r maintain, / That hand on which no plighted vows were ever vain."[43] The new king must be what the old king had been: "Intrepid, pious, merciful, and brave" (206).

One function of the poem, then, is to advise James that being king entails responsibility as well as authority, piety as well as power. At the same time, however, Dryden's portrayal of James establishes an ideal for the people. Because James is not yet king at the time his piety is expressed, he himself becomes a model for the subjects of the new reign.[44] As in *Absalom and Achitophel* (though without the irony), Dryden again shows

43. *Threnodia Augustalis*, 229–232. The combination here of war and peace suggests a specific version of the more general *augustus/amabilis* ideal. Likewise the hand image suggests Waller, *A Paneyric To My Lord Protector*, 1–2, and Jonson, *A Panegyre*, 121–123.

44. This idea is touched on by Earl Miner in the California Dryden, III, 409. See also, John Wallace, *Destiny His Choice: The Loyalism of Andrew Marvell* (Cambridge, 1968), pp. 88–89.

piety to be a subject's virtue as well as a king's. In his behavior toward Charles, James promotes love and duty toward the monarch as the desired norm for his own subjects.

Later in the poem Dryden directly addresses these subjects on behalf of the new king. "View then a *Monarch* ripen'd for a Throne" (446). The purpose of this address, as the preceding lines indicate, is to convince the people that James is indeed the perfect prince.

> *But e'r a Prince is to Perfection brought,*
> *He costs Omnipotence a second thought.*
> *With Toyl and Sweat,*
> *With hardning Cold, and forming Heat,*
> *The Cyclops did their strokes repeat,*
> *Before th' impenetrable Shield was wrought.*
> *It looks as if the Maker wou'd not own*
> *The Noble work for his,*
> *Before 'twas try'd and found a Masterpiece.* (437–445)

Thus moving somewhat uneasily and defensively toward the role of spokesman for the king, Dryden attempts to bolster his appeal to the nation by enlisting divine aid. Whereas *Astraea Redux* had ended with an enthusiastic prophecy, affirmed in *To His Sacred Majesty*, the prophecy at the end of *Threnodia Augustalis* is complicated and severely qualified by the distressful prayer that precedes it.

> *For once, O Heav'n, unfold thy Adamantine Book;*
> *And let his wondring* Senate *see,*
> *If not thy firm Immutable Decree,*
> *At least the second Page, of strong contingency;*
> *Such as consists with wills, Originally free:*
> *Let them, with glad amazement, look*
> *On what their happiness may be:*

Let them not still be obstinately blind,
Still to divert the Good thou hast design'd,
Or with Malignant penury,
To sterve the Royal Vertues of his Mind.
Faith is a Christian's and a Subject's Test,
Oh give them to believe, and they are surely blest! (491–503)

Although the invocation of the gods on behalf of the monarch is not in itself new, Dryden's emphasis is strikingly different from what we find in earlier poems. Following panegyrists both in Latin (like Walter Haddon) and in English (like Samuel Daniel), Dryden defines disobedience to the king as disobedience to God and equates established government with divine providence. But the future of this government, and of the English nation, does not here rest directly on God but rather on the people's "faith" in God, and "faith" has a strong adversary in the blind obstinance of the people.

The test Dryden poses for the future is to "believe" in God and the king. Yet, in reading these lines, it is possible to wonder how long Dryden himself can continue to believe in the metaphor which links the king with God. This traditional analogy expresses the reconciliation of actual and ideal in the political sphere, a reconciliation challenged during the interregnum, recaptured at the Restoration, and now during the reign of James II asserted with more hope than conviction. The almost-pleading voice of Dryden's address to God, "O give them to believe," exposes the unbridged gap between the political realities of 1685 and the political ideals of traditional panegyric.

Britannia Rediviva is sufficient proof that Dryden did

not see his prayer answered in the years between 1685 and 1688. The poem celebrates the birth of Prince James and thus represents a variation on traditional panegyric which classical writers referred to as a *panegyricus genethliacus*.[45] In the panegyrics of Claudian, Erasmus, Cowley, and in the early panegyrics of Dryden himself, the poet draws a parallel between the day of celebration and the day of the prince's birth. In *Astraea Redux*, for example, Dryden, developing the parallel by allusion to the king's birth star, celebrates the Restoration of the prince as a new birth for the nation. In *Britannia Rediviva* Dryden reverses the analogy and celebrates the birth of the prince as symbolic of national restoration. Indeed this occasion is actually perfect for panegyric as the poet is not hampered by biographical fact; the baby prince can easily become the symbolic focus of whatever ideals the orator wishes to persuade the king and people to accept. However, given this perfect occasion, Dryden's oratory is more complicated and more strained than in any of the previous panegyrics. Sometimes he is the people's spokesman and sometimes the king's, but ultimately he is neither. Moreover, this shifting rhetorical stance is accompanied by a new rigidity, a firmness of tone and diction not to be found in *Threnodia Augustalis*.

The poem opens with Dryden in his old role as the people's orator. The very first word of the poem is the corporate "Our" so characteristic of Dryden's public poetry of the 1660's. But this "Our" turns out to be an exclusive rather than an inclusive pronoun, referring

45. This is also, of course, the ancestor of the infamous birthday odes of the eighteenth century.

only to those who came to pray for the child. The interests of the rest of the nation Dryden considers not as "ours" but as "yours."

> *O still repining at your present state,*
> *Grudging your selves the Benefits of Fate,*
> *Look up, and read in Characters of Light*
> *A Blessing sent you in your own Despight.*
> *The Manna falls, yet that Coelestial Bread*
> *Like* Jews *you munch, and murmure while you feed.*
> *May not your Fortune be like theirs, Exil'd,*
> *Yet forty Years to wander in the Wild:*
> *Or if it be, may* Moses *live at least*
> *To lead you to the Verge of promis'd Rest.*[46]

Dryden, dissociating himself from that "Headstrong, Moody, Murmuring race," sees the nation threatened by a new period of exile for which the hoped-for survival of this new Moses is but small consolation. To prevent this disaster and to counter public disbelief, Dryden attempts to revive the voice of *Threnodia Augustalis* and to address the nation once again on behalf of James.

> *Now view at home a second* Constantine;
> *(The former too, was of the* Brittish *Line)*
> *Has not his healing Balm your Breaches clos'd,*
> *Whose Exile many sought, and few oppos'd?*
> *Or, did not Heav'n by its Eternal Doom*
> *Permit those Evils, that this Good might come?*
> *So manifest, that ev'n the Moon-ey'd Sects*
> *See* Whom *and* What *this Providence protects.* (88–95)

Although the repeated negatives disclose the increased difficulty of Dryden's task, he is at least trying to fill the role of spokesman for the monarch.

46. *Britannia Rediviva, A Poem On The Birth Of The Prince,* 61–70, *Poems,* II, 543.

From this perspective, speaking to the people for the king, Dryden attempts to refute the notorious "warming-pan" story. Hercules (55), Jesus (127), and Aeneas (128), who figure so prominently in heroic panegyric, are now trundled out to prove the legitimacy of the prince. The comparison of the child to "the Saviour" suggests, moreover, the ritualistic element of traditional panegyric. In Samuel Daniel's address to James I, in particular, there is a passage that anticipates the rhetoric of *Britannia Rediviva*.

> *And all for thee, that we the more might praise*
> *The glory of his [God's] powre, and reverence thine,*
> *Whom he hath rais'd to glorifie our dayes,*
> *And make this Empire of the North to shine*
> *Against all th'impious workings, all th'assayes*
> *Of vile disnatur'd Vipers, whose designe*
> *Was to embroile the State, t'obscure the light,*
> *And that cleere brightnesse of thy sacred right.*[47]

Daniel's "Vipers" become Dryden's "Fiends."

> *Fain wou'd the Fiends have made a dubious birth,*
> *Loth to confess the Godhead cloath'd in Earth.*
> *But sickned after all their baffled lyes,*
> *To find an Heir apparent of the Skyes:*
> *Abandon'd to despair, still may they grudge,*
> *And owning not the Saviour, prove the Judge.* (122–127)

Dryden's oration, like Daniel's, is designed to counter those who would "embroile the State." It should be noted, however, that Dryden omits the loaded word "impiety" and instead defines opposition to the monarchy

47. Samuel Daniel, *A Panegyrike Congratulatorie*, lines 97–104, *The Complete Works in Verse and Prose of Samuel Daniel*, ed. Alexander B. Grosart, 5 vols. (New York, 1963), p. 147.

as willful disbelief, a failure in faith, a failure to pass the test proposed at the end of *Threnodia Augustalis*. What *Britannia Rediviva* demonstrates is the denial of Dryden's plea for belief uttered three years earlier. Dryden as poet-orator has reached an impasse, his ideal way into the future blocked by the nation's unwillingness to believe in their monarch.

But it is also evident that Dryden himself no longer believes in the monarch either. The closing line of the above citation, "And owning not the Saviour, prove the Judge," besides referring to the dual nature of Christ, anticipates Dryden's address to James. "The Name of Great, your Martial mind will sute, / But Justice, is your Darling Attribute" (333–334). The merciful king of *Astraea Redux*, challenged in *Absalom and Achitophel*, gives way to the just king of *Britannia Rediviva*.[48] The substitution of justice for mercy is double-edged; justice is all the people deserve but, as the subsequent lines reveal, it is possibly more than they can expect from the king. Having lectured the people, Dryden turns around and lectures James.

> *Some Kings the name of Conq'rours have assum'd,*
> *Some to be Great, some to be Gods presum'd;*
> *But boundless pow'r, and arbitrary Lust*
> *Made Tyrants still abhor the Name of Just;*
> *They shun'd the praise this Godlike Virtue gives,*
> *And fear'd a Title, that reproach'd their Lives.*
> *The Pow'r from which all Kings derive their state,*
> *Whom they pretend, at least, to imitate,*
> *Is equal both to punish and reward;*
> *For few wou'd love their God, unless they fear'd.*

48. For a brief discussion of this point, see the California Dryden, III, 482–483. See also Blair, 392.

> *Resistless Force and Immortality*
> *Make but a Lame, Imperfect Deity:*
> *Tempests have force unbounded to destroy,*
> *And Deathless Being ev'n the Damn'd enjoy,*
> *And yet Heav'ns Attributes, both last and first,*
> *One without life, and one with life accurst;*
> *But Justice is Heav'ns self, so strictly He,*
> *That cou'd it fail, the God-head cou'd not be.* (399–356)

Although Dryden invokes the tradition of the genre by rejecting "boundless pow'r," these lines have an ironic edge that expresses the orator's deep disillusionment with royalty. Dryden here views kings as a presumptuous lot who have claimed ties with divinity but have not acted in accordance with divine laws. As a critique of the fundamental royalty-divinity metaphor of panegyric, this passage shows that the traditional virtues—mercy, patience, and piety—are now beyond Dryden's hopes. Even if James were to live up to the reduced ideal of justice, he would be but a momentary exception to the general rule of less-than-ideal monarchs. Dryden can no longer speak for the people, but he can no longer speak for the monarchy either.

The frustration of Dryden's attempt to influence power with poetry is strongly expressed in his address to God.

> *Enough of Ills our dire Rebellion wrought,*
> *When, to the Dregs, we drank the bitter draught;*
> *Then airy Atoms did in Plagues conspire,*
> *Nor did th' avenging Angel yet retire,*
> *But purg'd our still encreasing Crimes with Fire.*
> *Then perjur'd Plots, the still impending Test,*
> *And worse; but Charity conceals the Rest:*
> *Here stop the Current of the sanguine flood,*
> *Require not, Gracious God, thy Martyrs Blood* . . . (152–160)

This summation of recent English history, from one rebellion to the eve of another, suggests the full extent of Dryden's disillusionment with events and the inadequacy of the traditional ideals of panegyric in writing about contemporary English politics. Rebellion, plague, fire, plot, martyrdom are the actualities that, by their persistence and progress, undermine belief in the ideals of panegyrical oratory. *Britannia Rediviva* represents, finally, the collapse of the persuasive purpose that had sustained Dryden's political poetry during the preceding three decades.

The futility of continuing to assert the old ideals is most evident in Dryden's elaboration of conventional image patterns. The poem begins with a sequence of commonplace metaphors, as Dryden celebrates the occasion by reference to the day, the season, and the liturgical calendar. To trace these images through the rest of the poem, however, is to discover Dryden's recognition that such poetic comparisons no longer make political sense.

Dryden's initial celebration of the "day" of the prince's birth includes the conventional image of *le roi soleil*.

> *Just on the Day, when the high mounted Sun*
> *Did farthest in his Northern Progress run,*
> *He bended forward and ev'n stretch'd the Sphere*
> *Beyond the limits of the lengthen'd year;*
> *To view a Brighter Sun in* Britaine *Born* ... (5–9)

Later in the poem, however, the solar imagery is developed in a strikingly unconventional way.

> *Born in broad Day-light, that th' ungrateful Rout*
> *May find no room for a remaining doubt:*
> *Truth, which it self is light, does darkness shun,*
> *And the true Eaglet safely dares the Sun.* (118–121)

The extension of the image to include the additional comparison between the king and the eagle is itself nothing new. Claudian, for example, had used the same complex metaphor to demonstrate the worth of Honorius.[49] What is new is the apparent purpose of the image in *Britannia Rediviva*. Neither demonstrative nor deliberative in function, this passage is designed to prove the child's legitimacy. Dryden thus forces the ceremonial image of the sun to serve a quasi-judicial purpose, to function as factual proof. The conventional, hyperbolic language of panegyric simply cannot bear this kind of strain and still be taken seriously. As proof of the prince's parentage this image—and this poem—will convince no one.

Like the sun image, the related imagery of the seasons is developed in an initially conventional but ultimately strained manner. At the outset Dryden celebrates the child by allusion to spring, summer, and fall. "Betwixt two Seasons comes th' Auspicious Heir, / This Age to blossom, and the next to bear" (17–18). Eventually, however, this image of seasonal transition gives way to a harvest image set in the context of the familiar tempest metaphor. The focus of this later passage is the rumored death of the prince, an event which suggests to Dryden's mind all the old horrors of rebellion.

> *Down fell the winnow'd Wheat; but mounted high,*
> *The Whirl-wind bore the Chaff, and hid the Sky.*
> *Here black Rebellion shooting from below*
> *(As Earth's Gigantick brood by moments grow)*
> *And here the Sons of God are petrify'd with Woe . . .*
>
> (234–238)

49. Claudian, *III Cons.*, "Praefatio," lines 1–18, Platnauer, I, 268.

Although reminiscent of passages in Dryden's previous panegyrics, these conventional metaphors do not here suggest reconciliation either now or in the future, but rather indicate a permanent national division: wheat and chaff. Although Dryden further extends the harvest imagery, shaping it into the usual pattern of restoration, his voice expresses at best a temporary victory of good over evil.

> *As when a sudden Storm of Hail and Rain*
> *Beats to the ground the yet unbearded Grain,*
> *Think not the hopes of Harvest are destroy'd*
> *On the flat Field, and on the naked void;*
> *The light, unloaded stem, from tempest free'd,*
> *Will raise the youthful honours of his head;*
> *And, soon restor'd by native vigour, bear*
> *The timely product of the bounteous Year.* (259–266)

Although the prince is here "restor'd," there is nothing in this passage to persuade the "chaff" of Dryden's audience that national restoration is symbolized by the fortune of the child.

That Dryden himself no longer believes in the political reconciliation of actual and ideal through metaphor is strikingly evident in his development of the third major image pattern initiated in the opening lines: religious ritual. The celebration of the prince's birth is initially linked to the celebration of Whitsuntide. "Last solemn Sabbath saw the Church attend; / The Paraclete in fiery Pomp descend; / But when his Wondrous Octave rowl'd again, / He brought a Royal Infant in his Train" (19–22). The significance of the descent of the Holy Spirit is subsequently focused by the ceremony of baptism.

> Let his Baptismal Drops for us attone;
> Lustrations for Offences not his own.
> Let Conscience, which is Int'rest ill disguis'd,
> In the same Font be cleans'd, and all the Land Baptiz'd.
>
> (188–191)

The penitential pattern of *Astraea Redux* and the national baptism implicit in the flood imagery of *To His Sacred Majesty* are revived in the spiritual birth of the prince. As Dryden's definition of conscience suggests, however, he no longer believes in the political significance of ceremony. As he had observed earlier in the poem, "To mend our Crimes whole Ages wou'd require" (38). This one symbolic day cannot eradicate past and persistent evils; this festival ceremony cannot bring national reconciliation. The enthusiastic prophecies of the 1660's end in 1688 with a very tentative vision of the future, a vision in which ideals have surrendered to actualities. "By living well, let us secure his days, / Mod'rate in hopes, and humble in our ways" (298–299).

In *Britannia Rediviva* Dryden abandons his belief in the essential functions of panegyric. Although he opens the poem by celebrating a public festival, he admits that this occasion does not symbolize national restoration: "Nor yet conclude all fiery *Trials* past, / For Heav'n will exercise us to the last" (267–268). As this pessimism extends to both the people and the king, as there is no ground left between his two audiences, Dryden gives up the traditional posture of mediator and the traditional goal of reconciliation. In effect, what Dryden recognizes in the course of this poem is that a poet's advice concerning the responsible exercise of political power means nothing in the face of royal presumption and recurrent popular rebellion. In sum, what is called for by 1688 is not panegyric, but rather its opposite, polemic.

After 1688, although Dryden occasionally threatens to adopt the stance of the polemicist, he never carries out that threat. Instead, he abandons the role of public orator, forsaking both the prince and the people. In his poem on the death of *Eleonora*, Dryden formally steps down from the podium he had occupied since the interregnum. In doing so, however, he takes a retrospective look at the genre that—more than any other—illuminates his career as a public poet.

Like most of Dryden's poems of the 1690's, *Eleonora* is concerned with private rather than public life. There is, nevertheless, a metaphoric relationship between *Eleonora* and the classical tradition of panegyric that fully explains Dryden's subtitle: *A Panegyrical Poem*. Metaphorically, the occasion for the poem is a public festival or assembly, which Dryden celebrates in the familiar processional *topos*.

> *As when in glory, through the publick place,*
> *The Spoils of conquer'd Nations were to pass,*
> *And but one Day for Triumph was allow'd,*
> *The Consul was constrain'd his Pomp to crowd;*
> *And so the swift Procession hurry'd on,*
> *That all, though not distinctly, might be shown;*
> *So, in the straiten'd bounds of life confin'd,*
> *She gave but glimpses of her glorious Mind:*
> *And multitudes of Vertues pass'd along;*
> *Each pressing foremost in the mighty throng;*
> *Ambitious to be seen, and then make room,*
> *For greater Multitudes that were to come.*[50]

50. *Eleonora: A Panegyrical Poem Dedicated to the Memory Of The Late Countess of Abingdon*, 274–285, *Poems*, II, 592.

The virtues thus publicly displayed are, moreover, specifically those that define the ideal subject and the ideal
king. As subject she evinces "Love" (176) and "Obedience" (176) and is guiltless of "Crime" (170). As king
she cares for the poor (12–64), manages the economy
(65–82), provides a model for the settlement of religious
disputes (106–115), loves and educates her subjects (193–
239), and thus at death assumes a position as a star near
"Heav'ns Imperial Face" (267). These specific virtues
are contained by the traditional panegyrical emblem of
national harmony, namely marriage. Eleonora as ideal
wife is analogous to the ideal subject, Eleonora as parent
is analogous to the ideal king.[51]

Dryden's elaboration of these analogies typically involves a pattern of elevation from local to universal, as
for example in the passage "Of her prudent Manage-
ment," where Eleonora is portrayed as king.

> *Yet was she not profuse; but fear'd to wast,*
> *And wisely manag'd, that the stock might last;*
> *That all might be supply'd; and she not grieve*
> *When Crouds appear'd, she had not to relieve.*
> *Which to prevent, she still increas'd her store;*
> *Laid up, and spar'd, that she might give the more:*
> *So* Pharaoh, *or some Greater King than he,*
> *Provided for the sev'nth Necessity:*
> *Taught from above, his Magazines to frame;*
> *That Famine was prevented e're it came.*
> *Thus Heav'n, though All-sufficient, shows a thrift*
> *In his Oeconomy, and bounds his gift:*
> *Creating for our Day, one single Light;*
> *And his Reflection too supplies the Night:*
> *Perhaps a thousand other Worlds, that lye*

51. For a brief discussion of the analogies in this poem, see
Roper, pp. 111–113.

> *Remote from us, and latent in the Sky,*
> *Are lighten'd by his Beams, and kindly nurst;*
> *Of which our Earthly Dunghil is the worst.* (65–82)

Here Dryden unites home economy with national economy and then with the economy inherent in God's universe.[52] As the last lines of this passage indicate, however, the smooth progression from human to divine is undermined by Dryden's perception of the actual world. We find the same progression and the same undercurrent of disillusionment in passages that portray Eleonora as subject.

> *Love and Obedience to her Lord she bore,*
> *She much obey'd him, but she lov'd him more.*
> *Not aw'd to Duty by superior sway;*
> *But taught by his Indulgence to obey.*
> *Thus we love God as Author of our good;*
> *So Subjects love just Kings, or so they shou'd.* (176–181)

Although Eleonora emerges here as the ideal subject to husband, king, and God, all three of whom are encompassed by the word "Lord," the skepticism of the last phrase again evokes the gulf between actual and ideal worlds that panegyric traditionally attempts to bridge.

In this "panegyrical" poem Dryden affirms the verdict of *Britannia Rediviva* by acknowledging the impossibility of uniting the two domains of the genre. The tension in the poem between the symbol of Dryden's ideals, Eleonora, and the actual world culminates in her fortunate escape to heaven.

52. The same pattern of elevation can be seen in the passage shoulder-noted "Of her love to her Children," only here the allusions are classical, Anchises and Cybele.

> Let this suffice: Nor thou, great Saint refuse
> This humble Tribute of no vulgar Muse:
> Who, not by Cares, or Wants, or Age deprest,
> Stems a wild Deluge with a dauntless brest:
> And dares to sing thy Praises, in a Clime
> Where Vice triumphs, and Vertue is a Crime:
> Where ev'n to draw the Picture of thy Mind,
> Is Satyr on the most of Humane Kind:
> Take it, while yet 'tis Praise; before my rage
> Unsafely just, break loose on this bad Age;
> So bad, that thou thy self had'st no defence,
> From Vice, but barely by departing hence. (359–370)

Dryden, who in 1660 had celebrated the return of justice and the golden age, here brings his career full circle by praising Eleonora, whose Astraea-like flight signifies the advent of a new iron age. The same "wild deluge" that had subsided in *To His Sacred Majesty* now rises again and Dryden stands alone against it. The pronouns in this passage are indicative of Dryden's new stance; "my" and "thy" have replaced "our" and "you." No longer the voice of a public constituency or public institution, Dryden now speaks as a private man to private individuals, praising them as exceptions to the general and apparently unalterable reign of viciousness and crime.[53]

In tracing the course of Dryden's career as poet-orator, we move from a Renaissance to an Augustan perception of the relationship between literature and politics. To stress the historical significance of the dynamics in Dryden's career as a public poet, we can juxtapose two very

53. For a good discussion of the changing nature of Dryden's subjects of praise, see Blair, pp. 388–393.

fine assessments of the problem, the first by Arthur W. Hoffman writing on Dryden and the second by Maynard Mack writing on Pope.

In continuation of Renaissance tradition, Dryden, like Milton, conceives his role as a poet as entailing the responsible consideration of those at the head of society and the issues and events in which theirs is the leading role. Throughout his life whether in the vein of satire or of compliment, Dryden undertakes to fulfill this traditional social responsibility of the poet.[54]

The time was past when any serious writer could find his place to stand beside the throne. Dryden had managed this . . . . But for Pope, after the death of Anne, the throne as center of the dream of the civilized community has become absurd. . . . Dryden's angle of vision was no longer available to a serious poet . . .[55]

I wish to suggest that Dryden does not "stand beside the throne," but rather that he stands between the throne and the people—until that position becomes untenable. Dryden preserves the "Renaissance tradition" not "throughout his life" but only as long as he is able. The Renaissance conception of the public poet begins to crumble in the course of Dryden's career. What Pope recognizes after 1714, Dryden had already seen by 1688.[56] Unlike Pope, however, Dryden does not turn

54. Arthur W. Hoffman, "Dryden's Panegyrics and Lyrics," *Writers and Their Background, John Dryden*, ed. Earl Miner (London, 1972), p. 121.

55. Maynard Mack, *The Garden and the City: Retirement and Politics in the Later Poetry of Pope 1731–1743* (Toronto and Buffalo, 1969), pp. 234–235. This passage is cited by Hoffman, "Dryden's Panegyrics and Lyrics," p. 122.

56. Hoffman acknowledges this in his brief discussion of *Britannia Rediviva*. "Dryden's Panegyrics and Lyrics," p. 122.

to antigovernment satire. Instead he simply turns away from "the throne as center of the dream of the civilized community."

The celebration of the early panegyrics places Dryden alongside Erasmus, More, and Jonson, if not (as he would have wished) next to Spenser and Milton. The disillusionment of the later panegyrics, on the other hand, anticipates the posture of Pope, of Byron, and of many modern poets who find themselves alienated from the institutional centers of political power.

5: Dryden and the Conventions of Panegyric

DRYDEN CAN BE distinguished from the other panegyrists of the seventeenth century in two ways. First, he attempts to preserve the traditional functions of panegyrical oratory within the popular forms of Pindaric ode and heroic narrative. More conscious than his immediate predecessors of the oratorical origins of panegyric, Dryden adopts the innovations of Cowley and Waller not to obscure, but rather to emphasize the ancient themes and topics of the genre. Second, Dryden ingeniously adapts these very themes and topics for purposes of satire. In *Mac Flecknoe*, *Absalom and Achitophel*, and *The Hind and the Panther*, Dryden combines heroic poetry and oratory to create a brilliant kind of satire that is structured on the well-defined values of panegyric.

The movement from heroic panegyric to varieties of mock-heroic panegyric confirms the central importance of this genre in Dryden's career. Although he came to recognize the futility of writing serious panegyric in Restoration England, Dryden also discovered new and highly original uses for the old conventions. Indeed, until the time of his death in 1700, Dryden was still experimenting with these conventions, thereby illuminating, transforming, even re-creating his own heritage.

HEROICS AND PINDARICS

In the preface to *Eleonora* Dryden describes the versification of his "panegyrical poem" as both "heroic" and "Pindaric." Although written in heroic couplets, the verse is characterized by its Pindaric qualities: copious imagery and quick transitions. The influence of heroic and Pindaric poetry on Dryden's concept of panegyric is not, however, restricted to techniques of versification. A second look at *Astraea Redux* and *Threnodia Augustalis*, in the context of Dryden's criticism, will show how carefully he adopted the innovations of Waller and Cowley.

Dryden's unwritten epic is the hollow center of his achievement. At various moments in his literary life he referred not only to panegyric but also to historical poetry, tragedy, and satire as branches or kinds of epic. To some degree Dryden's epic-centered criticism is probably disingenuous. Unable to write an epic, he therefore tended to label the poems he was capable of writing as types of epic. Taking Dryden's criticism on its own terms, however, it is evident that his theory of epic explains these surprising correlations with other genres. At least we can see in his criticism of epic in general, and of the *Aeneid* in particular, ample justification for his reference to panegyric as a "branch of epic."

Dryden holds at once an exalted belief in the importance of epic poetry and a rather narrow conception of

its appeal. For Dryden an epic poem is "the greatest
work of human nature," but it appeals almost exclusively
to the public side of "human nature."[1] In effect, Dryden
really hears only one of what Adam Parry has called
"The Two Voices of Vergil's *Aeneid*."

Vergil continually insists on the public glory of the Roman
achievement, the establishment of peace and order and civilization. . . . But he insists equally on the terrible price. . . .
More than blood, sweat, and tears, something more precious
is continually being lost by the necessary process; human freedom, love, personal loyalty, all the qualities which the heroes
of Homer represent, are lost in the service of what is grand,
monumental, and impersonal.[2]

Dryden's response to the impersonal, public voice of the
epic has been generally recognized and has been demonstrated at some length by L. D. Proudfoot in his book on
*Dryden's Aeneid and Its Seventeenth Century Predeces-
sors*. Proudfoot concludes that Dryden makes us "vividly
conscious of Virgil as a court poet," but "in his responses
to pathos" Dryden proves "unsatisfactory."[3] Dryden's
perception of Vergil as "a court poet," however partial
this perception may be, suggests the possible correlation
between epic and panegyric. In fact, a closer look at Dryden's criticism of epic reveals precise functional similarities between the two genres.

1. John Dryden, "The Author's Apology for Heroic Poetry and
Poetic Licence" [Preface to *The State of Innocence: an Opera*], *Of
Dramatic Poesy and Other Critical Essays*, ed. George Watson, 2
vols. (London and New York, 1962), I, 198. Hereafter cited as
Essays.

2. Adam Parry, "The Two Voices of Vergil's *Aeneid*," *Arion*,
II (1963), 78.

3. L. D. Proudfoot, *Dryden's Aeneid and Its Seventeenth Century Predecessors* (Manchester, 1960), pp. 276–277.

For Dryden, epic has two basic functions: political education and political propaganda. First, as education, the epic poem "forms a hero, and a prince," to whom Dryden ascribes certain specific virtues.[4] "The shining quality of an epic hero, his magnanimity, his constancy, his patience, his piety . . . raises first our admiration; we are naturally prone to imitate what we admire . . ."[5] The phrase "shining quality" recalls Davenant's epic theory of "emulation," while the word "admire" suggests Dryden's own discussion of the branches of epic in the "Account" of *Annus Mirabilis*.[6] The theory, in either case, is that the prince is educated in virtue by admiring and emulating the epic hero. Second, as political propaganda, the epic poem can persuade the people to accept a pious ruler even, as in Vergil's time, at the cost of adjusting to a changed polity. "[The] Roman Commonwealth, being now changed into a Monarchy, Virgil was helping to that design, by insinuating into the people the piety of their new conqueror, to make them the better brook this innovation . . ."[7]

These two functions of epic as defined by Dryden parallel exactly the two functions of panegyric as defined by Erasmus. Of the first Erasmus had written: "By having the image of virtue put before them, bad princes might be made better, the good encouraged, the ignorant instructed, the mistaken set right, the wavering quick-

4. *A Discourse Concerning the Original and Progress of Satire*, in *Essays*, II, 96.

5. "To the Right Honourable Hugh, Lord Clifford, Baron of Chudleigh" [Preface to the *Pastorals* in *The Works of Virgil*], *Essays*, II, 228.

6. See above, chap. 1, "Critical Definition."

7. "The Character of St. Evremond," *Essays*, II, 58.

ened, and even the abandoned brought to some sense of shame." And of the second: "[It] is for the public advantage, that even when a sovereign is not the best of men, those over whom he rules should think the best of him."[8] In short, Dryden's theory of epic is functionally identical with the theory of panegyric as it had developed since the sixteenth century.

This helps to explain why Dryden persistently refers to Edmund Waller, the most prolific panegyrical poet of the seventeenth century, in the context of remarks on epic poetry. Dryden names Waller in the company of Tasso's translator Fairfax, Spenser, and Milton. "Milton was the poetical son of Spenser, and Mr Waller of Fairfax . . ."[9] Elsewhere Dryden praises Waller for being more harmonious than Spenser, mentions Waller's love for Chapman, and like Rymer refers to Waller's fractional translation of *Aeneid* IV.[10] The drift of Dryden's criticism of Waller may at first seem surprising, as Waller wrote nothing that we would call an epic (if we exclude the mock-epic *The Battle Of The Summer Islands*). But this criticism begins to make sense if we remember that Dryden measured every other kind of literature against epic and was inclined to call almost anything written in heroic couplets "a kind of epic." It makes very good sense when we consider in addition Dryden's functional

8. Erasmus, "Epistle 176," *The Epistles of Erasmus*, ed. and trans. Francis Morgan Nichols, 3 vols. (London, 1901), I, 366–367.

9. "Preface to *Fables Ancient and Modern*," *Essays*, II, 270.

10. *A Discourse Concerning . . . Satire*, in *Essays*, II, 83–84; "To the Right Honourable My Lord Radcliffe" [Preface to *Examen poeticum*], *Essays*, II, 167; "The Preface to *Ovid's Epistles*," *Essays*, I, 268.

identification of panegyric with epic. To see how this theoretical correlation works in practice for both Waller and Dryden, we can juxtapose *Astraea Redux* first with Waller's early poem on the king's escape and then with his panegyric to Cromwell.

Vergil's *Aeneid* provides the heroic background in the return poems of both Waller and Dryden. Charles I in Waller's poem and Charles II in Dryden's are both compared to the storm-tossed Aeneas of Vergil's first book. Waller establishes the epic context of the prince's heroism by emphasizing the storm itself: "Great Maro could no greater tempest feign . . ."[11] Although Waller continues by showing how the intrepid Charles surpasses Aeneas in heroic bravery, he also shows his modern hero to be concerned less about the potential demise of empire than about the loss of "love's untasted joys" (100). Waller incorporates the romantic theme from *Aeneid* IV into his allusion and soft-pedals the public or impersonal dimension of Vergil's poem. That Waller had the fourth book in mind is particularly suggested by the line, "Neptune's smooth face, and cleave the yielding deep" (42), which he later adopted unchanged to translate *Aeneid* IV, 583 ("adnixi torquent spumas et caerula verrunt").[12] Like Waller, Dryden initially sees the English monarch as Aeneas, *fato profugus*.

11. Edmund Waller, *Of The Danger His Majesty (Being Prince) Escaped In the Road At Saint Andrews*, line 85, *The Poems of Edmund Waller*, ed. George Thorn-Drury (New York, 1968), p. 4. For mention of this poem in connection with *Aeneid* I and *Astraea Redux*, see Arthur W. Hoffman, *John Dryden's Imagery* (Gainesville, Fla., 1962), p. 19, fn. 12.

12. This has been noted by Thorn-Drury, p. 282.

> *He toss'd by Fate, and hurried up and down,*
> *Heir to his Fathers Sorrows, with his Crown,*
> *Could tast no sweets of youths desired Age,*
> *But found his life too true a Pilgrimage.*[13]

Dryden's Aeneas suffers as a public man; the "sweets" of youth are readily sacrificed to the necessities of the "Crown." Appropriately, then, the early allusion to *Aeneid* I gives way at the end of the poem to *Aeneid* VI, as Dryden echoes Vergil's prophecy of the Augustan golden age. Dryden, responding to the impersonal voice of the *Aeneid,* directs us from book 1 to book 6, whereas Waller, responding to the personal voice of the poem, takes us from book 1 to book 4. Unlike Waller, Dryden echoes Vergil to reassert public themes that are consistent with the tradition of panegyric.

But Waller himself had already achieved a similar union of epic and panegyric in his poem to Cromwell by initially alluding to the storm in *Aeneid* I and subsequently to Anchises' advisory speech in book 6.[14] Like Dryden in *Astraea Redux,* Waller in *A Panegyric To My Lord Protector* develops the Vergilian echoes to emphasize the reconciliation of heroic and monarchical ideals. Even at this point of strong similarity, however, there is an important difference between Waller's method and Dryden's. Throughout his career as a public poet and especially in the Cromwell panegyric, Waller celebrates active heroism. "Praise of great acts he scatters as a

13. John Dryden, *Astraea Redux*, lines 51–54, *The Poems of John Dryden,* ed. James Kinsley, 4 vols. (Oxford, 1958), I, 17. The allusions to the *Aeneid* have been carefully identified by the editors of the California Dryden, I, 215. See also, Hoffman, *John Dryden's Imagery*, pp. 16–17.

14. See above, chap. 3, "Transformation."

seed, / Which may the like in coming ages breed."[15]
Dryden, on the other hand, characteristically celebrates
passive heroism. Charles in *Astraea Redux* is not only
Aeneas, but also Christ.[16] "How Great were then Our
Charles his Woes, who thus / Was forc'd to suffer for
Himself and us" (49–50). Complementing the allusive
pattern that elevates Charles from Aeneas to Augustus
is a second pattern that elevates Charles from the suffering, human Christ to the divine "Prince of Peace" (139).
If Charles thus restores England as Aeneas restored Troy,
he also redeems England as Christ redeemed the world.
Whereas Waller sees action as the motive force in political history, Dryden distrusts action and looks instead
for evidence of a divine historical order. Combining allusions to the *Aeneid* and allusions to the gospel, Dryden
celebrates the Restoration as a renewal of faith in divinely sanctioned institutions and as a renewal of trust in the
providential design of history.

The background of this design is displayed in the opening paragraph of the poem. Here Dryden distinguishes
two outlines of the historical process. The first is man-
centered and is identified with war, tempests, and irra-
tionality. Its appropriate illustration is the reign of
Charles X in Sweden.

> *Th' Ambitious* Swede *like restless Billowes tost,*
> *On this hand gaining what on that he lost,*
> *Though in his life he Blood and Ruine breath'd,*
> *To his now guideless Kingdome Peace bequeath'd.* (9–12)

15. Waller, *Upon The Earl Of Roscommon's Translation Of
Horace*, 35–36.

16. For the king as Christ, see Steven N. Zwicker, *Dryden's Political Poetry: The Typology of King and Nation* (Providence,
1972), especially pp. 61–71.

In contrast, Dryden envisions history as a divine creation.

> *And Heaven that seem'd regardless of our Fate,*
> *For* France *and* Spain *did Miracles create,*
> *Such mortal Quarrels to compose in Peace*
> *As Nature bred and Int'rest did encrease.* (13–16)

Human action, although unpredictable in its results, is divisive, whereas inaction leads to reconciliation, which is the desired goal of traditional panegyric. Dryden, in effect, attributes the evils of history ("Blood and Ruine") to men and its blessings ("Peace") to God. In this providential design, active heroism of the kind celebrated by Waller is a form of rebellion against God's will.

In *Astraea Redux* the active heroes are the Puritans.

> *Th' incensed Pow'rs beheld with scorn from high*
> *An Heaven so far distant from the sky,*
> *Which durst with horses hoofs that beat the ground*
> *And Martial brass bely the thunders sound.*
> *'Twas hence at length just Vengeance thought it fit*
> *To speed their ruine by their impious wit.* (195–200)

The distance between "sky" and "ground," between power and impiety, condemns the Commonwealth government as at best a misguided parody of divine rule and exposes the militant religion of the Puritans as an instance when "Religions name against it self was made" (191). The association of the Puritans with "Martial brass" represents the traditional panegyrist's rejection of military heroism; the censure of their "impious wit" associates the Puritans with the villains of the genre and foreshadows Dryden's portrayal of the arch villain, Achitophel. Here, moreover, Dryden stresses the self-defeating nature of Puritan heroics by allusion to figures from modern and ancient history, the Milanese Duke

Lodovico Sforza and the Roman Emperor Otho. Sforza is like Sweden's Charles X; both aspire to personal power but find their successes cancelled by their failures, as if the act of pursuing such power were in itself defeating. "Thus *Sforza* curs'd with a too fertile brain / Lost by his wiles the Pow'r his wit did gain" (201–202). An even better—indeed a perfect—exemplum of self-defeating action is provided by the brief reference to Otho, whom Dryden specifically contrasts with Charles II. "He would not like soft *Otho* hope prevent / But stay'd and suffer'd Fortune to repent" (67–68). The allusion to Otho's suicide complements the allusions to Sforza and Charles X and confirms the historical perspective of the narrative: the power of individual men is momentary, self-destructive, and in the long run of history insignificant. The source of enduring power is God, and it is the recognition of this truth that Charles brings with him at the Restoration.

In contrast to Charles X, Sforza, Otho, and especially the Puritans, Charles II is not an active hero. He does not will his own Restoration nor act to encourage it. His Restoration is instead a natural, even a divine event.

> *Frosts that constrain the ground, and birth deny*
> *To flow'rs, that in its womb expecting lye,*
> *Do seldom their usurping Pow'r withdraw,*
> *But raging floods pursue their hasty thaw:*
> *Our thaw was mild, the cold not chas'd away*
> *But lost in kindly heat of lengthned day.* (131–136)

The seasonal imagery and the implied vegetation myth present a conception of the historical process that is characteristic of virtually every panegyric we have considered from Claudian to Cowley, but Dryden adds some nice touches of his own. By identifying winter "frost" as a "usurping Pow'r," in contrast to the "kindly heat of lengthned day," Dryden persuasively uses the death and life forces in nature to establish the difference between the rule of a usurper and the rule of a king. He then adapts this natural imagery to define the proper exercise of kingly power. The phrase "raging floods" in particular suggests the recurrent river image as it had been developed by poets like Claudian and Daniel to restrain the power of the ruler. Here too the ideal is *tranquilla potestas*, as Dryden praises the moderation of the king and simultaneously admonishes him to stay on the same course. Latent in this passage is one final metaphor, that of the hunt, implied by the words "pursue" and "chas'd." By refusing to hunt down his father's enemies, by rejecting revenge, by not acting, Charles lives up to the ideal of true piety as explicitly defined by Claudian in his last panegyric to Honorius. In this respect Charles must surpass even Augustus, who did take vengeance on his "father's" murderers. The piety of Charles, implicit in the comparison with Aeneas, is here refined by reference to the conventions of traditional panegyric.

Considerably more visible than the shadow of Aeneas in this heroic panegyric, however, is the image of Christ.

> *That Star that at your Birth shone out so bright*
> *It stain'd the duller Suns Meridian light,*
> *Did once again its potent Fires renew*
> *Guiding our eyes to find and worship you.* (288–291)

The Christian significance of the allusion to Charles's famous birth star has frequently been pointed out, and as Professor Swedenberg has shown, other poets besides Dryden adopted this image for their Restoration panegyrics.[17] It should be recognized, however, that the midday star also appears in Claudian's pagan *Panegyricus De Quarto Consulatu Honorii Augusti.*

> *stella die, dubitanda nihil nec crine retuso*
> *languida, sed quantus numeratur nocte Bootes,*
> *emicuitque plagis alieni temporis hospes*
> *ignis et agnosci potuit, cum luna lateret . . .*[18]

Even at midday did a wondering people gaze upon a bold star ('twas clear to behold)—no dulled nor stunted beams but bright as Boötes' nightly lamp. At a strange hour its brilliance lit up the sky and its fires could be clearly seen though the moon lay hid.

Dryden adapts the conventional divine augury to connect the Restoration with the resurrection, as Christ-Charles reclaims England from sin: "your Edicts some reclaim from sins, / But most your Life and Blest Example wins" (316–317). But this passage is almost certainly imitated from another, more familiar passage in the same poem by Claudian:

> *componitur orbis*
> *regis ad exemplum, nec sic inflectere sensus*
> *humanos edicta valent quam vita regentis.* (299–301)

The world shapes itself after its ruler's pattern, nor can edicts sway men's minds so much as their monarch's life.

Although Daniel, Jonson, and Drummond had appropriated the same passage, Dryden's paraphrase is closer to the original by one key word, his literal rendering of

17. H. T. Swedenberg, "England's Joy: *Astraea Redux* in its Setting," *SP*, L (1953), 30–44.

18. Claudian, *IV Cons.*, lines 185–188, *Claudian*, trans. Maurice Platnauer, 2 vols. (Cambridge, Mass., and London, 1963), I, 300.

edicta. In this couplet, then, Dryden reconciles heroic panegyric with a traditional version of the genre. Specifically, he unites the image of Charles as Christian hero with the traditional image of the ideal monarch, who always rules by "Example."

The heroic allusions in *Astraea Redux* serve finally to place Charles in the line of ideal monarchs found in panegyric long before Waller. Dryden modifies Waller's concept of heroic panegyric to define the royal virtues necessary for national reconciliation: mercy, expressed by comparison with Christ, and piety, expressed by allusion to Aeneas. When, moreover, we recall the close association of mercy and piety in the tradition of panegyric, we can appreciate just how carefully Dryden has chosen his heroic comparisons to reassert the essential values of the genre.[19] Charles, a suffering hero at the beginning of *Astraea Redux,* emerges at the conclusion as the *optimus princeps.* The poem itself, initially a heroic narrative, ends (as we have seen) in the combination of demonstrative and deliberative oratory that defines classical panegyric.

In *Threnodia Augustalis* Dryden again attempts to reconcile heroic and monarchical ideals, this time against the distant background of the Pindaric ode and by specific allusion to the example of Abraham Cowley. As Robert Hinman has pointed out, Cowley was held in very high esteem by Dryden, who once wrote that Cowley's "authority is almost sacred to me."[20] In *An Essay of*

19. See above, chap. 4, "The Early Poems."

20. "Of Heroic Plays: An Essay" [Preface to *The Conquest of Granada*], *Essays,* I, 162. See Robert Hinman, *Abraham Cowley's World of Order* (Cambridge, Mass., 1960), chap. 1.

Dramatic Poesy, Dryden specifically indicates his approval of Cowley's most ambitious verse. "[There is] nothing so elevated, so copious, and full of spirit, as Mr Cowley . . ."[21] "Elevated" suggests that Dryden is referring to the Pindaric odes and perhaps the *Davideis* rather than to Cowley's works of a smaller scale. "Copious" points to the Pindarics alone, as this is the same term that Dryden usually applies to Pindar himself.[22] "Spirit" is harder to pin down, although this term presumably alludes to the freedom that Dryden found characteristic of Cowley's verse in general and of the Pindaric odes in particular. In sum, this description of Cowley tends to restrict Dryden's evaluation to the poet's most important and distinctive achievement. Dryden, who sees Waller primarily as an epic poet, sees Cowley, more accurately, as primarily the author of Pindaric odes.

In Dryden's later discussions of Cowley, he largely ignores everything except the odes, and these he defends vigorously. "I acknowledge myself unworthy to defend so excellent an author . . . only in general I will say that nothing can appear more beautiful to me than the strength of those images which they [Cowley's detractors] condemn."[23] Although consistent in his praise for the Pindarics, Dryden believes that in these poems Cowley has pushed "poetic license" to its acceptable limits.

Yet I dare not say that either of them [Cowley and Denham] have carried this libertine way of rendering authors (as Mr Cowley calls it) so far as my definition [of imitation] reaches;

21. *Of Dramatic Poesy: An Essay*, in *Essays*, I, 24.

22. See, for example, "Preface to *Sylvae*," *Essays*, II, 32.

23. "The Author's Apology for Heroic Poetry and Poetic Licence," *Essays*, I, 203.

for in the *Pindaric Odes* the customs and ceremonies of ancient Greece are still preserved. But I know not what mischief may arise hereafter from the example of such an innovation, when writers of unequal parts to him shall imitate so bold an undertaking.[24]

Dryden's defense of Cowley's "innovation" does not, however, rest entirely on that poet's boldness. Dryden justifies his older contemporary most effectively by pointing to the example of Pindar himself. "So wild and ungovernable a poet [Pindar] cannot be translated literally, his genius is too strong to bear a chain, and Samson-like he shakes it off. A genius so elevated and unconfined as Mr Cowley's was but necessary to make Pindar speak English . . ."[25]

The same qualities that Dryden finds in Cowley can also be found in the odes Dryden wrote himself. Although these odes are more disciplined and regular than those of Cowley, they too can be accurately described as "elevated," "copious," and "full of spirit." By defending Cowley, Dryden also defends himself.

To see how Dryden uses the example of Cowley, we can compare *Threnodia Augustalis* with Cowley's *Ode Upon His Majesties Restoration and Return*. It may be recalled that in his Restoration Pindaric, Cowley defines rebellion as paradise lost and the Restoration as paradise regained. To amplify this historical and mythical pattern, Cowley alludes to both *Genesis* and *Exodus*, casting Cromwell in the role of Satan and Charles in the composite role of Moses and Joshua. Metaphorically uniting

24. "The Preface to *Ovid's Epistles*," *Essays*, I, 270.
25. "The Preface to *Ovid's Epistles*," *Essays*, I, 271.

Eden, Canaan, and England, Cowley represents 1660 as
the return to an earthly paradise.

> *'Twas a right* Season, *and the very* Ground
> *Ought with a face of* Paradise *to be found,*
>   *Then when we were to entertain*
> Felicity *and* Innocence *again.*[26]

The commingling of Biblical allusions in this ode is
duplicated, though with significantly less freedom, in
Threnodia Augustalis. Looking back on the reign of
Charles, Dryden too sees the Restoration as paradise
regained.

> *Amidst the peaceful Triumphs of his Reign,*
> *What wonder if the kindly beams he shed*
> *Reviv'd the drooping Arts again,*
> *If Science rais'd her Head,*
> *And soft Humanity that from Rebellion fled;*
> *Our Isle, indeed, too fruitful was before;*
> *But all uncultivated lay*
> *Out of the* Solar *walk and Heav'ns high way;*
> *With rank* Geneva *Weeds run o're,*
> *And Cockle, at the best, amidst the Corn it bore:*
> *The Royal Husbandman appear'd,*
> *And Plough'd, and Sow'd and Till'd,*
> *The Thorns he rooted out, the Rubbish clear'd,*
> *And blest th' obedient Field.*
> *When, straight, a double Harvest rose;*
> *Such as the swarthy* Indian *mowes;*
> *Or happier Climates near the Line,*
> *Or Paradise Manur'd, and drest by hands Divine.*[27]

26. Abraham Cowley, *Ode Upon His Majesties Restoration and
Return,* lines 32–35, *The English Writings of Abraham Cowley,*
ed. A. R. Waller (Cambridge, 1905), p. 421.

27. *Threnodia Augustalis,* 346–363, *Poems,* I, 451–452.

Dryden's basic metaphor of husbandry creates an ideal of "culture" that depends on political order. In this stanza Dryden describes the ideal polity in the terms that Cowley had defined twenty-five years before. In both poems we have a prince who is an image of the divine and a people who are obedient to him. This political paradise, for both Cowley and Dryden, is England in the reign of Charles II.

But Dryden, writing in 1685, has an additional problem to face, the accession of James II. If Charles has already restored the nation to paradise, what can there possibly be left for James to do? Dryden begins to answer this question by qualifying his earlier conception of the period from 1660 to 1685. Turning to the *Exodus* story (with supplementary echoes from *Absalom and Achitophel*), Dryden now suggests that the Restoration was not the entry into Canaan.

> *For Twelve long years of Exile, born,*
> *Twice twelve we number'd since his blest Return:*
> *So strictly wer't thou Just to pay,*
> *Even to the driblet of a day.*
> *Yet still we murmur, and Complain,*
> *The Quails and Manna shou'd no longer rain;*
> *Those Miracles 'twas needless to renew;*
> *The Chosen Flock has now the Promis'd Land in view.*
> (421–428)

Charles II as Moses gives way to James II as Joshua, who will lead the nation into the "Promis'd Land" in 1685. From this vantage point, Dryden portrays the reign of Charles as both the return to paradise and the continued exile of the chosen people. Thus, the Biblical allusions which reinforce each other in Cowley's ode, verge on contradiction in Dryden's.

It is against this background of apparent contradiction that Dryden attempts his reconciliation of heroic and monarchical ideals in the figure of James, the "Warlike Prince [who] ascends the Regal State" (429). Whereas Cowley had stopped short of comparing Charles with Hercules in his Restoration Pindaric, Dryden does compare James with Hercules in *Threnodia Augustalis*. Moreover, the literary source for his heroic portrayal of James is the comparison between Hercules and Chromius in Cowley's translation of Pindar's first Nemean ode.

How early *has young* Chromius *begun*
The Race of Virtue, *and how swiftly run,*
   And born the noble Prize *away,*
Whilst other youths yet at the Barriere *stay?*
None but Alcides *e're set earlier forth then* He;
The God, *his* Fathers, *Blood nought could restrain,*
   'Twas ripe at first, *and did disdain*
The slow advance of dull Humanitie,
The big-limm'ed Babe *in his huge* Cradle *lay,*
Too weighty to be rockt by Nurses *hands*
   Wrapt in purple swadling-bands.
When, Lo, by jealous Juno's *fierce commands,*
   Two dreadful Serpents *come*
Rowling and hissing loud into the roome.
To the bold Babe *they trace their* bidden *way,*
Forth from their flaming eyes *dread* Lightnings *went,*
Their gaping Mouths *did forked* Tongues *like* Thunderbolts
   present.[28]

In *Threnodia Augustalis* Dryden condenses and restrains Cowley's comparison for application to James.

28. Cowley, *The First Nemean Ode of Pindar,* lines 75–91.

> *View then a* Monarch *ripen'd for a Throne.*
> Alcides *thus his race began,*
> *O'er Infancy he swiftly ran;*
> *The future God, at first was more than Man:*
> *Dangers and Toils, and* Juno's *Hate*
> *Even o're his Cradle lay in wait;*
> *And there he grappled first with Fate:*
> *In his young Hands the hissing Snakes he prest,*
> *So early was the Deity confest;*
> *Thus, by degrees, he rose to* Jove's *Imperial Seat;*
> *Thus difficulties prove a Soul legitimately great.* (446–456)

Although Dryden certainly did not require Cowley's translation as a source for the familiar story of Hercules strangling the serpents, there are enough parallel words and phrases in the two passages to indicate at least a strong probability that Dryden had Cowley in mind. And yet it is evident that the function of Dryden's adaptation differs from the function of his model. The focus of Cowley's translation is on the heroic deeds of Hercules, whereas the focus of Dryden's allusion is on Hercules' ascension to "Jove's Imperial Seat." Dryden thus adopts the heroic image of Cowley's translation, and then modifies it to serve the traditional panegyrical function of elevating a man into a king.

The ascension of James-Hercules in *Threnodia Augustalis* parallels the ascension of Charles-Christ in *Astraea Redux*. Line 454, "So early was the Deity confest," suggests that in fact Dryden is using the image of Hercules as a type of Christ and thus repeating the pattern of his earlier heroic panegyric. James is confronted by the same difficulties that plague Charles in the narrative section of *Astraea Redux*. If the early encounter with the serpents demonstrates (with a glancing blow at Monmouth) the legitimate greatness of James, it is the later encounter with the furies of rebellion that actually ripens him "for a Throne."

> *Like his, our Hero's Infancy was try'd;*
> *Betimes the Furies did their Snakes provide;*
> *And, to his Infant Arms oppose*
> *His Father's Rebels, and his Brother's Foes;*
> *The more opprest the higher still he rose:*
> *Those were the Preludes of his Fate,*
> *That form'd his Manhood, to subdue*
> *The* Hydra *of the many-headed hissing Crew.* (457–464)

The heroic picture of James finishing his labors by subduing the Hydra completes the comparison with Hercules, but at the same time acknowledges that there have been fundamental disorders in the state during the reign of Charles, again contradicting claims made earlier in the poem.

The contradictions in *Threnodia Augustalis* can, however, be explained in terms of panegyrical conventions. In this poem the traditional theme of restoration is applied simultaneously to successive monarchs, which means that both 1660 and 1685 represent a transition from bad times to good. The interval of history between these two ceremonial occasions is therefore described as peaceful when Charles is the subject of praise and as stormy when Dryden turns to James. Although fact and logic thus give way to convention, it is precisely the conventional theme of restoration that gives the poem its unity and conveys its persuasive purpose. In *Threnodia Augustalis* Dryden amplifies the theme of restoration to convince his popular audience that James will be like Charles, that is, like the *optimus princeps*, and to admonish his royal audience that the king must live up to this created expectation.[29] In sum, Dryden would persuade both audiences to make 1685 like 1660. He thus concludes *Threnodia Augustalis* with a distinct echo of *Astraea Redux.*

> *. . . there appears*
> *The long Retinue of a Prosperous Raign,*
> *A Series of Successful years,*
> *In Orderly Array, a Martial, manly Train.*
> *Behold ev'n to remoter Shores*
> *A Conquering Navy proudly spread;*
> *The British Cannon formidably roars,*
> *While starting from his Oozy Bed,*
> *Th' asserted Ocean rears his reverend Head;*
> *To View and Recognize his ancient Lord again:*
> *And with a willing hand, restores*
> *The Fasces of the Main.* (506–517)

Here Dryden invokes in Pindaric verse the conclusion of the narrative section of the earlier poem.

> *The British Amphitryte smooth and clear*
> *In richer Azure never did appear;*
> *Proud her returning Prince to entertain*
> *With the submitted Fasces of the Main.*[30]

Dryden's prophetic vision of "A Series of Successful years" beginning in 1685, similar to the prophecy of "times whiter Series" beginning in 1660, is strikingly different from the prophecy in Cowley's translation of Pindar.

29. For the instructive purpose of the poem, see above, chap. 4, "The Later Poems." Here I am concerned primarily with the demonstrative theme of the poem.

30. *Astraea Redux*, 246–249. The parallel has, of course, long been recognized by Dryden's editors.

> *When wise* Tiresias *this beginning knew*
>   *He told with ease the things t'ensue,*
>   *From what* Monsters *he should free*
>   *The* Earth, *the* Ayr, *and* Sea,
>   *What mighty* Tyrants *he should slay,*
>   *Greater* Monsters *far then* They. (113–118)

Chromius-Hercules is the dragon-slayer, the most primitive kind of hero, who is moreover allegorically cast in the role of rebel against tyranny. James-Hercules, on the other hand, is a king who restores royal authority just as Charles-Christ had done a generation earlier.

The image of this authority, the "Fasces," confirms the traditional function of *Threnodia Augustalis*. The insignia of official Roman authority, the fasces were ceremonially restored at the beginning of the new year, an event that coincided with the inauguration of the new consul. Claudian carefully alludes to the authority symbolized by the fasces in the opening sentence of his panegyric on Honorius's third consulship and again, more emphatically, in the opening of his panegyric on the fourth consulship:

exultant reduces Augusto consule fasces.[31]

[The] returning fasces rejoice in Caesar's consulship.

Like Claudian's poetic investiture of Honorius, Dryden's identification of James with the symbol of institutional authority signifies the restoration of power. But because the fasces (wooden rods bound together) also symbolize unity, this ceremony also captures the ideal of national reconciliation. Perhaps most importantly, however, this symbol functions in *Threnodia Augustalis* to recall

31. Claudian, *IV Cons.*, 4.

Astraea Redux. The most significant words in the final lines of Dryden's 1685 prophecy are "restores" and
"again." What was propaganda in 1660 is taken in retrospect as truth and used to create new propaganda appropriate to the conditions of 1685. The traditional theme
of Dryden's Pindaric panegyric is restoration, only in
this case what Dryden has in mind is the restoration of
the Restoration.

PANEGYRIC AND SATIRE

In *Astraea Redux* and *Threnodia Augustalis* Dryden
boldly adopts innovations in order to conserve a tradition. The heroic forms pioneered by Waller and Cowley
are modified by Dryden to serve the oratorical functions
of traditional panegyric. During the same period, from
1660 to 1688, however, the reverse is also true. Dryden
adopts the tradition of panegyric in order to perfect three
of the most innovative poems of the seventeenth century. Specifically, Dryden incorporates panegyrical oratory into the design of his own heroic or quasi-heroic
poems, *Mac Flecknoe, Absalom and Achitophel,* and *The
Hind and the Panther.*

At crucial moments in each of these poems, the themes
and values of Dryden's satire are defined by panegyrical
oratory. This is evident in Fleckno's orations, lines 29–
59 and 139–210 of *Mac Flecknoe,* in Achitophel's first
address to Absalom, lines 230–302 of *Absalom and
Achitophel,* and in the speech of the pigeon "more mature in Folly than the rest," lines 1108–1140 of *The Hind
and the Panther,* part 3. In each of these instances Dry-

den unites deliberative and demonstrative oratory for satiric purposes. What these speeches reveal, in sum, is that Dryden's major satires depend in part on the conventions of panegyric.

Earl Miner has described *Mac Flecknoe* as " 'mock-heroic,' if the term may be applied beyond its strict generic meaning to include as well ironic versions of panegyric, of coronation, and of religion."[32] Although a variety of other influences have been discovered to bear on the poem, the metaphor linking the kingdoms of poetry and state does suggest an ironic version of panegyric.[33] Dryden ironically adopts panegyrical conventions for three basic purposes: (1) to establish the overall pattern of the poem, the movement from empire to exile, (2) to develop the two major "scenes" of the poem, procession and coronation, and most significantly, (3) to provide the topics for Fleckno's two orations, the first demonstrative and the second deliberative.

The progress of dullness in *Mac Flecknoe* reverses the direction of the royal progress described, for example, in *Astraea Redux*. In serious panegyric the movement is traditionally from absence or exile to return; *Astraea Redux* begins with the suffering of Charles the exile and concludes with the return and triumph of Charles the king.

> *Oh Happy Age! Oh times like those alone*
> *By Fate reserv'd for Great Augustus Throne!*

32. Earl Miner, *Dryden's Poetry* (Bloomington, Ind., and London, 1968), p. 89. My own discussion of *Mac Flecknoe* has benefited significantly from chapter 3 of Professor Miner's book.

33. For the other influences on the poem, see H. T. Swedenberg's notes to the poem in the California Dryden, II, 299–327.

> *When the joint growth of Armes and Arts foreshew*
> *The World a Monarch, and that Monarch You.*[34]

The last lines of this heroic panegyric thus anticipate the famous first lines of Dryden's mock-heroic panegyric.

> *All humane things are subject to decay,*
> *And, when Fate summons, Monarchs must obey:*
> *This* Fleckno *found, who, like* Augustus, *young*
> *Was call'd to Empire, and had govern'd long . . .* [35]

The important words "Fate," "*Augustus*," and "Monarch(s)," which the passages have in common, function in both poems to create a classic image of the golden age. The difference, of course, is that *Astraea Redux* is about restoration, whereas *Mac Flecknoe* is about "decay." By the end of the poem we find Shadwell exiled to a literary Elba, "Some peacefull Province in Acrostick Land" (206); the once great "Empire" is ultimately reduced to "one poor word" (208). Prophetically extending this exile indefinitely into the future, Fleckno modifies the two-Indies *topos* to show the extent of his son's rule over the domains of nothingness. "Heavens bless my Son, from *Ireland* let him reign / To farr *Barbadoes* on the Western main . . ." (139–140).

Within this general pattern, Dryden concentrates on two familiar ceremonies, procession and coronation. In serious panegyric the processional *topos* expresses the idea of national reconciliation, as men and women, old and young, people and nobles unite in consent to the rule of the monarch. In *Mac Flecknoe*, too, the procession attracts the "Nations" (96), but this potentially human

34. *Astraea Redux*, 320–323.
35. *Mac Flecknoe*, 1–4, *Poems*, I, 265.

audience is reduced (in almost Swiftian fashion) to a pile of books, papers, and excrement.

> *No* Persian *Carpets spread th' Imperial way,*
> *But scatter'd Limbs of mangled Poets lay:*
> *From dusty shops neglected Authors come,*
> *Martyrs of Pies, and Reliques of the Bum.*
> *Much* Heywood, Shirly, Ogleby *there lay,*
> *But loads of* Sh—— *almost choakt the way.*
> *Bilk't* Stationers *for Yeomen stood prepar'd,*
> *And* H——*was Captain of the Guard. (98–105)*

This scene, cluttered with the works of dull authors, is a direct reflection of the poem's hero: "But loads of *Sh*—— almost choakt the way." Only at the very end of this passage does humanity reappear to set the stage for the second ceremony, coronation. In serious panegyric coronation signifies the union of ceremony and power, sometimes (as in *To His Sacred Majesty*) expressed as a union of church and state. In *Mac Flecknoe* the two worlds of panegyric are united in the figure of Fleckno, the modern jack-of-all-trades, who bequeathes his virtues to the new monarch. "The King himself the sacred Unction made, / As King by Office, and as Priest by Trade" (119–120). Within the overall movement from empire to exile, the ironic versions of traditional ceremonies—procession and coronation—separate Fleckno's two orations, confirming the demonstration of the first and anticipating the deliberation of the second.

The function of the first oration, placed before the ceremonies, is to elevate the man into a monarch. A demonstrative oration, the topics of praise demonstrate Shadwell's qualifications for the monarchy of dullness. This elevation through praise naturally includes inversions of conventional topics. For obvious example, instead of *le roi soleil*, Fleckno's speech presents *le roi brouillard*.

> *Some Beams of Wit on other souls may fall,*
> *Strike through and make a lucid intervall;*
> *But Sh——'s genuine night admits no ray,*
> *His rising Fogs prevail upon the Day . . .* (21–24)

The core of the first speech, however, is the extended but obscure allusion to Shadwell as some kind of royal bandmaster.

> *My warbling Lute, the Lute I whilom strung*
> *When to King* John *of* Portugal *I sung,*
> *Was but the prelude to that glorious day,*
> *When thou on silver* Thames *did'st cut thy way,*
> *With well tim'd Oars before the Royal Barge,*
> *Swell'd with the Pride of thy Celestial charge;*
> *And big with Hymn, Commander of an Host,*
> *The like was ne'er in* Epsom *Blankets tost.*
> *Methinks I see the new* Arion *Sail,*
> *The Lute still trembling underneath thy nail.*
> *At thy well sharpned thumb from Shore to Shore*
> *The Treble squeaks for fear, the Bases roar:*
> *Echoes from* Pissing-Ally, Sh—— *call,*
> *And* Sh—— *they resound from* A—— Hall. (35–48)

Although the biographical reference has never been discovered, the literary background of the passage has been identified as Waller's heroic panegyric on the king's escape at Santander.[36] In Waller's poem, however, Arion sings "of our Albion kings," and although this is presumably Shadwell's task as well, the name that "Echoes from *Pissing-Ally*" to "*A—— Hall*" is the poet's own. Shadwell, apparently, sings only of Shadwell. Beyond

36. See Kinsley, IV, 1916.

foggy stupidity and benighted somnolence, the essential qualification for monarchy in this poem is solipsism. The importance of the echo motif is confirmed by the ensuing processional ceremony where Shadwell's solipsism is revealed in the mirror figure, Shadwell reflected in the "loads of *Sh*——" that line the way of his procession.

The second speech, which follows both procession and coronation, is patently designed to instruct the newly crowned monarch. A deliberative speech, it takes the common form of a father educating his son. The initial rhetorical pattern of the speech resembles Theodosius's speech to Honorius in Claudian's *Panegyricus De Quarto Consulatu Honorii Augusti*. Theodosius begins by making a distinction between the empires of the east and the Roman empire, thereby offering his son a prescription for rule based on a Roman tradition:

> *altera Romanae longe rectoribus aulae*
> *condicio. virtute decet, non sanguine niti.*[37]

Very different is the state of Rome's emperor. 'Tis merit, not blood, must be his support.

Fleckno, similarly, establishes a contrast between the empires of wit and dullness, and delivers his own prescription for rule on the basis of this contrast. "Success let others teach, learn thou from me / Pangs without birth, and fruitless Industry" (147–148). He expands this contrast by naming various English writers as exempla, Jonson and Etherege from the empire of wit, himself and Ogilby from the realm of dullness. Just as Trajan and Theodosius are the instructive models for Honori-

37. Claudian, *IV Cons.*, 219–220.

us's rule of Rome, so Ogilby and Fleckno are the models
for Shadwell's rule over the realms of nonsense.

The balance of the speech is concerned specifically
with Shadwell's education as the ruler of dullness in
drama, but by the conclusion Fleckno is actually advising
Shadwell to quit the stage altogether.

> *Thy Genius calls thee not to purchase fame*
> *In keen Iambicks, but mild Anagram:*
> *Leave writing Plays, and chuse for thy command*
> *Some peacefull Province in Acrostick Land.* (203–206)

Advice to the prince becomes advice to the exile, as the
second speech undercuts the first one. The solipsism of
Shadwell revealed earlier is punctured by this final reve-
lation of his true insignificance. The two orations are
entirely contradictory; the first elevates Shadwell to the
throne, whereas the second admonishes him to go into
eternal exile. Satirically these two orations thus comple-
ment each other perfectly to create a unified impression
of Shadwell as a puffed-up nonentity.

By separating the demonstrative and deliberative functions of panegyric and then ironically playing them off
against each other, Dryden first creates and then negates
the hero of the poem.[38] There is, moreover, no doubt that
Shadwell is indeed a hero as well as a monarch. The famous allusions to the gospel and to Vergil which satirically define Shadwell's mock-heroic stature are staples of
English panegyric. Comparisons that appear ridiculous
or even blasphemous in the context of *Mac Flecknoe* are
taken very seriously in *Astraea Redux*, for example,
where Charles is both Christ and Aeneas. In the satire,

38. See Miner's discussion, *Dryden's Poetry*, 77–105.

Fleckno and Shadwell are first compared to John the Baptist and Christ and later to Aeneas and Ascanius. This means that Shadwell himself emerges as Christ and Ascanius rather than as Christ and Aeneas. The reason for this small shift from convention is evident enough, for Shadwell is consistently portrayed as the "filial dullness" (136), as *Mac* Flecknoe, as Christ the son, and logically then as Ascanius.

> *The hoary Prince in Majesty appear'd,*
> *High on a Throne of his own Labours rear'd.*
> *At his right hand our young* Ascanius *sate*
> Rome's *other hope, and pillar of the State.* (106–109)

But Dryden also had a Latin precedent on his side in sustaining the comparison between the young Ascanius and "the hopefull boy" (61) of *Mac Flecknoe*. Claudian in his panegyric on Honorius's fourth consulship, had seriously developed the same comparison to celebrate the young emperor.

> *ventura potestas*
> *claruit Ascanio, subita cum luce comarum*
> *innocuus flagraret apex Phrygioque volutus*
> *vertice fatalis redimiret tempora candor.*
> *at tua caelestes inlustrant omina flammae.* (192–196)

Clear was the prophecy of Ascanius' coming power when an aureole crowned his locks, yet harmed them not, and when the fires of fate encircled his head and played about his temples. Thy future the very fires of heaven foretell.

The image here of the light crowning the boy's head, adapted from the *Aeneid* (II, 682–684), is also suggested somewhat more obliquely in *Mac Flecknoe*. "His Brows thick fogs, instead of glories, grace, / And lambent dullness plaid arround his face" (110–111). Although the

word "lambent" in particular suggests that Dryden had
Vergil's line 684 ("lambere flamma comas, et circum tem-
pora pasci") directly in mind, the context of Dryden's
allusion closely parallels that in Claudian.

In *Mac Flecknoe*—and specifically in its heroic allusions, its combination of demonstrative and deliberative
oratory, and its metaphoric occasion—we can perceive
the conventions and defining characteristics of the genre
that Dryden had adopted for his serious public poetry.
The central irony of the poem, moreover, is derived from
the central concern of poems like *Astraea Redux*: the
use and abuse of power. *Mac Flecknoe* is finally a mock-
heroic panegyric because it celebrates impotence rather
than power. Dull poets are powerless poets, and this category includes both father and son.

> *Like mine thy gentle numbers feebly creep,*
> *Thy Tragick Muse gives smiles, thy Comick sleep.*
> *With whate'er gall thou sett'st thy self to write,*
> *Thy inoffensive Satyrs never bite.*
> *In thy fellonious heart, though Venom lies,*
> *It does but touch thy* Irish *pen, and dyes.* (197–202)

In *Absalom and Achitophel,* on the other hand, we have
a struggle between father and son for real political power,
and power is the subject of Achitophel's first speech.
This oration represents a second and far more menacing
combination of demonstrative and deliberative oratory
because it attempts to make incipient usurpation the new
occasion for panegyric. Fleckno as orator is no threat to
anyone. Achitophel as orator, however, is a very serious
threat to the whole nation.

Bernard Schilling has emphasized the importance of

eloquence in *Absalom and Achitophel* and, like others before him, has been explicit in pointing out the Miltonic influence on Achitophel's first speech.[39] But Achitophel's oratory should not be dismissed as a "temptation speech." It is that, but it is more than that, for the temptation is cast in the form of panegyric. The speech combines the elements of demonstrative and deliberative oratory; the first fourteen lines (230–243) are pure praise, while the rest of the speech (244–302) is Achitophel's advice to the would-be ruler.

The orator crowds into the demonstrative opening several of the most characteristic topics of panegyric.

Auspicious Prince! at whose Nativity
Some Royal Planet rul'd the Southern sky;
Thy longing Countries Darling and Desire;
Their cloudy Pillar, and their guardian Fire:
Their second Moses, *whose extended Wand*
Divides the Seas, and shews the promis'd Land:
Whose dawning Day, in every distant age,
Has exercis'd the Sacred Prophets rage:
The Peoples Prayer, the glad Deviners Theam,
The Young-mens Vision, and the Old mens Dream!
Thee, Saviour, *Thee, the Nations Vows confess;*
And, never satisfi'd with seeing, bless:
Swift, unbespoken Pomps, thy steps proclaim,
And stammerring Babes are taught to lisp thy Name. (230–243)

39. Bernard Schilling, *Dryden and the Conservative Myth: A Reading of Absalom and Achitophel* (New Haven and London, 1961), p. 45–65, 195–199. Although he does not deal specifically with Dryden's panegyrics, Schilling indirectly illuminates them through his discussion of *Absalom and Achitophel.* I am indebted to him generally for his discussion of the law, pp. 146–153, and particularly for his emphasis on the "cause"/"laws" rhyme in the poem, pp. 151–152.

The first couplet, and especially the first word, of the speech establish the optimistic orientation of the genre and echo a host of earlier poems. Claudian, for classical example, opens his panegyric on Honorius's fourth consulship:

> *Auspiciis iterum sese regalibus annus*
> *induit et nota fruitur iactantior aula.* (1–2)

Once more the year opens under royal auspices and enjoys in fuller pride its famous prince . . .

In the Renaissance Thomas More views the outset of Henry's reign in similar terms.

Rex init auspiciis regna Britanna bonis.[40]

The king undertakes amid happy auspices the rule of Britain.

In his Restoration panegyric Abraham Cowley uses the word "auspicious" in conjunction with a reference to Charles's nativity star.

> *Auspicious* Star *again arise,*
> *And take thy* Noon-tide station *in the skies,*
> *Again all* Heaven *prodigiously adorn;*
> *For loe! thy* Charles *again is* Born.[41]

Later Dryden himself was to extract significance from the position of the sun at the birth of Prince James, the "Auspicious Heir" and the "auspicious Infant."[42] In short, Achitophel is giving Absalom conventional, even exaggerated, treatment by locating the "auspicious"

40. Thomas More, *Carmen Gratulatorium*, line 42, *The Latin Epigrams of Thomas More*, ed. and trans. Leicester Bradner and Charles Arthur Lynch (Chicago, 1953), p. 17.

41. Cowley, *Ode Upon His Majesties Restoration and Return*, 20–23.

42. *Britannia Rediviva*, 17, 321, *Poems*, II, 541, 550.

planetary sign that ruled his birth and forecast his reign. The irony is that Absalom's birth was anything but "auspicious." It is precisely because he is a bastard that he has no right to the throne. The first couplet of Achitophel's oration thus gives us a clue to the whole; the speech begins with a *topos* that is true to tradition, but entirely false to the occasion and the man.

From this starting point Achitophel multiplies demonstrative topics in line after line. Absalom becomes Moses, the sun, the answer to national prayers, the savior who unites the people in celebration, "The Young-mens Vision, and the Old mens Dream!" In this panegyric, however, the traditional praise of the new prince as redeemer is effectively negated by the poem's Biblical context. It is obvious that Absalom is not the "second *Moses*," is not the *"Saviour,"* as Jesus is Christ, the true messiah. Allegorically, moreover, Shaftesbury's praise of Monmouth is refuted by Dryden's own praise of Charles II, the true king. In *Astraea Redux* Dryden had already compared Charles to both Moses and Christ: "Thus when th' Almighty would to *Moses* give" (262); "The Prince of Peace would like himself confer" (139). If, in Biblical history Absalom is not Jesus, in English history Monmouth is not Charles. In this speech Dryden places panegyrical conventions in the mouth of Achitophel to illuminate the false premise on which both the speech and the plot are based: that the bastard should be king.

Dryden provides ample authority for viewing this passage of *Absalom and Achitophel* in light of earlier panegyrics and especially in light of his own *Astraea Redux*. Later in the speech, after he has shifted from demonstrative to deliberative oratory, Achitophel describes the Res-

toration in terms that demand comparison with Dryden's
first Stuart panegyric.

> *He is not now, as when on* Jordan's *Sand*
> *The Joyfull People throng'd to see him Land,*
> *Cov'ring the* Beach, *and blackning all the* Strand:
> *But, like the Prince of Angels from his height,*
> *Comes tumbling downward with diminish'd light;*
> *Betray'd by one poor Plot to publick Scorn,*
> *(Our only blessing since his Curst Return:)*
> *Those heaps of People which one Sheaf did bind,*
> *Blown off and scatter'd by a puff of Wind.* (270–278)

What had been described as the "white" clothing of
penitence in 1660 is now dyed black. The Restoration
has become the King's "curst Return," as Achitophel re-
peals the "blessings" of 1660 and appropriates the word
"blessing" to describe the "Plot." In this process of inversion, Charles, the Christ of the earlier poem, here
becomes Lucifer; the political world of *Astraea Redux*,
defined in the traditional terms of panegyric, is turned
upside down to make the usurper Christ and the legitimate monarch Satan.

In his revision of *Astraea Redux*, however, Achitophel
does more than simply change the metaphoric identifica-
tions. He also changes the theory of history on which the
earlier poem is based. It should be recalled that the Restoration was achieved, according to Dryden, by "delay."
" 'Twas not the hasty product of a day, / But the well
ripened fruit of wise delay" (169–170). Achitophel
adapts the imagery of ripeness to convey a very different
moral. "Believe me, Royal Youth, thy Fruit must be, /
Or gather'd Ripe, or rot upon the Tree" (250–251). This

image defines the theory of history that is adduced to justify Absalom's usurpation.

> *Heav'n, has to all allotted, soon or late,*
> *Some lucky Revolution of their Fate:*
> *Whose Motions, if we watch and guide with Skill,*
> *(For humane Good depends on humane Will,)*
> *Our Fortune rolls, as from a smooth Descent,*
> *And, from the first Impression, takes the Bent:*
> *But, if unseiz'd, she glides away like wind;*
> *And leaves repenting Folly far behind.* (252–259)

The providential order restored in *Astraea Redux* is now replaced by a man-centered idea of history based on "humane Will" and expressed by human action. "Now, now she meets you, with a glorious prize, / And spreads her Locks before her as she flies" (260–261). Urging Absalom to act, Achitophel repeats one of the catchwords of panegyric, only "now" is no longer the occasion for restoration but has become instead the occasion for usurpation.[43] To follow Achitophel's advice is to follow the

43. "Now" or the Latin *nunc* often initiates the demonstrative theme of restoration. Erasmus's verse panegyric to Philip includes the line, "Nunc nunc videor mihi reddita demum." *Gratulatorium Carmen*, line 7, *The Poems of Desiderius Erasmus*, ed. C. Reedijk (Leiden, 1956), p. 273. Thomas More echoes Erasmus in lines 21–26 of his *Carmen Gratulatorium* to Henry VIII, where the word *nunc* is repeated three times. The opening words of Ammonius's poem on the same occasion are "Nunc, nunc. . . ," *Elegia De Obitu Regis Henrici VII Et Felici Successione Henrici Octavi*, line 1, *Andreae Ammonii Carmina Omnia*, ed. Clemente Pizzi (Florence, 1958). In Haddon's poem to Elizabeth, *nunc* introduces the characteristic weather imagery which defines the theme of restoration: "Nunc Zephyrus mollis iucundas commovet auras, / Anglia vere novo nunc recreata viret." *In auspicatissimum*, lines 13–14, *The Poetry of Walter Haddon*, ed. Charles J. Lees (The Hague, 1967), p. 169.

self-defeating course of Charles X, Sforza, and the Puritan revolutionaries.

If Absalom does pick the fruit, as Achitophel advises, then he falls as Adam fell. Dryden leaves no room for doubt on this score, for Achitophel is modeled partially on Milton's Satan. By defining the *ethos* of the panegyrist in Satanic terms, Dryden exposes Achitophel's perversion of one of the conventional patterns of Renaissance panegyric: paradise lost in usurpation and regained in restoration. Achitophel perverts panegyric from its traditional function of celebrating redemption to that of encouraging the fall. In political terms, the orator invites the would-be monarch to place his "cause" above the "laws," to become king by violating the institution of kingship.

Achitophel's panegyric does, then, function as a temptation speech and the bauble that tempts Absalom is power.

> *What may not* Israel *hope, and what Applause*
> *Might such a General gain by such a Cause?*

"Now" emphatically introduces the demonstrative theme in the English panegyrics of Daniel, Jonson, Cowley, and Waller. It appears in the first stanza of the panegyrics by Daniel and Cowley (*Ode Upon His Majesties Restoration and Return*) and in the first line of those by Jonson and Waller (*Of the Danger His Majesty . . . Escaped in the Road at Saint Andrews*). Moreover, in *Astraea Redux* Dryden implicitly contrasts the "Now" that is the first word of the poem to the "now" that initiates the concluding prophecy. Although its significance varies somewhat from poem to poem, the emphatic recurrence of this word suggests the historical perspective of panegyric. "Now" is the fulcrum on which history turns, as evil gives way to good, usurpation to restoration. Achitophel reverses this historical pattern and makes the "now" in his oration a time for usurpation.

> *Not barren Praise alone, that Gaudy Flower,*
> *Fair only to the sight, but solid Power:*
> *And Nobler is a limited Command,*
> *Giv'n by the Love of all your Native Land,*
> *Than a Successive Title, Long, and Dark,*
> *Drawn from the Mouldy Rolls of Noah's Ark.* (295–302)

Here the orator concentrates on the fundamental concern of panegyric: "Not barren Praise alone . . . / . . . but solid Power." Like many a panegyrist before him, Achitophel insists on the ideal of "a limited Command" ensured by "the Love of all your Native Land." He thus ingeniously and outrageously works his inverted, perverted panegyric around to the traditional theme of limitation. The ideal of "a limited Command" is traditional and unobjectionable. What this rhetoric ignores, however, is that this ideal has already been realized in the person of David, a fact which Absalom himself confirms.

> *My Father Governs with unquestion'd Right,*
> *The Faiths Defender, and Mankinds Delight:*
> *Good, Gracious, Just, observant of the Laws;*
> *And Heav'n by Wonders has Espous'd his Cause.* (317–320)

The "cause"/"laws" rhyme here recalls the limitations placed on the king in *Astraea Redux*. "Your Pow'r to Justice doth submit your Cause, / Your Goodness only is above the Laws" (266–267). As monarchical power is already limited by the law, the ideal of a limited command is an insufficient argument for "innovation." The real issue is not limitation, but simply power.

> *Desire of Power, on Earth a Vitious Weed,*
> *Yet, sprung from High, is of Caelestial Seed:*
> *In God 'tis Glory: And when men Aspire,*
> *'Tis but a Spark too much of Heavenly Fire.* (305–308)

In these lines, softened to exculpate Absalom, Dryden calls on divine authority to refute the Satanic argument. Power is derived from God, not from men. A more complete answer to Achitophel's argument is permanently embodied in Dryden's serious panegyrics, of which this speech is a clever but self-evident mockery.

Later in the poem, after completing his gallery of rebel portraits, Dryden lists the names of those who resisted rebellion. "These were the chief, a small but faithful Band / Of Worthies, in the Breach who dar'd to stand" (914–915). By identifying himself with this "small but faithful Band" Dryden foreshadows the demise of his political constituency that occurs after 1688. Even more indicative of Dryden's changing relationship with his national audience, however, is *The Hind and the Panther*. The speech of the pigeon "more mature in Folly than the rest" (III, 1108–1140), Dryden's third satiric combination of demonstrative and deliberative oratory, indirectly suggests the increasing futility of Dryden's serious attempts at persuasive oratory.

The alternating speeches of the Hind and the Panther have been discussed as oratory by Phillip Harth. "Dryden's problem," Harth writes, "is one of creating an objective *ethos* for each speaker which is appropriate to his purpose of making the Hind's arguments credible to the audience, and those of the Panther unconvincing. The character and motivation of the two combatants are as opposite as the positions they adopt in their dispute."[44] Although the "domestic conversation" of part 3 is rather far removed from pure classical oratory, it may

44. Phillip Harth, *Contexts of Dryden's Thought* (Chicago and London, 1968), p. 43.

still be profitable to discuss these speeches in traditional rhetorical terms.

For the first almost nine hundred lines of part 3 we are given a blend of judicial and deliberative oratory. The forensic element, carried over from the theological debate of part 2, makes it clear that the ultimate judge of this long argument is God. In one of the more heated moments of the debate, the Hind pauses, having "suppress'd / The boiling indignation of her breast," to remind herself and the Panther of this very fact. "Be vengeance wholly left to pow'rs divine, / And let heav'n judge betwixt your sons and mine . . ."[45] But because the issues in part 3 are predominantly ecclesiastical and political, rather than theological, this legal language is more often applied to temporal concerns, such as the Test Act. In this judicial contest the Hind is the plaintiff, the Panther the defendant, as even the Panther admits.

> *To this the* Panther *sharply had reply'd,*
> *But, having gain'd a Verdict on her side,*
> *She wisely gave the loser leave to chide;*
> *Well satisfy'd to have the But and peace,*
> *And for the Plaintiff's cause she car'd the less,*
> *Because she su'd in formâ Pauperis . . .* [46]

Behind these judicial roles, moreover, are related political ones. The Hind's arguments have a clear political purpose: reconciliation between Anglicans and Catholics. Her speeches are thus deliberative, designed to persuade the recalcitrant Panther to a kind of peaceful

45. *The Hind and the Panther*, III, 261–262, 279–280, *Poems*, II, 510–511.
46. *The Hind and the Panther*, III, 756–761. See Miner's note in the California Dryden, III, 435.

coexistence, if not to the national reconciliation desired by the Lion.

If as you say, and as I hope no less,
Your sons will practise what your self profess,
What angry pow'r prevents our present peace?
The Lyon, *studious of our common good,*
Desires, (and Kings desires are ill withstood,)
To join our Nations in a lasting love . . . (III, 672–677)

The Panther, however, rejects all of the Hind's conciliatory proposals and refuses to be persuaded. The Hind, as a result, abandons her attempt to persuade.

The Matron *woo'd her Kindness to the last,*
But cou'd not win; her hour of Grace was past.
Whom thus persisting when she could not bring
To leave the Woolf, *and to believe her King,*
She gave Her up, and fairly wish'd her Joy
Of her late Treaty with her new Ally:
Which well she hop'd wou'd more successfull prove,
Than was the Pigeons, *and the* Buzzards *love.* (III, 892–899)

Here the Hind turns away from both the judicial and the deliberative and toward the one kind of oratory that requires no persuasion, the demonstrative. What follows this turning point is demonstrative oratory in its negative form of censure. Yet the whole of this speech is taken up by the fable of the Pigeons and the Buzzard, and within this fable Dryden gives us a splendid set piece of deliberative oratory, the speech of the most foolish pigeon. Here, then, Dryden unites the two types of oratory that define panegyric in a new and highly original way: he encloses a deliberative speech within a demonstrative one.

Although the speech of the pigeon begins as indirect

discourse, it becomes direct discourse as soon as he mentions the Buzzard. The argument is that the pigeons should confer the kingship on "Some Potent Bird of Prey" who will take up their cause against the "encreasing race of *Chanticleer*." The nominee of the orator is the "noble *Buzzard*." As this argument from circumstance satisfies the pigeons, the oration is followed by a brief glimpse of the immediate result, procession and coronation.

> *After a grave Consult what course were best,*
> *One more mature in Folly than the rest,*
> *Stood up, and told 'em, with his head aside,*
> *That desp'rate Cures must be to desp'rate Ills apply'd:*
> *And therefore since their main impending fear*
> *Was from th' encreasing race of* Chanticleer:
> *Some Potent Bird of Prey they ought to find,*
> *A Foe profess'd to him, and all his kind:*
> *Some haggar'd* Hawk, *who had her eyry nigh,*
> *Well pounc'd to fasten, and well wing'd to fly;*
> *One they might trust, their common wrongs to wreak:*
> *The* Musquet *and the* Coystrel *were too weak,*
> *Too fierce the* Falcon, *but above the rest,*
> *The noble* Buzzard *ever pleas'd me best;*
> *Of small Renown, 'tis true, for not to lye,*
> *We call him but a* Hawk *by courtesie.*
> *I know he haunts the* Pigeon-House *and Farm,*
> *And more, in time of War, has done us harm;*
> *But all his hate on trivial Points depends,*
> *Give up our Forms, and we shall soon be friends.*
> *For* Pigeons *flesh he seems not much to care,*
> *Cram'd* Chickens *are a more delicious fare;*
> *On this high Potentate, without delay,*
> *I wish you would conferr the Sovereign sway:*
> *Petition him t' accept the Government,*
> *And let a splendid Embassy be sent.*

This pithy speech prevail'd, and all agreed,
Old Enmity's forgot, the Buzzard *should succeed.*
  Their welcom Suit was granted soon as heard,
His Lodgings furnish'd, and a Train prepar'd,
With B's *upon their Breast, appointed for his Guard.*
He came, and Crown'd with great Solemnity,
God save King Buzzard, *was the gen'rall cry.* (III, 1108–1140)

Although the speech retains something of the comic pretentiousness of Fleckno's orations, the issues involved here are closer to those raised by Achitophel.

Both Achitophel and the pigeon would have a monarch chosen by the people. Although in both poems Dryden's opinion of this electoral procedure is succinctly expressed by the repeated phrase, "the dregs of a democracy," the later poem expresses greater intransigence.[47] In the essay on innovation in *Absalom and Achitophel,* Dryden concedes Shaftesbury's premise for the sake of argument. "Yet, grant our Lords the People Kings can make, / What Prudent men a setled Throne would shake?" (795–796). In *The Hind and the Panther,* on the other hand, Dryden passes over the democratic argument with evident contempt.

The Hind *thus briefly, and disdain'd t' inlarge*
On Pow'r of Kings, *and their Superiour charge,*
As Heav'ns Trustees before the Peoples choice:
Tho' sure the Panther *did not much rejoyce*
To hear those Echo's *giv'n of her once Loyal voice.*
                                        (III, 887–891)

This passage, placed just before the Hind's fable, refutes the very premise of the pigeon's oration before he even stands up to suggest his "desp'rate Cures."

47. See *Absalom and Achitophel,* 227; *The Hind and the Panther,* I, 211.

Condemned from the start by the Hind, the pigeon nevertheless condemns himself by his choice of the Buzzard to be king. As Earl Miner has shown by reference to the tradition of sacred zoography, the buzzard, as a member of the hawk family, is a typological representation of impiety. Drawing on Wolfgang Franzius's *Historia Animalium Sacra*, Miner writes: "Not only was the buzzard (*butaeo*) related to the hawk family, but also Franzius noted in this genus a *palumbaris accipiter*, or pigeon hawk. The hawk family is a type of all impious creatures (*omnium impiorum*), according to Franzius . . ."[48] The pigeon, then, would confer power on impiety, in effect, directly violating the traditional ideal of monarchy. Moreover, as Franzius points out and Miner emphasizes, the bird's impiety was conventionally specified by comparison with the devil. The Buzzard, then, is not a king, but a usurper. The deliberative oration of the pigeon finally calls for nothing less than the overthrow of the political values defined by the tradition of panegyric. Piety will be replaced by impiety; the divinely sanctioned monarch will be supplanted by the popularly chosen usurper.

Although the political issues are thus very similar to those raised in Achitophel's speech, the *ethos* of the speaker himself is very different. Achitophel is cunning; the pigeon is just a fool. By enclosing the pigeon's deliberative speech within the Hind's demonstrative one, Dryden censures the whole proceeding of the pigeons from the outset. "For Fools are double Fools endeav'ring to be wise" (III, 1107). The purpose of providing this

48. Miner, note to lines 1141–1194 in the California Dryden, III, 451.

context is not only to ridicule the pigeon's speech, but also to reveal the dangerous folly of being persuaded by such oratory. Consequences unforeseen by the pigeons are foreseen by the Hind.

> *'Tis said the Doves repented, tho' too late,*
> *Become the Smiths of their own Foolish Fate:*
> *Nor did their Owner hasten their ill hour:*
> *But, sunk in Credit, they decreas'd in Pow'r:*
> *Like Snows in warmth that mildly pass away,*
> *Dissolving in the Silence of Decay.*
>
> *The* Buzzard *not content with equal place,*
> *Invites the feather'd* Nimrods *of his Race,*
> *To hide the thinness of their Flock from Sight,*
> *And all together make a seeming, goodly Flight:*
> *But each have sep'rate Int'rests of their own,*
> *Two* Czars, *are one too many for a Throne.*
> *Nor can th' Usurper long abstain from Food,*
> *Already he has tasted Pigeons Blood:*
> *And may be tempted to his former fare,*
> *When this Indulgent Lord shall late to Heav'n repair.*
>   (III, 1267–1282)

Dryden thus relies on the conventions of panegyric not, as customary, to affirm royal piety, but rather to satirize the efforts of others to crown impiety.

In *The Hind and the Panther,* as in *Mac Flecknoe* and *Absalom and Achitophel,* Dryden's satire is sustained in part by normative values derived from the tradition of panegyric. Dryden's creative combinations of deliberative and demonstrative oratory in these three poems reveal the importance of panegyric as a source of topics and ideals for his poetry. The recurrent adaptation of panegyrical conventions for satiric purposes, however, also reveals a waning faith in panegyric as a serious kind of poetry. By placing panegyrical oratory in the mouths of Fleckno, Achitophel, and a fool of a pigeon, Dryden undermines the very genre he was still attempting to write seriously as late as 1688. After the revolution Dryden follows the path already staked out by his own Hind and abandons persuasive oratory.

CONCLUSION

Political oratory requires not only an audience, but also a constituency. The orator speaks for others, voicing the convictions and aspirations of a nation, as Dryden had done in the 1660's, or of a party, as other poets were doing with increasing vigor toward the end of the seventeenth century. Immobilized by his past political commitments and isolated by his religion, Dryden has no constituency after 1688. Nor does he attempt to create one from the remnants of that "small but faithful Band" catalogued in *Absalom and Achitophel*. In the poems of the 1690's Dryden does not address the nation or the king, nor does he speak for a party. His most characteristic poems of this final period are not orations at all, but rather epistles to private individuals, usually other artists like Southerne, Congreve, Kneller, Motteux, and Granville. Although these poems have a delicate rhetoric of their own, the poet's voice is that of a private man, or more accurately, that of a public man now resigned to a private role. The immediate audience in each of these epistles is a private individual, who is elevated by achievement above Dryden's former—and now forsaken—audience, the nation as a whole.

Although he abandons the traditional oratorical functions of panegyric, advising the prince and pacifying

the people, Dryden continues until his death to draw
on the store of topics provided by this genre. The conventions of panegyric are now absorbed into the metaphoric structure of his complimentary poems and used
not to persuade but primarily to embellish. The transition
from a functional to a purely formal kind of panegyric is
already evident in *Britannia Rediviva*. Here Dryden, addressing at various times people, prince, and God, takes
up convention after convention only to discard each one
as politically useless. But in the same poem he also addresses Mary of Modena, and in this passage he experi-
ments with less political versions of the familiar topics.

> *But you, Propitious Queen, translated here,*
> *From your mild Heav'n, to rule our rugged Sphere,*
> *Beyond the Sunny walks, and circling Year:*
> *You, who your Native Clymate have bereft*
> *Of all the Virtues, and the Vices left;*
> *Whom Piety, and Beauty make their boast . . .* [49]

The occasion for celebration, the "Triumphant Day"
(315) of the prince's birth, recalls the "triumphant Day"
celebrated in *Astraea Redux* but also looks forward to
the "Triumphant Day" of the Duchess of Ormonde's return to Ireland, celebrated in Dryden's poem from the
preface to the Fables.[50] On the one hand, Dryden praises
Mary in terms very similar to those he had used to praise
Charles II in the panegyrics of the 1660's. "Virtues un-
known to these rough Northern climes / From milder
heav'ns you bring, without their crimes . . ."[51] On the

49. *Britannia Rediviva*, 304–309.

50. The similarity between this passage of *Britannia Rediviva*
and the later poem addressed to the Duchess of Ormonde has been
noted by Miner in the California Dryden, III, 481.

51. *To His Sacred Majesty*, 89–90, *Poems*, I, 27.

other hand, Dryden forecasts the complimentary poetry of the 1690's by expressing the union of divine and human as a reconciliation, not of power and piety, but rather of beauty and piety. In the later panegyrics political concerns are subordinated to esthetic ones, as beauty takes the place of power. "Vouchsafe, Illustrious *Ormond*, to behold / What Pow'r the Charms of Beauty had of old . . ."[52] No longer able to believe in the political union of actual and ideal, Dryden re-creates the conventions of panegyric to express this union esthetically.

To Her Grace The Dutchess Of Ormond completes the preface and dedication of *Fables Ancient and Modern* to the Duke of Ormonde and specifically introduces the first fable of the collection, "Palamon and Arcite, from Chaucer." Yet the metaphoric occasion establishes this poem as a descendant of the "return poems" that had been so popular earlier in the century.

> *Now in this Interval, which Fate has cast*
> *Betwixt Your Future Glories, and Your Past,*
> *This Pause of Pow'r, 'tis* Irelands *Hour to mourn;*
> *While* England *celebrates Your safe Return,*
> *By which You seem the Seasons to command,*
> *And bring our Summers back to their forsaken Land.*
> *The Vanquish'd Isle our Leisure must attend,*
> *Till the Fair Blessing we vouchsafe to send;*
> *Nor can we spare You long, though often we may lend.*
> *The Dove was twice employ'd abroad, before*
> *The World was dry'd; and she return'd no more.* (90–100)

The seasonal imagery and the allusion to the flood recall Dryden's panegyrics of the 1660's, *To His Sacred Majesty*

52. *To Her Grace The Dutchess Of Ormond, With the following Poem of Palamon and Arcite, from Chaucer*, lines 7–8, *Poems*, IV, 1463.

in particular. Moreover, this occasion is placed in the special context of a previous occasion when the Duchess had returned from England to Ireland; in his description of this analogous event Dryden develops the theme of restoration in significant detail. He begins by adapting a couplet from *Astraea Redux*. "The Land, if not re-strain'd, had met Your Way, / Projected out a Neck, and jutted to the Sea."[53] This revised version of the earlier "approaching cliffes of *Albion*" leads to a recollection of the evils of civil war.

> *The Waste of Civil Wars, their Towns destroy'd,*
> Pales *unhonour'd,* Ceres *unemploy'd,*
> *Were all forgot; and one Triumphant Day*
> *Wip'd all the Tears of three Campaigns away.*
> *Blood, Rapines, Massacres, were cheaply bought,*
> *So mighty Recompence Your Beauty brought.*
>
> *As when the Dove returning, bore the Mark*
> *Of Earth restor'd to the long-lab'ring Ark,*
> *The Relicks of Mankind, secure of Rest,*
> *Op'd ev'ry Window to receive the Guest,*
> *And the fair Bearer of the Message bless'd;*
> *So, when You came, with loud repeated Cries,*
> *The Nation took an Omen from your Eyes,*
> *And God advanc'd his Rainbow in the Skies,*
> *To sign inviolable Peace restor'd;*
> *The Saints with solemn Shouts proclaim'd the new accord.*
>
> (64–79)

The processional *topos,* introduced in the traditional con-text of a contrast between past and present, focuses the ideals of reconciliation and peace. Ireland is miraculously restored, but the human focus of the event is neither a

53. *To Her Grace The Dutchess Of Ormond,* 51–52. The parallel has been noted by Kinsley, IV, 2065.

king nor a hero, but instead a beautiful woman. It is now
beauty that brings redemption.

The challenge to the power of beauty in the poem takes
the same form as it had in Dryden's very first published
poem, the Hastings elegy.

> *Now past the Danger, let the Learn'd begin*
> *Th' Enquiry, where Disease could enter in;*
> *How those malignant Atoms forc'd their Way,*
> *What in the faultless Frame they found to make their Prey?*
> *Where ev'ry Element was weigh'd so well,*
> *That Heav'n alone, who mix'd the Mass, could tell*
> *Which of the Four Ingredients could rebel;*
> *And where, imprison'd in so sweet a Cage,*
> *A Soul might well be pleas'd to pass an Age.*
>
> *And yet the fine Materials made it weak;*
> *Porcelain by being Pure, is apt to break:*
> *Ev'n to Your Breast the Sickness durst aspire;*
> *And forc'd from that fair Temple to retire,*
> *Profanely set the Holy Place on Fire.*
> *In vain Your Lord like Young* Vespasian *mourn'd,*
> *When the fierce Flames the Sanctuary burn'd:*
> *And I prepar'd to pay in Verses rude*
> *A most detested Act of Gratitude:*
> *Ev'n this had been Your Elegy, which now*
> *Is offer'd for Your Health, the Table of my Vow.* (111–130)

This episode of illness, metaphorically defined as rebellion, adds a final dimension to the poem's demonstrative
theme of restoration and introduces the deliberative
theme that brings the poem to a close, putting the ideal
in touch with the actual.

> *The soft Recesses of Your Hours improve*
> *The Three fair Pledges of Your Happy Love:*
> *All other Parts of Pious Duty done,*

> *You owe Your* Ormond *nothing but a Son:*
> *To fill in future Times his Father's Place,*
> *And wear the Garter of his Mother's Race.* (163–168)

Beauty is qualified by piety, as Dryden invokes the traditional virtue of the consort in panegyric, fecundity. The "Pious Duty" of the Duchess, the only obligation of her power, is to produce a male heir. As in earlier panegyrics by Claudian, More, Daniel, and in Dryden's own *To His Sacred Majesty*, present ideals are here extended into the future by allusion to the responsibilities of marriage and parentage. The difference is that the anticipated birth of this son, however significant for the Ormonde family, will have no symbolic significance for the nation as a whole. Having excluded that larger audience from his concern, Dryden preserves the traditional form of panegyric but relinquishes its traditional function.

This does not mean, however, that Dryden has relinquished his political principles. Although he abandons public oratory in favor of addresses to private individuals, Dryden nevertheless clings to the essential values of traditional panegyric, reconciliation and peace. These ideals, defined in the metaphors of *To Her Grace The Dutchess Of Ormond*, are recorded more directly, for one final time, in *To my Honour'd Kinsman, John Driden*. The unifying idea of the poem is concord, expressed by the life of Dryden's cousin, who has studied "Peace" and shunned "Civil Rage."[54] Although the vocabulary of the poem reflects the conditions of William's reign, the normative values are fundamentally the same as those expressed four decades earlier.

54. *To my Honour'd Kinsman, John Driden, Of Chesterton In The County Of Huntingdon, Esquire*, 3, *Poems*, IV, 1529.

> *A Patriot, both the King and Country serves;*
> *Prerogative, and Privilege preserves:*
> *Of Each, our Laws the certain Limit show;*
> *One must not ebb, nor t'other overflow:*
> *Betwixt the Prince and Parliament we stand;*
> *The Barriers of the State on either Hand:*
> *May neither overflow, for then they drown the Land.*
> *When both are full, they feed our bless'd Abode;*
> *Like those, that water'd once, the Paradise of God.* (171–179)

Here "we"—Dryden the poet and Driden the MP—stand "Betwixt the Prince and Parliament," defining the limits of royal and popular power. It is this position between the people and the prince that Dryden had occupied from 1660 to 1688 and that he now describes as the stance of a "Patriot."

When Dryden stepped down, without invective, from his position as poet-orator, he left the way clear for a host of younger poets ready and willing to celebrate the accession of the new Dutch king. The significance of Dryden's achievement as a panegyrist can be measured by considering briefly the panegyrics of his successors. The best examples for comparison are Swift's *Ode to the King on his Irish Expedition* and Addison's *To the King*. Swift, like Dryden, was influenced by the Pindaric model for panegyric; Addison, also like Dryden, was influenced by the epic concept of the genre. The successors of Dryden are, in truth, the descendants of Cowley and Waller.

Swift's ode is patently modeled on Cowley's *Ode Upon His Majesties Restoration and Return*. It has been recognized in particular that Swift's famous celebration of Louis XIV's *fistula in ano* is a reductive version of Cowley's treatment of Cromwell. Cowley, it may be recalled, had written of Cromwell in astronomical metaphors.

> *Wher's now that* Ignis Fatuus *which e're while*
>   *Mis-lead our* wandring Isle?
>   *Wher's the* Imposter Cromwel *gon?*
> *Where's now that* Falling-star *his* Son?
> *Where's the* large Comet *now whose raging flame*
> *So fatal to our* Monarchy *became?*
> *Which o're our heads in such proud horror stood,*
> *Insatiate with our* Ruine *and our* Blood?
> *The* fiery Tail *did to vast length extend;*
> *And twice for want of* Fuel *did expire,*
> *And twice renew'd the dismal* Fire;
> *Though long the* Tayl *we saw at last its end.*[55]

In Swift this becomes:

> *That* Restless Tyrant, *who of late*
> *Is grown so impudently Great,*
>   *That Tennis-Ball of Fate;*
> *This Gilded Meteor which flyes*
> *As if it meant to touch the Skies;*
>   *For all its boasted height,*
> *For all its Plagiary Light,*
> *Took its first Growth and Birth*
>   *From the worst Excrements of Earth;*
> *Stay but a little while and down again 'twill come,*
> *And end as it began, in Vapour, Stink, and Scum.*
>   *Or has he like some fearful Star appear'd?*
> *Long dreaded for his* Bloody Tail *and* Fiery Beard,
>   *Transcending Nature's ordinary Laws,*
>   *Sent by just Heaven to threaten Earth*
>   *With War, and Pestilence, and Dearth,*
> *Of which it is at once the Prophet and the Cause.*[56]

55. Cowley, *Ode Upon His Majesties Restoration and Return,* 207–218.

56. Jonathan Swift, *Ode to the King on His Irish Expedition,* lines 119–135, *Swift's Poems,* ed. Harold Williams, 3 vols. (Oxford, 1937), I, 10.

Louis XIV here assumes the characteristic attributes of the villain in panegyric. He is a *"Restless Tyrant"* who considers himself above the "Laws," the prophet of a "Cause" that brings to earth the evils of plague and war. In contrast Swift celebrates William as the poem's hero, who combines *"Valour"* and *" Virtue."*

> *This made the Ancient Romans to afford*
> *To* Valour *and to* Virtue *the* same Word:
> *To shew the Paths of both must be together trod,*
> *Before the* Hero *can commence* a God. (27–30)

William thus emerges as the Herculean hero, whom Swift praises, however, far more for his valor than for his virtue.

> *For strait I saw the Field maintain'd,*
> *And what I us'd to laugh at in* Romance,
> *And thought too great ev'n for effects of Chance.*
> *The Battel almost by* Great William's *single Valour gain'd* . . .
> (61–64)

Comparing him to Tamburlaine as well as Hercules, Swift celebrates William as a military hero of titanic proportions. "He trampled on this Haughty *Bajazet*, / Made him his Footstool in the War, / And a Grim Slave to wait on his Triumphal Car" (42–44). Leaving the traditional conjunction of valor and virtue far behind, Swift expands the heroic dimension of Pindaric panegyric beyond anything dreamed of by Cowley.

Addison does the same for Waller's conception of heroic narrative. Although he begins by describing William as the "auspicious Prince," Addison defines William's duty in distinctly imperialist terms: "To bind the

Tyrants of the Earth with laws, / And fight in ev'ry Injur'd nation's cause . . ."[57] To develop the narrative Addison borrows his topics directly from Waller.

> *Where-e'er the Waves in restless errors rowle,*
> *The Sea lies open now to either Pole:*
> *Now may we safely use the* Northern *gales,*
> *And in the* Polar Circle *spread our sails;*
> *Or deep in* Southern *climes, Secure from wars,*
> *New Lands explore, and sail by Other stars;*
> *Fetch Uncontroll'd each labour of the Sun,*
> *And make the product of the World our own.*[58]

This passage, for example, is an elaboration of a quatrain from *A Panegyric To My Lord Protector*: "The taste of hot Arabia's spice we know, / Free from the scorching sun that makes it grow; / Without the worm, in Persian silks we shine; / And, without planting, drink of every vine."[59] Against this background, Addison portrays William as a hero more active than any of Waller's.

> *Thus when the forming Muse wou'd copy forth*
> *A perfect Pattern of Heroick worth,*
> *She sets a Man Triumphant in the field,*
> *O'er Giants cloven down, and Monsters kill'd,*
> *Reeking in blood, and smeer'd with dust and sweat,*
> *Whilst Angry Gods conspire to make him Great.* (91–96)

William now appears as the contemporary hero of an epic poem.

Both Swift and Addison thus cut themselves free from

57. Joseph Addison, *To the King*, lines 57–58, *The Miscellaneous Works of Joseph Addison*, ed. A. C. Guthkelch, 2 vols. (London, 1914), I, 42.

58. Addison, *To the King*, 115–122.

59. Waller, *A Panegyric To My Lord Protector*, 57–60.

the tradition that had anchored Dryden. In both of these poems the original, oratorical function of panegyric is obscured by its novel form. Whereas Dryden had adapted the transformations of Cowley and Waller in order to emphasize the themes of restoration and limitation, his successors adopt these innovations for their own sake. Verse oratory thus gives way to the rising popularity of the Pindaric ode and the heroic narrative, both of which endure well beyond Swift and Addison. Shadwell, in his later bursts of laureate verse, chose the form of the ode, and in this choice he was followed by a long and inglorious line of successors. Indeed, by the mid-eighteenth century the genre is treated with so little seriousness that Colley Cibber had to pretend his birthday odes were written in jest.[60] Although the heroic narrative never became so popular or infamous as the ode, it too was taken as an especially appropriate form for panegyric. Thus Elijah Fenton in his eighteenth-century edition of Waller observes that the heroic narrative of Charles I's escape at Santander can be taken as a model "panegyric." "This Poem may serve as a model for those who intend to succeed in Panegyric; in which our Author illustrates a plain historical fact with all the graces of poetical fiction."[61] The seventeenth-century transformation has thus become the eighteenth-century tradition.

To see how this formal shift toward Pindaric ode and

60. This, at least, was Johnson's opinion. See James Boswell, *The Life of Samuel Johnson*, ed. G. B. Hill, rev. L. F. Powell, 6 vols. (Oxford, 1934), I, 402.

61. Elijah Fenton, ed. *The Works of Edmund Waller, Esq. in Verse and Prose* (London, 1729), p. iii. This passage is cited by Ruth Nevo, *The Dial of Virtue*, p. 21.

heroic narrative signifies a basic shift in the function of panegyric as well, we can compare Fenton's prescription for panegyric with Dryden's. "[On] all occasions of praise, if we take the Ancients for our patterns, we are bound by prescription to employ the magnificence of words, and the force of figures, to adorn the sublimity of thoughts. Isocrates amongst the Grecian orators, and Cicero, and the younger Pliny, amongst the Romans, have left us their precedents for our security."[62] Dryden adorns "the sublimity of thoughts," whereas his successors illustrate "a plain historical fact." Traditionally the panegyrist's concern is for the nation's future. Although Dryden uses the past as a source of contrast, illustration, analogy, or warning, his panegyrics are designed to ensure the future stability and harmony of the nation. His is a poetry of ideals. The panegyrists who succeed him are concerned instead with the immediate past. Although Swift and Addison dress up contemporary history in the mirror of Cowley and Waller, theirs is essentially a poetry of facts. Clearly, moreover, it was Fenton's rather than Dryden's conception of this genre that Johnson had in mind when he objected to Restoration panegyric. "Charles had yet only the merit of struggling without success, and suffering without despair. A life of escapes and indigence could supply poetry with no splendid images."[63] Originally a kind of oratory, panegyric has become a kind of journalism.

It is this eighteenth-century conception of panegyric,

---

62. "Dedicatory letter prefixed to *Eleonora*," *Essays*, II, 61.
63. Samuel Johnson, *The Life of Waller*, in *Lives of the English Poets*, ed. G. B. Hill, 3 vols. (Oxford, 1905), I, 272.

"plain historical fact" embellished with "poetical fiction," that invites satiric inversion. If panegyric must now depend on the actual deeds of monarchs and statesmen, it is clear that the genre cannot always be taken seriously, and cannot often be taken seriously in the Georgian age. By exposing the discrepancies between "fiction" and "fact," political satirists like Pope and Byron destroy panegyric once and probably for all. The comic-satiric effect of Pope's epistle "to Augustus" depends heavily on the actual facts of George II's rule. Whereas Jonson, Drummond, Waller, and Dryden had all compared the various rulers of the seventeenth century to Caesar Augustus, thus defining an ideal of successful government, Pope suggests that such "Praise undeserv'd is scandal in disguise."[64] Likewise in Byron's *The Vision of Judgment*, the fate of George III at the gates of Heaven depends on his "deeds" as king. "He is what you behold him, and his doom / Depends upon his deeds . . ."[65] Whereas the panegyrist attempts to unite actual and ideal, the individual man with the *optimus princeps*, the satirist subverts the genre by reveling in the gulf between traditional fiction and contemporary fact.

Both Pope and Byron extend their ridicule to include the authors as well as the subjects of panegyric. Toward

64. Alexander Pope, *The First Epistle of The Second Book of Horace Imitated,* line 413, *Imitations of Horace,* ed. John Butt (New Haven and London, 1939), in the Twickenham Edition of Pope's *Poetical Works,* IV, 229.

65. George Gordon, Lord Byron, *The Vision of Judgment,* stanza 69, lines 1–2, *The Works of Lord Byron: Poetry,* ed. E. H. Coleridge, 7 vols. (London, 1898–1904), IV, 509.

the end of his epistle, Pope steps from behind his ironic
mask to belittle those poets who had written in praise
of kings.

> *And when I flatter, let my dirty leaves*
> *(Like Journals, Odes, and such forgotten things*
> *As Eusden, Philips, Settle, writ of Kings)*
> *Cloath spice, line trunks, or flutt'ring in a row,*
> *Befringe the rails of Bedlam and Sohoe.* (415–419)

The "multo-scribbling Southey" is given even harsher
treatment by Byron, who allows George to slip into
heaven during the confusion caused by the recitation
of the laureate's eulogy. We now have two "parties" of
poets: the "court" poets like Eusden and Southey, and
the "country" poets like Pope and Byron. The shift from
an oratorical to a journalistic mode is thus accompanied
by a movement toward polemic, toward strictly party
verse. Moreover, it is quite evident that if facts are the
issue, then the rhetorical advantage rests entirely with
the opposition. Factually, it is far more difficult to prove
that the present is a golden age than to prove that it is
not.

Although party verse was often ferocious during
Dryden's lifetime, Dryden himself cannot be considered
a political polemicist. He persistently, and sometimes
against great odds, attempts to speak for and to the whole
nation, not for any faction or extreme. Behind this effort
is the heritage of panegyric and its traditional purpose,
national reconciliation. Even Dryden's political satires
are typically conciliatory. His ironic versions of panegyric do not, like those of Pope and Byron, emphasize the
gap between actual and ideal. Rather they expose the

danger of perverting the traditional ideals to serve factional goals.

As the seventeenth century comes to an end, however, and the national orator is supplanted by the party polemicist, Dryden's inherited conception of the public poet's responsibility to the whole nation becomes an anachronism. In place of traditional panegyric the eighteenth century offers a kind of public poetry that is at once factual and partisan. The post-Revolution verse of writers like Halifax and Prior even inspired William Courthope to devote a chapter in *A History of English Poetry* to "The Whig Victory: Panegyrical Poetry."[66] But Courthope's concept of "whig panegyric," however familiar it may have been to Pope, would surely have seemed a contradiction in terms to Dryden. For Dryden "panegyric" continues to mean what it had meant to writers like Pliny and Erasmus, More and Jonson, a kind of literature that attempts to unite all (*pan*) the people (*gyris*) behind an ideal monarch. The political poets who succeed Dryden have much more realistic, and therefore much more limited ambitions.

66. W. J. Courthope, *A History of English Poetry*, 6 vols. (London, 1905), V, 20–43. Courthope's study has since been extended much later into the eighteenth century by Cecil A. Moore, "Whig Panegyric Verse: A Phase of Sentimentalism," in Moore, *Backgrounds of English Literature, 1700–1760* (Minneapolis, 1953). For further consideration of "panegyric" in the eighteenth century, see Kenneth Hopkins, *The Poets Laureate* (London, 1954).

Index